The Visit of the Angels, *by the Master Bertram* (date about 1390)
"The Knitting Madonna"
(*see page* 6)

[*Frontispiece*]

Mary Thomas's
KNITTING
BOOK

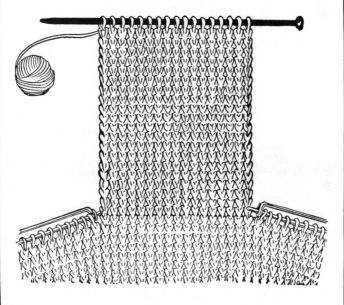

DOVER PUBLICATIONS, INC.
NEW YORK

This Dover edition, first published in 1972, is an unabridged republication of the work originally published in 1938 by Hodder and Stoughton, Ltd., London. It is reprinted by special arrangement with Hodder and Stoughton, Ltd., Warwick Lane, London, E.C.4.

International Standard Book Number: 0-486-22817-7
Library of Congress Catalog Card Number: 72-188814

Manufactured in the United States of America
Dover Publications, Inc.
180 Varick Street
New York, N.Y. 10014

DEDICATION

This book is dedicated with
gratitude and affection

To my Uncle

MR. J. W. LOVEGROVE

for all his many kindnesses, help
and encouragement

CONTENTS

PREFACE

OF ALL THE LOOMS in the world ceased to produce cloth, and the art of spinning and knitting alone remained, we could still be clothed, both warmly and fashionably.

Such is knitting, which without doubt is the most resourceful and inventive method of fabric construction in the world, being made without loom or machine, without warp or weft, shaped as it is constructed, patterned as whim requires, and divided without being cut!

All things are possible in knitting. Women knit almost by instinct, men now for pleasure, though not so long past it provided him with a means of livelihood.

To understand something of the vast and resourceful scope of the art it appears necessary to know something of its past history, when knitting meant so much to the world in general. Such has been attempted in this book. The different methods of knitting practised by other nations, familiar and unfamiliar, have been collected, sorted and assembled into position. These will provide a wealth of ideas for either novice or adept.

All the diagrams have been made with care, and selected so that less familiar forms of knitting can be followed and learned with accuracy.

Detail to some length has been devoted to the subject of knitting implements and yarns, the making of which was at one time an integral part of a knitter's education. Needles and yarn are the implements of the knitter, and all implements are better used and appreciated when they are understood. This knowledge also ensures a more reasonable comprehension of that mysterious thing—tension!

In teaching a child to knit, begin right. Let her learn how to hold her needles, wind her yarn, cast-on and cast-off in tension. Pair her stitches when forming an increase or decrease. Turn. Create different triangular shapes, learning their use. Knit-up, and so forth. These are the technique of knitting, upon which the whole structure is built; and, learnt young, will never be forgotten.

Knitting should be done thoughtfully. It should not be hurried. That is its charm to our generation, who live surrounded with a wild helter-skelter of speed. It is creative, and that is its supreme satisfaction. If things go wrong, don't get impatient. Remember, it took six years to make a master knitter!

All ages have contributed their quota to the progress of knitting, and that contributed by the modern knitter is style. A modern knitted garment is not a thing to be dragged on for extra warmth, but has, in its own right, a place in the world of fashion.

This new desire for style, as now in evidence, demands new methods of treatment, and the suggestion that all knitters should construct a basic pattern to their own measurements, and so make their garments to a definite *known* size, appears more reasonable. This, at least, will ensure fit, and fit IS style. Design is another thing and decided upon before-hand, and for knitted garments should be simple, as variety is obtained by change of fabric, which lies literally at the finger tips.

For this purpose of simplicity the pattern suggested here is that of the body-line, as this can be used for all purposes, whether the garment is being originated by the knitter herself, or constructed from written directions.

Style also demands precision of details, shaping, etc., and these in turn demand a precise knowledge and methods of increasing and decreasing and of refining the fabric by change of needles. These subjects have therefore been treated in great detail so that the best results can be obtained, while the different methods of casting-on as detailed will yield a never-ending source of dainty edges.

At first I had hoped to present the whole story of knitting in one volume only, but this eventually proved impossible, as the subject was too vast. So, with the greatest reluctance, a division had to be made, leaving the fascinating art of fabric construction, which rose to such heights of beauty in the brocade and lace periods of knitting, and which is now rapidly being multiplied, for a later book. This is already in preparation.

These two books will, I hope, give a wider interest to this great and fascinating work.

△ This mark (the well-known danger signal to travellers) is used throughout this book to indicate points of vital importance where beginners are likely to falter. It should be heeded, and so save a lot of trouble. It's there to say "Look out."

MARY THOMAS

ACKNOWLEDGMENTS

IN PRESENTING this first book on the subject of knitting, I would like to acknowledge with my sincere thanks and gratitude the brilliant and painstaking work of the artists Miss Margaret Agutter, Miss H. Lyon-Wood, Miss Dorothy Dunmore, and Miss Mary Kirby. The delightful little caricatures which flavour the text with atmosphere and humour are the work of Miss Margaret Agutter.

My thanks are also due to the many people of different countries, Europe, Asia and America, not forgetting the Shetland Isles, who have forwarded me much valuable information; also to Dr. Fritz Ikley, Dr. Hans Haug, Mrs. Gertrude Mason, for their kindly help, and Miss Dorothy Moss for typing the MS.

The great kindness of various people and museums who have loaned articles for illustrations is acknowledged with thanks beneath the pictures respectively reproduced.

MARY THOMAS

WHENEVER YOU SEE THIS SIGN

STOP!

CAUTION!!

GO!!!

Fig. 1.   A Knitted Masterpiece.   Initials P. I. E.   Dated 1713

HISTORY

KNITTING, like other of its kindred arts, came from the East, from the Arabian peninsula, whence it spread eastwards to Tibet, westwards as far as Spain, carried thence and to other Mediterranean ports by the Arabs, who were the great traders of those days. A superb specimen of Arabian knitting silk of the 7th to 9th centuries is shown about actual size in *Fig.* 82.

Egypt learned her knitting from the Arabs, and it is only in Coptic Egypt, and where Arabian influence could penetrate, that Egyptian knitting discoveries dating from the 4th and 5th centuries have been found (*see Fig.* 209). At what date knitting actually originated no one knows, but in the ancient city of Yemen, in Arabia Felix, earlier known as Shabwa, the city of the Queen of Sheba, it is said to have been known for ever, and that the pattern on the serpent's back was knitted by Eve. Such is Eastern chronology.

Historians place the date about A.D. 200, but legend claims that the seamless garment of Christ was knitted and so could not be cut or divided; and lots were cast for it.

Legend again provokes a claim to Penelope's web which she wrought by day and unravelled so quickly by night, saying it was knitted! Was this Frame knitting?

But legend is a whimsical handmaid, and, though facts are rare, and knitting relics even more rare than those of any other textile, historians generally agree that knitting had but one common source, Arabia, and that from thence it has penetrated to the far corners of the earth, carried hence by the traders, sailors and settlers of different nations.

SCALE PATTERN

MEN KNITTERS

Knitting, then, in its earlier history, would appear to have been taught to

1

the outer world by men—the traders of Arabia and the sailors of the Mediterranean—and right up to the end of the 19th century men as well as women plied the knitting needles.

MASTER KNITTERS

In the heyday of the Guilds, when knitting was as much an industry as weaving, men served an

ARAB KNITTING

apprenticeship in its cause. This needed six years: three years to learn, three years to travel, after which the apprentice made his Masterpieces in thirteen weeks. These were:

(1) To knit a carpet 4 ells square, the design to contain flowers, foliage, birds and animals, in natural colours. (Existing carpets are mainly about 6 ft. × 5 ft.)

(2) To knit a beret.
(3) To knit a woollen shirt.
(4) To knit a pair of hose with Spanish clocks.

The details varied a little. In some Guilds it was specially stated, "stockings to be made after the English style," others that the beret, stockings and shirt were to be knitted and afterwards felted, but the knitted carpet, as principal masterpiece, was acknowledged by most Guilds after 1602.

For this, the prentice first submitted his design in colour, as a chart (*see page* 93), swearing on oath, or by clasping the hands if a Protestant, that it was his own work. This approved, he asked to be informed of the workshop in which he must execute the work, and upon being named, the candidate made here all four of his appointed works in thirteen weeks, and upon approval, was received as Master and member of the Guild.

These carpets are magnificent specimens of knitted fabric. They are in wool, and as full of detail and colour as many Persian carpets, and obviously, like most of these, are intended as wall hangings or covers. *Fig.* 1 contains twelve different colours, red, green, blue, violet, pale blue, black, yellow, dark red and light brown, the yarn being stranded from colour to colour on the back (*see page* 96), and the gauge about five stitches to the inch. The fabric is in one piece, and may have been done on extra long needles, with some mechanical support for the increasing weight of the fabric, or could with ease have been done on a frame, as described in Frame Knitting (*see page* 114). The date—1713—is knitted at base of central ornament, and the initials of the Master, P. I. E., either side. Some of the carpets bear full name and date as part of the design.

These carpets can be classified as follows: 1. Knitted carpets. 2. Knitted and felted carpets. The first come mainly from the Upper Rhine, embracing Alsace, where the Guilds held their charters from the Hapsburgs (*see* the double-headed eagle, *Fig.* 1). These are more square and floral in design.

The second come mainly from Silesia, and are larger, about 7 to 10 feet, with central panel containing figures and landscapes of religious nature, surrounded with texts and wide floral frame-like border.

SILK KNITTING

Knitting and Hosiery Guilds as formed in the 15th and 16th centuries both on the Continent and in England, brought the standard of knitting to great perfection, especially after the introduction of silk to Europe, when garments would be knitted in several colours and in designs that resembled brocaded fabrics; often outlined or part knitted with gold or silver (*see Fig.* 83, *page* 92). This was knitting fit for kings and courtiers, and by such was it worn.

ADDISON KNITTING
GARTERS

The knitted shirt worn by King Charles on the day of his execution in 1649, and now in the London Museum, belongs to this great period, and was no doubt the work of a master knitter.

Silk completely changed the appearance and objective of knitting. Hitherto woollen fabrics had striven to imitate woven cloth even to the extent of disguising its appearance through a process of felting, a treatment which completely obliterated the stitches and gave the effect of solid fabric.

Fig. 2. Prentice Cap, knitted and felted, with double brim, the under one cut as loops
From the London Museum

FELTING

A few felted woollen caps of early Tudor period are to be seen in the London Museum. Two are shown in *Figs.* 2 and 3, and reveal that the fabric could be cut with safety, after the felting process had been applied.

Fig. 3. Knitted and Felted Cap with perforations cut in the fabric
London Museum

The last surviving use of felting, as applied to knitting, can be seen to-day in the French beret and the Eastern fez, both of which carry in the middle of the crown the knitter's end of wool, showing how the work commenced. In early days it was the custom to knit the article in the natural colour of the wool, and then dye and felt it in one process by leaving it to soak for some four or five days. When the wool had thickened, the hat or cap would be blocked to any shape, brushed with a teasle brush and even cut, since there was no fear of the knitting unravelling.

FELTED SLIPPERS

Thus disguised, it is difficult to ascertain at this stage to what extent knitted articles or garments were worn in early days, but in England an Act of Parliament passed during the reign of Henry VII in 1488 speaks of knitted caps, and later another Act of 1553, in the reign of Edward VI, enumerates "knitte peticotes, knitte gloves, knitte sleeves and knitte hose," and it is quite certain that before any Act of Parliament could be passed, knitting as an industry would be well established.

The object of felting was to induce a rainproof fabric, as weather conditions have ever been the problem of man and his clothes. The fisher-folk of Aran, in Ireland, still knit and felt their socks. The Russians knit and felt slippers, boots and thigh hose.

The old Greeks and Romans felted for the same purpose, though whether the fabric they felted was woven or knitted is not known, but felting is said to have been invented before weaving by a process of matting wool together.

Herodotus describes the Persian soldier as wearing light flexible caps of felt, and those worn by the ancient Greek fishermen bear a strong resemblance to the fez, even to the point in the middle of the crown.

WOMEN KNITTERS

Knitting was always highly regarded as a feminine accomplishment in the home, and in old documents a bride's ability to knit was quoted as part of her dowry.

A Knitting Cup was one drunk at a medieval wedding feast, and the word knit seems to have played an important part in the language of the people, who up to the end of the 19th century would talk of "knitting a hedge" or to "knit the gate." A surgeon still talks of "knitting a broken bone

THE "KNITTING" CUP

together." The Anglo-Saxon word for knitting is *cnyttan, cnotta*—a knot.

The beautiful picture shown in the Frontispiece, entitled "The Visit of the Angels," was part of the inside right wing of the Buxtehuder Altar, painted by the Master Bertram between the years 1390 and 1400. This was originally erected in the Buxtehuder Abbey, and would suggest that the homely occupation of knitting was revered and encouraged by the nuns of this abbey. It is an historical picture and of great interest to knitters, as the artist reveals that knitting then was much as it is to-day, even to the manner of picking up the stitches and forming the neck of a garment.

Shakespeare makes mention of knitting in his plays as a common accomplishment, while Knitting Bees, we read, were then a means of whiling away the long winter evenings.

Mistress Lee, the wife of William Lee, the inventor of the Stocking machine (1589), was a great knitter, and helped to swell the family funds with her earnings, and we read it was to lighten her task that Lee invented his machine. This is one of the earliest records of a woman, mentioned by name as earning money by knitting.

Thus it would appear that knitting had two sources of development: (1) The Guilds, which brought the art to such a high degree of perfection; (2) the home and convents.

In Scotland the order of knitting has always been high, and at one time it was reputed the Scottish lay claim to its invention, St. Fiacre, the son of a Scottish King, being adopted as the patron saint of a Guild of Stocking Knitters formed in Paris about 1527. But knitting began earlier than this, though the beautiful lace knitting of Scotland has, like their openwork embroidery, ever been a source of wonder and admiration.

SHETLAND KNITTERS

In the Shetlands, knitting remains an industry of the islands, and this small community, situated on the edge of civilisation, has something unique to offer a post-war, machine-minded generation; as here survives a knitting industry such as might have thrived in the days of the Guilds.

Children are taught to knit from their earliest childhood, and are given a pair of knitting needles at the tender age of four years, but not for knitting. The child holds these needles as she sees her mother hold her needles, and *pretends* to knit, beating the needles up and down as though making stitches, and so acquires rhythm and speed, for a Shetlander knits at the rate of 200 odd stitches a minute!

This incredible pace is attained to-day in much the same way as the master knitters of old must have knitted, with the aid of a knitting stick or sheath (*see page* 19). Into this he inserted the end of his right needle and the stick itself into a belt on the right hip. The Shetland knitter, prompted by the same impulse, inserts her needle into a knitting pouch (*see page* 21) and so frees her right hand, which is then held over the extreme point of the right needle, operating the wool with the forefinger only, while the fingers of both hands "play" the stitches to and from the needle points as though playing a musical instrument. (*See also page* 20.)

The quick staccato music of the 17th and 18th centuries must surely have found its inspiration in the rapid rhythmical "click" of the knitting needles.

But while the technique of a Shetland knitter rekindles ideas of the Guilds, her spinning and carding of the wool rekindles ideas still more ancient.

The Shetland knitter still uses her distaff and spinning wheel. Her wool is plucked from the backs of her own sheep, and these she tends and breeds herself, nursing the tiny lambs through the difficult period of their early months, and often rescuing them, at danger to herself, from snow, sea or bog. The sheep are so small and their wool so delicately long that, when the time comes, the fleece can be "lifted" from the backs of the sheep by the simple process of running the hand, with fingers spread apart, along the back of the animal and "lifting" or "roeing" it away.

SPINNING

The fleece is then cleaned to remove dirt, heather, twigs, etc., placed before a large fire, and covered with a dressing of seal oil. This must be equally distributed by mixing and turning the wool about in this fire-heated atmosphere. When thoroughly soaked, the "combing" or "carding" begins, and as the wool is combed it is made into "rourers" (rolls) ready for spinning. The finest spun is a single hair, which is reeled off into a two-ply wool and hanked. This is then washed, as it is still permeated with oil, but for the very finest fabrics it is not washed until it has been knitted up, as by this means the delicate gossamer hair is stronger, though the knitting process is rather a messy one.

In early days, some such long procedure as this would have been the work of every knitter, and here in our midst to-day exists this medieval knitting sanctuary, free of the sound of machinery, kept alive by the women of these little islands.

WORLD-WIDE ACTIVITY

Over the world in general, knitting spread with persistent speed. Within the home it was part of the daily work. In the fields, shepherds ever had their knitting in their hands, gathering their precious wool from the thickets, twigs and bushes against which the animals brushed in passing. Wool-gathering had another meaning then. They, too, would spin and make their own yarns, and knit socks, scarves and caps for themselves and their families, and as we approach the 18th century it is to find all Europe and western Asia to Tibet, knitting.

But while the story of knitting in Europe is difficult enough

"LLAMA-HERD" KNITTING

to follow, it is still more difficult in Asia. The knitting of Bokhara is brilliant in colour and magnificent in design, being similar in pattern to their embroideries. Colour knitting had, and still has, a great vogue in the East. The long thigh-length hose worn by the Tibetans scintillated in colour and pattern, and, curiously enough, the knitting of the Corvichan Indians of Vancouver bears similar designs.

There seems no early trace of knitting in China, and little in India until European influence is felt, for these great

countries, which gave such magnificent woven textiles and embroideries to the world, seem to
have specialised in other forms
of work, plaiting, etc., and since,
perhaps, as they did not wear
hose, never felt the urge to knit.
Neither is there early trace of
knitting in Africa except along
the fringes of the Mediterranean,

but things were soon to change. Europe, who had
learnt the art from the East, was colonising. The British,
French, Dutch, Spanish, and Portuguese were all acquiring
colonies, and the settlers were spreading the cult over the seas
of the world. Soon a grand panorama of world-wide activity
was to respond in accord to that which had previously actuated
the countries of Europe and Asia. We find the shepherds of

DUTCH KNITTING

Peru knitted as they tended
their llama-herds, in common
with the lonely Dutch settler in
the Cape, or the impish donkey-
boy of Morocco.

Knitting, because of its practical use, made its appeal in the
new world, as it did in the
old, to all classes, and perhaps
why so little remains of all this activity is because of its too
general acceptance and obvious utility.

WHITE KNITTING

But silk knitting, which made such a stir in Europe and in
England when Good Queen Bess decided she would never
again wear woollen hose, was to be superseded in the early
18th century by white knitting in linen and cotton yarns.
With the importation of white Eastern muslins, the craze for
cotton surpassed that of silk, and white knitting, just as white
embroideries, became fashionable. The knitting was ambitious,
and aspired to be regarded no longer as fabric or brocade, but
lace, and so fine and open in pattern did it grow that the

finest lace thread was used, knitted upon needles known as "wires."

Here, with the advent of cotton, dawned another great period of knitting. The lacemakers seized the art, and used knitted backgrounds as a cheaper and more expedient way upon which to embroider their lace stitches (*see Fig.* 146, *page* 142). Hosiery, too, was changing, and fine stockings of cotton were knitted with openwork fronts; mittens that rose up above the elbow bore openwork designs; bonnets, coats, scarves and fichus, all in finest openwork knitting, were the order of the day and fashion, while the knitting samplers as exemplified in *Fig.* 4 reveal what wealth of pattern and diversity of design was then in use. This sampler contains 150 different stitch patterns, and the stitches of the final pattern are not cast-off, but left ready for more! So the collection was never finished. The strip is mounted on pink sarsenet ribbon, the patterns being numbered in tens, with embroidered figures.

There is good reason to suppose that the graceful knitting of this period was mainly the work of women.

This grand epoch of white knitting was enjoyed by all nations, though the finest of its kind in Europe matured in those districts not engaged in the making of needlepoint or embroidered laces. The white knitting of Germany, Holland and Scandinavia is renowned unto this day, and in Britain, where the lace tariffs almost prohibited the use of Continental lace, white knitting became a work of art and utility.

BEAD KNITTING

About this time beads as well as embroidery stitches were added to the fabric (*see Fig.* 135, *page* 132). The work was ingenious, and the bead-knitted bags of Vienna delighted the Courts of Europe and the grand ladies of fashion. They were as fine and delicate in colours as miniature paintings, and, indeed, this was their objective, for the knitter had found in the romantic paintings of the 18th century yet another source of inspiration. Here is adventure indeed. From the humble beginning of imitating thick woollen cloth and woven patterns, knitting had progressed first to brocade effects in silk, later to lace, and finally paintings.

Fig. 4. Knitting Sampler of 150 different patterns

By kind permission of Mrs. John Jacoby

THE DECLINE

This was the last heyday of knitting, for the machine age which swept Europe, and England in particular, during the early 19th century did not hesitate to include knitting in its wake; indeed, it was one of the earliest to suffer, as the stocking machine invented by Lee of Cambridge as long ago as 1589 was now to become the parent of the Jacquard loom in France (1790) and the Heathcote machine in England (1809). Together they banished hand knitting from the industrial world. The work of the Master was finished. The fine, delicate knitting gradually became coarser, and ultimately petered out altogether.

KNITTING BOOKS

Happily for us, knitting continued in the home, though the flow of young and virile blood poured into its progress had stopped; the work went on, but without invention or inspiration. Knitting samplers grew more rare and knitting books began to appear, recording now in written word the glories of those old patterns. (The earliest knitting books were in chart form.) Some of these books print "receipts" known then to be nigh on two hundred years old. But books were expensive and couched in genteel language. They were for "ladies," and by the middle of the last century knitting books excused their appearance on the plea that knitting was a suitable pastime for the "aged and feeble-minded!" How had the mighty fallen!

RURAL KNITTING

On peasant soil and among the country-folk the work had a better fate. Knitting still remained an industry in isolated spots. The end of the 18th century found hand knitting in Wales a flourishing means of livelihood, and we read that the children learned to knit as they learned to walk and that the women could knit a whole stocking in a day. A pair in Merioneth wool cost 10s. 6d. to buy, the knitters selling their work to travellers at coach stops.

In Ireland, hand knitting remained an industry until well into the 19th century, and also in Scotland. In England, the knitters of Gayle, in the dales of Yorkshire, were famed for

From " Richmondshire," by Edmund Bogg. By kind permission

Fig. 5. The Knitters of Gayle

The position of the hands indicates that both knitters are using knitting sheaths

their work, and one of the all too rare pictures of knitters at work is shown here in *Fig.* 5, depicting Gayle knitters of about 1878. Such a domestic scene as this must have been a common sight during those days, and Edmund Bogg says in his book *Richmondshire*: "Up to 1880, and perhaps even later, at Hawes and other places in the dale, the industry of hand knitting engaged the fingers of many persons of both sexes. Men in charge of carts, or herding sheep or cattle, would ply their needles, and on a visit to other dales carry their unfinished work with them to fill in the time and pauses in conversation." Even lovers went courting with their knitting, and it was a thing well understood in the dales that when a young couple married, if both were expert knitters, no matter what were their shortcomings in housewifery or husbandry, they would "do all right and get on in the world."

Dr. Lees informs us how, calling at Carperby as late as 1880, he found Thomas Willis, father of the noted sheep farmer, knitting a quilt, and that during the long winter evenings, in kitchen and parlour alike, callers would congregate, and both music and song, or gossip and tale-telling, would be punctuated by the click-click of the bright steel needles, one of which rested in a (holder) sheath affixed to the waist-belt of the knitter. (*See Fig.* 5.)

But, while little communities such as these survived to tell a story that must have been all too familiar in other centuries, the general state of knitting throughout the country was such that in 1872 a law was passed in England obliging it to be taught in schools, and a half-hearted renaissance occurred. This was followed, at the end of the century, by an avalanche of instructive literature, the quality of which was fading when the sound of war broke in 1914, for the great story was dying. It needed to be born again—born of a new generation, one content to love it as a means of personal expression. Knitting for knitting's sake.

So knitting, together with her sister arts, weaving, embroidery and lace-making, begins a new post-war cycle, but with this difference: the machine is servant and not master. Wools are carded, spun and dyed, needles polished and coloured to match a whim of fashion. The tyrant has become a willing slave. Almost, perhaps, too willing a slave!

KNITTING IMPLEMENTS,
ANCIENT AND MODERN

ANCIENT

THE earliest knitting needles were made with a hook at one end, like crochet hooks, and these, fashioned of copper wire, were used by the old Arabs; and can still be found in use

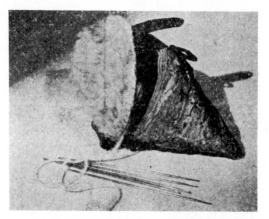

Fig. 6.   Knitting Pouch and Hooked Knitting Needles
from Landes (France)
By kind permission of Mrs. Josephine Whittingham

round the Mediterranean and in places where Arab influence penetrated. The hooked needles shown in *Fig.* 6 are modern, being made by a shepherd of Landes, in the South of France, from old umbrella ribs. They are hand filed and shaped, as they have always been made in this district, though earlier needles of this type were made from the young shoots of briar bushes. Five needles make a set.

These shepherds are great knitters, and spin their own wool, which is mainly gleaned from the straggling tufts left by the sheep on hedge or bush, for wool-gathering has yet a real meaning in these parts. They knit as they watch their sheep, erect on stilts the better to keep guard over their straggling flocks (*Fig.* 7). The younger shepherds do their folk-dances on stilts.

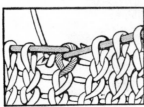

Fig. 7
The
Shepherds
of
Landes

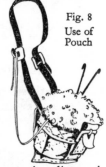

Fig. 8
Use of
Pouch

The ancient weather-beaten knitting pouch in *Fig.* 6 is also from Landes, and is the same as that still used by all the shepherds in this district. It is made from five double layers of sheepskin sewn together with red wool in decorative diagonal lines. The lid is circular and made of sheepskin, complete with wool. The knitting is kept in this pouch, which is worn slung round the neck with a long leather strap, to which is affixed a hook in the front. In knitting, the yarn is passed over this hook, as shown in *Fig.* 8, and then round the left thumb, and in and out the fingers of the left hand, for these shepherds operate the wool with the left thumb, in what we might assume was the orthodox method used when hook needles were in vogue.

Both needles are grasped horizontally in the full hand, at waist level, and the knitting movement is made like a concertina, inwards, outwards, and at great speed. The fabric is Crossed Stocking Stitch, knitted in the Eastern way. They make socks and berets, the latter being felted, as in the 15th century.

Fig. 9.   Hooked Knitting

While one end of the needle is hooked, the other end is quite blunted, and in Round Knitting the hooked ends never meet, as the stitches from the needle of the left hand are hooked off the blunted end. Perhaps this is why Round Knitting was more popular in the old days. In Flat Knitting the hooks must meet, and then the needles are held straight with the business ends inwards facing each other, so that the hook does not impede the transference of the stitch (*see Fig.* 9).

In the Basque districts of Spain, just the other side of the Pyrenees, similar hand-made hooked needles are also in use. Also in Bolivia, and other countries in South America where Spanish influence could penetrate.

FROM HOOK TO SMOOTH POINTS

At what date the hook needle was superseded by the smooth-pointed needle is not known, but a half-finished sock of the 12th century found in a Turkish tomb reveals that the knitter was then working with five hooked needles, similar in pattern to those yet made by the shepherds of Landes. The date of the frontispiece is 1390, and here the artist has painted smooth-pointed needles, so the invention may have been European. A smooth point would certainly be much easier to use with knitting sticks and for flat knitting, but history leaves no record either of their invention or advent. There appears no trace of hooked needles in Britain, yet Lee's first knitting machine was fitted with hooked needles.

NEEDLES, PINS AND WIRES

The old knitting needles were made of wood, bone, ivory, briar, bamboo, copper, wire, amber and, according to some records, iron. Steel was of later use. They were made by the knitters themselves, and were known by such divers names as knitting woods, needles, skewers or wires.

The old craftsfolk treated their needles with care and affection, wrapping them in leather to preserve their polish when not in use, and grinding the points as they became blunted in work. Bone and ivory needles were often spliced in order to obtain the required length, a task which needed the utmost precision in order to achieve a smooth surface and avoid fraying the working yarn.

The straight knitting needle appears to have been that

generally accepted, though needles with curved points were not unknown. These are said to be more convenient in work to peasants who knit as they walk, balancing heavy loads upon their heads. The knitters of Gayle are also reputed to have worked with curved needles.

The addition of knob ends to knitting needles is comparatively modern, and before their advent little stoppers made of wood or cork were used to prevent the stitches falling off either end. With the addition of the knob, the knitting Needle became a knitting Pin, and this practical distinction might well be revived.

The old knitting needles were graded in sizes, much as they are graded to-day, but in the 17th and 18th centuries the finer needles were the more popular, the finest being no thicker than sewing needles and justly described as "wires."

CURVED
NEEDLES

GUARDS AND CASES

When not in use, both points of the needle would be guarded with stoppers of wood or cork, a custom which led to a pretty fashion of decorative guards. These might be carved and studded with precious or semi-precious stones, or made of miniature horns, such as those of the Swiss chamois (*Fig.* 10). These guards fitted over the ends of the needle points, and were, before the advent of elastic, connected with a small spring or leather thong. In the Victor-ian era, little corks were covered with knitted caps for the same purpose. Carved fig-ures, such as Dutch dolls (*Fig.* 11), Darby and Joan, Punch and Judy, brought humour to the habit.

Long cylindrical needle cases for containing the needles became

Fig. 10
Swiss Needle Guards

Fig. 11. Needle Guards

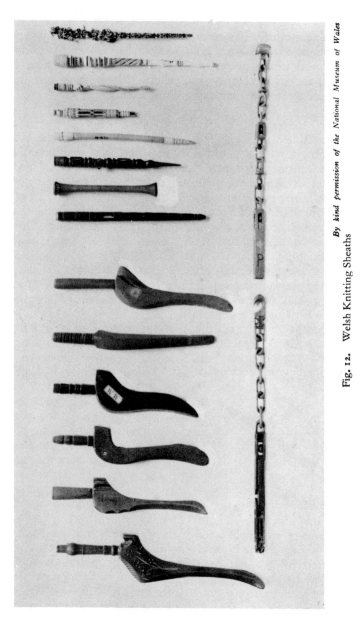

By kind permission of the National Museum of Wales

Fig. 12.   Welsh Knitting Sheaths

another vogue. These might be made of carved ivory or wood, and were often gold mounted. Skin cases, made of sheepskin complete with wool, or of sealskin or sable, also exist, and in the hands of a jeweller these objects were made the excuse for rare and expensive presents.

SHEATHS, STICKS AND POUCHES

Knitting sheaths, or sticks, as they were sometimes called, are now a feature of museum interest, but at one time, when hand knitting was a vast and flourishing industry and speed a matter of pence, every knitter owned and used these implements. The group of Welsh knitting sheaths shown in *Fig.* 12 are typical of the designs in universal use, those with the chains and hooks at the bottom being the most interesting. One of these, from Caerphilly, bears the date 1733–4. This hook had a special use, as will be explained.

The lengthened sheath was known as a knitting stick, and *Fig.* 13 shows three of German origin. Each sheath or stick had a small bore down the middle of the narrow end, large enough to admit a knitting needle.

Sheaths or sticks were used by both men and women knitters, and were worn on the right hip, tucked into a leather

belt or through the strings of the apron. Those of scimitar shape in *Fig.* 12 take the form of the body when slipped through the apron strings. The right needle was placed into the bore, and the right hand, thus freed of supporting the needle, was placed close up over the needle point, the forefinger acting as a shuttle, making the least possible movement and attaining a speed of 200 odd stitches a minute. (*See Fig.* 5.)

Fig. 13
German Knitting Sticks

Balance was maintained with the thumb and other fingers, and these "played" the stitches downwards as they were knitted off the left needle with a rhythmical movement, similar to playing a flute, while the left hand in turn played the stitches up to the point of the left needle.

There seems no record of the knitting stick being worn on

the left hip, by which we might suppose the introduction of the knitting stick (perhaps a Guild invention) inspired the transference of the working yarn to the right hand, and made obsolete the older left-handed hook technique.

The Shetland knitter to this day uses a knitting pouch as shown in *Fig.* 14. This is a sort of oval pad stuffed with horse-hair, covered with leather, and perforated with little holes, large enough to take the point of the needle. Into any of these holes the end of the needle is inserted (*Fig.* 15), and the same incredible speed of 200 odd stitches a minute is attained, the hand working in the same way as with the knitting stick.

As the knitting grows in length it is attached to the left hip with a safety-pin, and until it is long enough for this purpose a length of wool is threaded through the base and wound

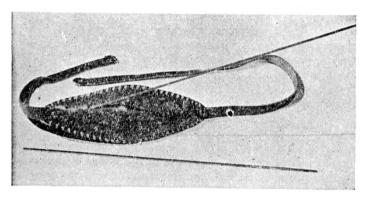

Fig. 14. Shetland Knitting Pouch and Needles

round a safety-pin. The old workers had a hook, suspended from the belt or the end of the knitting sheath, for the same purpose (*see Fig.* 12). By attaching the work to the back of the body in this way the necessary "pull," which is such an aid to speed, is obtained. (*See Fig.* 5.)

This habit reflects some light on the old story that certain so-called "odd-minded" old women walked about with their knitting dangling from their backs! They did, and because this was a handy way of carrying the knitting. A Shetland knitter will drop her work at any moment and

Fig. 15
Pouch in use

attend to other business, and, the job completed, resume her knitting with no loss of time. So well does she gauge her tension that the needles never fall out. On larger fabrics, cork guards will prevent this disaster.

But, though the use of the knitting sheath may be obsolete to the modern knitter, the idea still survives in the rural districts of Britain and Europe. In northern Scotland the countrywomen will fix their right needle into a bunch of feathers thrust through the belt, while the Devonshire and Cornish women will use a twist of straw tucked through their apron strings, or make a

long, narrow straw cushion which they call a knitting Cushion or Truss. These cushions measure about 10 in. × 3 in., and the straw envelopes of champagne bottles are now eagerly sought as stuffing, since they keep the cushion stiff and shapely. The envelope is cut across the middle and is sufficient for two cushions. The knitting pouch is

Fig. 16.   Spool Knitting

still used in the Scandinavian countries and is exported from there, to the Shetlands. Old knitting sheaths and sticks were often handsomely carved, and decorated with mottoes or the initials of the owners. Luxurious ones were made of carved ivory or amber. Both Belgium and France (Boulogne) have very fine collections. Tin knitting sticks were made as an experiment in America during the Great War.

FRAMES AND SPOOLS

Other implements used in knitting were oval and circular frames, fitted with pegs, over which the stitches were lifted with a bent nail fixed into a wooden handle, or with the fingers. The number of pegs would vary from 40 to 200, according to purpose. (*See page* 114.) The most familiar relic of this form of knitting is the Cotton-Spool Knitting (*Fig.* 16) done by children to make reins or whipcords.

MODERN NEEDLES AND PINS

Every sort of material, from steel to powdered milk, is now used to make the modern knitting needle or pin: wood, briar, bone, steel, nickel-plated steel, aluminium, lacquered aluminium, erinoid, casein, galalith, vulcanite, tortoiseshell, etc., etc. All these, and in every conceivable colour, are at the command of the modern knitter, who in making her choice should remember the old axiom: "The business end of the pin is the point," and see that this is long and tapering. In fancy knitting, when "knit 2 together" is the order of the pattern, a good point is most essential.

Any kind of pin or needle will grow blunt in use, and when it is realised that a jumper will contain as many as 20,000 stitches, and that the point of the needle will dig as many times, this can be appreciated. The old knitters ground their points because they loved their old needles, which they considered more "comfortable." To-day it is simpler to buy another pair. A blunt needle will fray the yarn and diminish speed.

The modern tendency to knit with thicker yarns has necessitated the introduction of extra large sizes in both needles and pins. These should be selected for their lightness, as heavy pins in large sizes are tiring to use.

Pins can be stiff or flexible according to preference, but a bent pin will cause an irregularity of tension.

Stiff pins were used for speed when knitting sticks were worn, and are still preferred by quick knitters for this purpose. Flexible pins of composition have a certain intimate comfort which pleases many workers, who must back their choice by learning to knit lightly and so avoid bending the pins.

When buying knitting pins or needles, always choose the best. They last longer, and give greater pleasure in working. The novice will find the work so much easier. The adept does not need this advice.

Knitting Pins are sold in pairs, but knitting Needles are sold in packets containing four or five needles. The latter is Continental in custom, as there Round knitting is worked with five instead of four needles. The needles used on any one piece of work must all be of the same thickness;

otherwise an irregularity of gauge will occur. Freak gauges, when needles are deliberately mixed, for pattern effect is another matter.

CIRCULAR NEEDLES

These are made in several lengths and of flexible wire, which is developed either end into a pointed knitting needle whereby a circular garment, such as a skirt or a vest, can be knitted in an endless spiral. New circular pins should never be bent to shape. They take their own natural curvature as the work progresses, and in bending a pin it is often misshapened.

NEEDLE AND PIN GAUGES

Needle gauges are made of steel, tin, celluloid, or cardboard, and are a means of measuring the different sizes in knitting needles. An interesting collection of needle gauges, as used in different countries, is shown in *Fig.* 17: No. 1, British (bell gauge), which has been in use 100 odd years; Nos. 2 and 3, modern French gauges; Nos. 4 and 5, American gauges; No. 6, German; and No. 7, Swedish. The shapes all vary. The means of ascertaining the measurements also vary. In the bell gauge the needle is passed between a regulated open aperture. In the French, American and German the needle passes through a regulated hole, and in the Swedish gauge the measurement is made by means of a graduated open space.

METHOD OF MEASURING

To measure the size of a needle, pass it sideways through the aperture or vertically through a hole, according to the type and make of gauge. The space which the needle clears represents the size. This will be numbered upon the gauge. Remember it is △ the body part of the pin which gives the measurement, and not the point, so make the measurement about halfway up the needle or pin. Occasionally the fit is a little close, but providing the needle will not enter the previous aperture, and runs loosely through the succeeding space, the size will be as the gauge records. "Tight fits" are rare, but they do occur, as a decimal in the thickness or thinness of a wire will cause ease or slight resistance, in making the measurement.

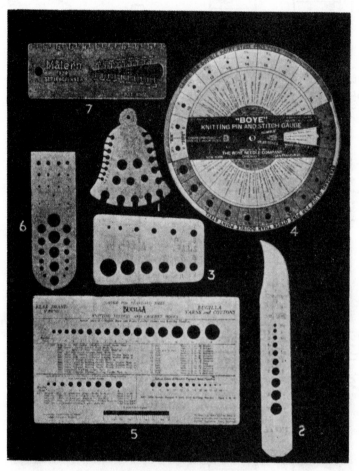

Fig. 17. Knitting Needle Gauges

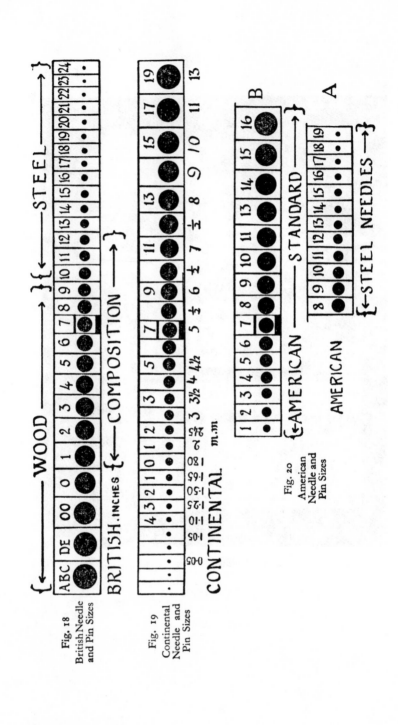

Fig. 18
British Needle
and Pin Sizes

Fig. 19
Continental
Needle and
Pin Sizes

Fig. 20
American Needle and
Pin Sizes

Composition pins are apt to vary a little more, though every effort is made to keep the gauge, needle or pin as accurately standard as bulk production will permit.

SIZES: NEEDLES AND PINS

The sizes of British knitting pins and needles are based on the inch measurement and given in numbers, sizes 1 to 24, the same measurements being used for △ all types of needles or pins. (*See Fig.* 18.) The numbers commence with the large sizes and diminish to the smallest size, those before Size 1 being extra large wooden needles.

Continental needles and pins are based on the millimetre measurement, and given in numbers (sizes) and decimal (mm.) measurement. On a Continental knitting gauge, therefore, each aperture will have two methods of numbering, the size being recorded in numbers above the hole, and the measurements (millimetre) beneath. These sizes will not tally with the British sizes, as the numbering commences in the opposite direction, with the small sizes, and increases in size with the numbers (*see Fig.* 19).

In America both inch and millimetre measurements are used. Steel needles (i.e. double pointed) are measured and numbered the same as British steel needles, the small sizes △ being the higher numbers (*see Fig.* 20 A). Pins (or other than double pointed steel needles) are measured in millimetres, the small sizes △ being the lower numbers, according to the Continental principle (*see Fig.* 20 B).

If these differences in needle measurements are remembered, there will not be so much confusion in working from the knitting instructions of other countries; also a needle gauge of any country can always be obtained by special order, and thus eliminate all possible doubt. Size No. 7, it should be noted, is common to all countries.

A FULL RANGE AND USES

Every knitter should own a complete range of knitting pins and needles, as in *Fig.* 21, as these are the mechanical means of controlling the size of the stitch and in consequence the dimensions of the fabric, which can thus be increased or decreased in size by a change of needle and without a change to the number of stitches. No one needle size will produce every effect desired, even on one garment. Each yarn demands its own particular size in needles, certain technical effects can only be obtained by change of needle and, with a complete set to choose from, the best results are automatically achieved.

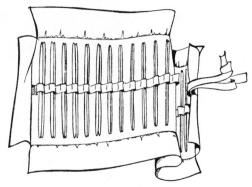

Fig. 21.   Needle Case

Needles, correctly used, are a lively means of shaping and refining the fabric, and by keeping a complete set in orderly arrangement, as in *Fig.* 21, the right size can be selected intelligently and quickly.

"FREAK" GAUGE PATTERNS

Needles in their own right can become a means of pattern

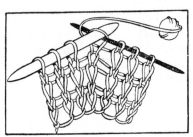

Fig. 22.   Freak Gauge Knitting

formation, and the idea of using one large needle and one small needle (*Fig.* 22) together on the same row in order to vary the gauge of the stitch was a trick well known to the old workers. They developed the idea, and to good effect, in open lace patterns. The odd needle might be used every fourth or sixth row, or perhaps every other row, according to pattern and effect required.

KNITTING YARNS

K NITTING YARNS are spun from wool, hair, silk, rayon, flax, hemp, cotton and metal, and each is subjected to so many various treatments and mixtures that the number of different knitting yarns now on the market is legion. The most important modern yarn is rayon. The others appear known to the old world. Modern knitting yarns are purchased ready for knitting, dyed in fast colours and unshrinkable. Think of the labour saved, and of the long process doing this at home, as was once the custom. Yet, in spite of machine perfection, there is still a desire for hand-made yarns.

The finest and softest of these come from the Shetland Isles, where the hair or staple of the sheep is so fine and long that it permits of the finest spinning, a single hair alone being used for the very best. (*See page 6.*)

With the departure of spinning from the home, the knitter lost some intrinsic interest of her craft, which can now only be regained by understanding the methods as carried out by the manufacturers. This knowledge gives a reasonable understanding of tension control.

OLD MARKETS

The ancient Saxon centre of the wool industry in Britain was Kent, and later Dorset, where the small town of Wool in that county yet reminds us of this forgotten fame. Norwich, too, was a flourishing wool centre in Tudor days, and the village of Worsted, hard by, bestowed its name on the best wool then produced in this district. This name is still used in classifying knitting yarns.

With the advent of machinery, the wool centres migrated to Yorkshire, and homespun wool became almost unknown in England, though the craft still survived in Scotland, and still survives in the outlying districts.

RAW MATERIALS

Wool. The rearing of sheep for the sake of their fleece was already an established occupation in early biblical days, and a map of the ancient world, showing the production of raw

materials for clothing (Yates, *The Art of Weaving Among the Ancients*), reveals the activity ultimately extended from southern-most Arabia, Persia, north to the Rhine, west to Britain (Kent) and south to Spain, Arabia being the greatest of them all. The sheep were rarely used for meat (as a sheep reared for its fleece does not make good mutton) and were only killed for sacrifice; they existed in vast herds, with a shepherd, and several underlings, to whom each sheep was known by name.

MOUNTAIN SHEEP   Demosthenes mentions the care bestowed on the flocks, and the practice of covering the Attic sheep with skins to preserve and refine their fleece! Pan was the happy, nomadic god of the Arcadian shepherds.

Other raw materials then in use were flax from Egypt, the Persian Gulf, Dead Sea and Flanders; silk from China; hemp, north of the Rhine; and cotton from India. The range was extensive, and covered the world as then known.

To-day, the world has become larger, and, in addition to the old sources, our wool comes from Australia, New Zealand and the Argentine; cotton from South Carolina and Georgia (Sea Island), Peru and still India; flax from Ireland, New Zealand and northern Europe; hemp from China and Japan. Silk comes from China, Japan, India and southern Europe, though silkworms in varying quantities are bred in most countries. The finest silk is mulberry fed. Wild silk fed on oak and jujupa leaves in China is coarser. Floss is the residue of silk, rayon the produce of wood fibre.

All these various raw materials are used for knitting yarns, besides the fleece of other animals: the soft, silky hair of the Indian Cashmere goat; alpaca, the wool of the Peruvian llama; mohair, the long, glossy, silky hair of the Angora goat; angora, the unglossy hair of a rabbit; vicuna, the soft, silky wool of

the South American vicugna; yak
hair; camel hair. Lamb's wool is
that obtained from the first shearing.

WOOL YARNS

These yarns are classified under
two main headings: (1) Woollen
yarns and (2) Worsted yarns, in accordance with the general principles
of spinning. All wool yarns are
carded but after this operation wool-
en yarns are condensed direct into
rovings, from which the yarn is spun.

ANGORA

Worsted yarns, however, are gilled, combed and drawn before
being spun. Thus Worsted yarns are smoother, more regular
and may be spun into finer counts than Woollen yarns, the latter
being usually of thick 2 ply only. A comparison of fingering
and cashmere (both worsteds) with wheeling and cable yarns
(woollens) will show the difference in the results. Because of
the condensing process Woollen yarns can be spun from shorter
fibres, and cheaper kinds can be made from remanufactured
materials (shoddy) produced on a woollen principle. Few of
this type will stand unravelling and in wash tend to felt.

PREPARATION

There are many different qualities of wool in one fleece, as
shown in *Fig.* 23.
The best and
longest staples
come from the
shoulder, neck,
flank and rump.
The longest are
used for weaving.
The average
length staple used
in the best knitting
yarns is from 2½″
to 4″.

Fig. 23. The Values of a Fleece

The first process,

then, is sorting and grading the different qualities and lengths. Yarn carelessly sorted and spun with uneven staples would be rough, like some of the peasant yarns. The next process is cleaning, to remove all the twigs, thistles, etc. The wool is then scoured, dyed and made into rolls ready for spinning.

Other raw materials are in turn subjected to equally long and tedious processes.

Linen yarns, derived from flax, the fibrous covering of the linum plant, are rippled, retted, scutched and heckled. The coarse fibres, when separated, are called tow; the finer, line. These are sorted and graded and made ready for spinning.

Silk is unwound from the cocoon already spun by the silk-worm, though in order to obtain a long unbroken length the pupæ within the cocoon must be killed by immersion in hot water. It is then reeled and thrown. Certain pupæ must emerge for breeding purposes, and these eat their way out of the cocoon, reducing the silk to short lengths, which are prepared, spun and known as Spun silk. Floss silk is made from the soft external covering of the cocoon.

Cotton is derived from the cotton plant, and undergoes a long preparation of opening, scutching, carding, combing, drawing, spinning and doubling, all in a humid atmosphere.

SPINNING AND TWISTING

After this long preparation, yarn-making really begins. The first process is spinning, which converts the different raw

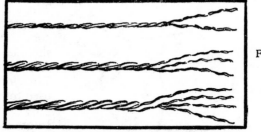

Fig. 24
Plys

materials into a single strand or one ply. This ply can be of any thickness, but it is not suitable to knit with a single ply yarn, so two or more plys must be folded by a second process in order to make it a workable yarn. This process is called doubling. A 2-ply is the least. Wool can be 2, 3, 4, 5, 6, 7, or 8 plyed, or even more. (*See Fig. 24.*)

A yarn can be lightly or firmly spun and twisted. The lightly spun and twisted yarns are soft and can be of any thickness. Those in pure wool of this description are delightful to feel, but not so hard-wearing as those more firmly spun and twisted. Fancy twisting is noted separately.

Cotton yarns are generally 3-fold, whether they be thick or thin, as in cotton it is the size of the ply and not the number which must be increased to make the yarn thicker. This is why cotton is sold in sizes, and not by the number of plys. Cotton yarns are first doubled or plyed and then corded. Mercerising is a strengthening process given to cotton; it also imparts sheen. Lightly twisted cotton yarns are called stranded.

Spun silk and rayon yarns are corded or pearled, and also sold by size. Some are loaded. Rayon yarns can be bright or delustred and are sensitive to climate.

QUALITY

All plys are not spun to the same size so that yarns vary with each different manufacturer. A yarn made by one may be thicker or thinner than that made by another, but this does not mean it is better in quality. Wool is of the same substance as hooves and teeth and can be coarse or fine according to climatic conditions and feed. A coarse hair may be rough or scaled, and so inclined to mat or felt. A fine wool hair is usually smooth and wavy and it is this wavy property which assists in the spinning of fine yarns, so that the term "quality" as understood, applies to the spinning properties of the fibres. Coarse yarns are produced from coarse fibres, devoid of crimp or curl, but fine yarns from fine wavy fibres. Short coarse fibres are used for cheap woollen yarns, and long coarse fibres for cheap worsted yarns, whilst soft high class yarns are spun only from the fine wools of specially selected sheep. Obviously then, a yarn required to be luxurious to handle and wear, may not possess the same wearing properties as one of a coarse and harsher material, but it will possess that extra quality of comfort. Length of staple improves the wearing properties of a yarn, and to ascertain this the individual fibres must be separated, first as in Fig. 24, and then to a single hair or staple, but the quality of softness and elasticity must remain the essential features of yarns which are to contact the skin, hence the selection of wool is governed by the purpose for which the yarn is required, and naturally the price at which it is to be sold.

FANCY YARNS

The spinning and twisting of different yarns permits of great variation and artistry in yarn-making. This is usually done in the folding process, when the plys are united. There are several methods and each manufacturer has his own processes

IRREGULAR TWISTING

Bouclé (a French term, meaning to curl). This is usually a 3-ply yarn. The process begins with two of the plys, one of which is fed into the machine faster than the other, the relative speed producing loops or curls of varying size. This 2-fold yarn is then twisted with a single ply in reverse direction to the other. The process can be applied to wool, cotton, silk, linen and mixtures, and has many kindred names and variations. Bouclette, small curls.

MIXTURES

This process can add a contrast of colour or of fabric to a yarn. (1) A mixture of colours is obtained by twisting together two or more matching plys and one of a contrasting colour, making a 3-ply yarn with a marled effect. (2) A mixture of fabric is obtained in the same way, making the third ply of silk, rayon or cotton in either a self or contrasting colour.

FLECKED YARNS

In the flecked variety, little knobs of wool or cotton in different colours are added (thrown in) during the spinning process, or, as in bouclé, two plys can be fed irregularly into the machine, one being suddenly released at intervals so that it winds on itself and forms a knob or knop. There is self knop and coloured knop. (Knop or Knopf, German term meaning head or knot.) Example: knop, homespun, tweed wools, etc.

In the hairy variety, tiny wisps of hair are added during the spinning process, usually white in colour. These added to a coloured wool produce misty effects called mist shades—morning mist, etc.

Another method is to add kemp wool during the spinning

process. Kemp is coarse, dead hair, and will not dye. After twisting, the yarn is dyed in the hank, the kemp hair always remaining white. Example: kempy, kemp knit, etc.

CRÊPE YARNS

These are given an extra twisting process, first 2-fold and then 4-fold. A 2-ply crêpe is therefore 4-fold, and a 3-ply 6-fold. Another method is to twist the different plys together in the opposite direction to that in which they were spun, producing a fancy cord. These methods are applied mainly to silk, rayon and cotton yarns. The process will delustre a wool and give what is known as a suède appearance.

Corded Yarn is obtained by twisting two yarns, already twisted, together in the opposite direction.

Pearl is a high twist 2-ply yarn the folding twist being in the opposite direction to that of the singles. Applied to silk, cotton or wool.

Floss hyphenated to a name implies a mixture: linen-floss, Shetland-floss, etc.

Lustre hyphenated to a name implies a mixture of rayon and some other yarn. Lustre or sheen are rayon yarns.

HOW TO USE YARNS

Such diversity of yarn production has complicated the question of tension very considerably, as each yarn has its own tension, which varies in common with the tension of the spinning. It is, therefore, necessary to understand a little of the different "twisting" processes in order to tension the different yarns with knowledge and understanding. Loosely spun and twisted yarn should be more loosely tensioned, firmer spun and twisted yarn more firmly tensioned.

A thick yarn will run through the fingers quicker than a fine one, as it has further to travel in making a stitch because of its size. It therefore needs an easy tension.

Over-tensioned wools, such as crêpe and suède, need a firmer tension than worsted yarns, as in the double twisting process they have lost much of their elasticity, and are but little more elastic than cotton.

Cotton yarns, which have not the elasticity of wool, need a much firmer tension, otherwise the fabric will drop, and, when washed, will need re-blocking. Silk, rayon and mercerised yarns, which have a polished surface, also need a firm control, otherwise they spring too readily through the fingers, causing the fabric to become uneven. Run the yarn through the fingers; its tension will soon be ascertained by the feel. (*See also page* 43.)

PATTERN

A fancy yarn limits the number of patterns in which the fabric can be knitted, as it is of itself decorative, and loses character when produced in elaborate stitches. Its beauty is greatly enhanced by style and fit.

A plain yarn, on the contrary, permits of elaborate stitchery, and with these the true art of knitting best finds expression.

TO WIND WOOL

All wool △ is naturally elastic, and is spun to retain this elasticity, which should not be lost in the process of winding the yarn from the hank into a ball, as to wind yarn too tightly is to stretch it beyond the natural tension set by the spinner. Different yarns need different methods of winding.

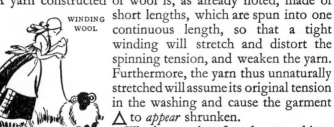

A yarn constructed of wool is, as already noted, made of WINDING WOOL short lengths, which are spun into one continuous length, so that a tight winding will stretch and distort the spinning tension, and weaken the yarn. Furthermore, the yarn thus unnaturally stretched will assume its original tension in the washing and cause the garment △ to *appear* shrunken.

Wool must, therefore, be wound into a soft pliable ball so that its original elastic quality is retained. Each ball must be wound to the same tension, and better wound by one person. Mixtures and cotton yarns, a few of which are still sold in hanks, can be wound tighter.

There are two ways of winding wool yarn into a ball.

BALL WINDING (1)

Lay the yarn lightly and several times round three fingers of the right hand, allowing the wool controlled by the left hand to pass lightly through the fingers. When sufficient turns have been made, slip the coils from the fingers, change the position, and continue to add more layers, winding over the fingers and slipping it on to the ball as shown in *Fig.* 25. This will avoid any strain. Continue winding until the entire hank has been formed into a nice, well-shaped, pliable ball.

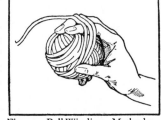

Fig. 25. Ball Winding. Method 1

This is the more usual method of winding wool, but should the ball be dropped it will roll far and quickly unwind. To prevent this, the ball should be wound so that the yarn is drawn from the centre, a method of winding particularly practical when knitting in several different coloured wools, as each ball "stays put" and does not △ roll and become entangled with the others.

BALL WINDING (2)

To draw from centre, hold the end of yarn in the palm of the hand as in *Fig.* 26 A, and wind the yarn over the thumb and forefinger in the form of a figure eight as shown. Make a good thick wad, and then with

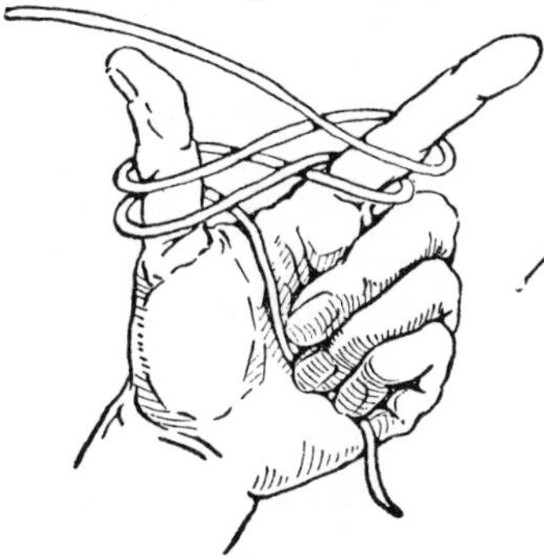

A

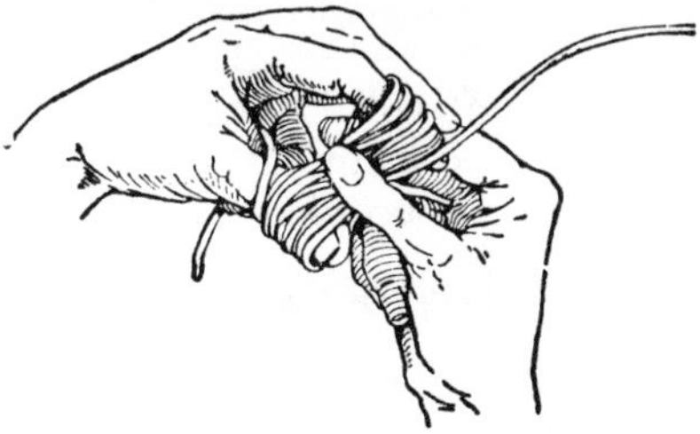

B

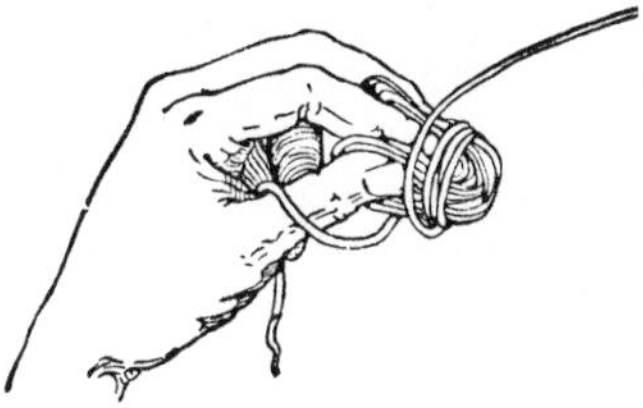

Fig. 26
Ball Winding
Method 2

C

D

the thumb and finger of the right hand grasp it in the middle as shown in *Fig.* 26 B. Slip this carefully off the fingers so as not to disturb the formation or the end of yarn still retained in the palm of the hand. Now fold the "eight" over the forefinger as in *Fig.* 26 C, and continue winding as shown. Note the original end of yarn, which must never be lost. Wind loosely, and, when sufficient turns have been added, change the position again and continue as in *Fig.* 26 D, and so on until the whole hank has been wound into a nice, well-shaped ball, the last few turns being made round the centre of the ball to form a band, into which the end is finally tucked away. The ball is now finished, and, providing the yarn has not been wound too tightly after the start, the original end of yarn can be conveniently pulled out from the centre, as in a ball of string.

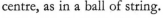

BALL WINDING (3)

WINDING WOOL
PRE-FLOOD

Silk and cotton yarns are usually purchased already balled, but artificial silks and mixtures are often hanked, and in winding these into a ball it is better to start on a foundation of cardboard, using two strips folded in the form of a cross. This keeps the centre of the ball firm. In winding, it will be found necessary to rotate the ball freely, since, if too many layers are added in one position, they will slip off and become entangled.

JOINING YARNS

Wool can be quite invisibly joined by splicing, but silk, cotton and rayon yarns are more conveniently joined at the beginning of a row. For silk yarns, leave the old end and start knitting with the new ball end, and, after knitting a few stitches, the two ends can be joined with a reef knot, and in seaming they will never show. In round knitting, all yarns should be spliced, and those which cannot conveniently be divided should be "woven" as in Colour knitting, adding and weaving in the new yarn before the old is quite exhausted and then knitting with the new yarn and weaving in the old end.

JOINING ANOTHER COLOUR

A new colour is usually introduced at the beginning of a row in flat knitting, or at the △ beginning of a round in round knitting. Knit the first stitch in the new colour, leaving an end of 3″ to 5″, according to pattern and thickness of yarn, and then take the two ends, the new and the old together, and proceed to weave them in as explained in weaving. Colour knitting, *Figs*. 99 to 101, *page* 101. If the yarn is extra thick it is better to weave in the new ball, or weave in the new first, as above, and weave in the old end later. Springy yarns, such as rayon (artificial silk), etc., are better always joined in this manner. Weave the knit rows.

SPLICING

Any join made in the middle of the row is more invisible when spliced. Separate the ply of the yarn on the new ball to a distance of about 5″ and cut away half the number of strands as in *Fig*. 27. Do the same on the knitting end of the yarn, and lay the two half-ply ends over each other so that they overlap, and then twist them together as shown in *Fig*. 27. Continue knitting with the twisted yarn, and on completion of the work trim the ends.

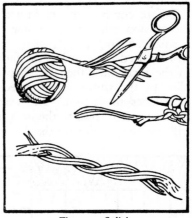

Fig. 27. Splicing

Woollen yarns should be frayed and the two ends laid together and twisted as explained. Very fine 2-ply wool can be rolled together without dividing. When working in open or lace patterns, △ avoid joining in the middle of a row. In round knitting △ avoid joining on a pattern line.

GAUGE AND TENSION

THE GAUGE, or size, of a stitch is determined by the size of the knitting pins or needles, and these in turn will be selected according to the size or thickness of the yarn.

Tension is the strain put upon the yarn by the knitter. Gauge then is mechanical, but Tension is personal control.

GAUGE

A knitted fabric is measured by counting the number of stitches to the inch, which gives the △ width measurement, and by counting the number of rows or rounds to the inch, which gives the △ depth measurement. (*See Fig.* 28.)

Before commencing to knit a fabric, both the gauge and the tension must be ascertained beforehand by knitting up a small square, 4″ × 4″, using the needles and yarn which will be used for knitting the fabric. The number of stitches to the inch must then be counted, and the number, multiplied by the width of fabric required, will give the number of stitches to cast-on. The vertical measurement will give the number of rows to the inch, and a multiplication of these will give the position for the shaping (increasing or decreasing).

In *Fig.* 28, there are six stitches to the inch, and eight rows to the inch.

Example:

Gauge. Pins size 8. American standard size 6.

Yarn 4-ply.

6 stitches to the inch.

8 rows to the inch.

Width required 20″.

6 × 20 = 120.

Cast-on 120 stitches.

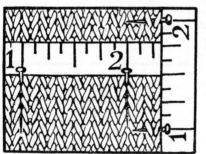

Fig. 28

Measuring the Gauge of a Fabric

The fabric will thus commence with a width of 20″, but is required to be 24″ wide, i.e. two extra inches either side, when it is a depth of 8″. There are 8 rows to the inch, so

$$8 \times 8 = 64 \text{ rows or } 8″ \text{ of fabric.}$$

The 4″ of extra stitches needed will be calculated so:

$$4 \times 6 = 24 \text{ extra stitches.}$$

As these are to be added either side, two increases must be made in a row, so we get:

12 increasing rows, with two increases in each.

Divide 12 into $64 = 5$ and 4 rows over.

Knit 3 rows and after this increase at the beginning and end of every fifth row 12 times. Knit the last 2 rows without increasing. This will equal 64 rows, and the fabric should now be 24″ wide.

RE-GAUGING

A gauge can be automatically varied as the fabric is knitted by using larger or smaller needles or pins. This is a mechanical change, like varying the stitch gauge on a sewing machine. Re-gauging in this manner is useful to tighten up or slacken a fabric

GAUGE!

as required, and, correctly used, can be of great value in refining and shaping a garment.

NEEDLE SIZES

The difference made to a fabric by a change in the size of needles is about half a stitch to the inch, providing the same yarn is used. For example, a fabric knitted on needles size 6 may have $5\frac{1}{4}$ stitches to the inch, on size 7, $5\frac{3}{4}$ stitches, size 8, $6\frac{1}{4}$ stitches, and so on. It is impossible to give any accurate decimal, as there is no standard of plying or cording a yarn, which makes it so necessary to gauge anew with every different yarn before commencing to knit. Otherwise there is no means of deriving accurate measurements.

Some guide to the correct size of needle to use with each different yarn can be obtained by folding the yarn once round the needle. Hold the two ends together, close to the needle, without straining, and then remove the needle. The aperture so revealed should about equal in size that of the united width of the two yarns. If the space closes up, try a larger needle; if it is too open, try a smaller. Take the selected needles and knit up a small square, and, if this proves satisfactory, carry on.

Fig. 28 reveals that in Stocking Stitch Fabric the yarn travels in an evenly waved journey from side to side. If the needle is too large, the fabric will be elongated, and, if too small, it will be over-broad. The number of rows to the inch (vertical) should average about one-third more than the number of stitches to the inch in Flat knitting. In Round knitting they will be fewer.

CORRECT GAUGE

Gauging is very fascinating, and every knitter should make the experiment. Choose a yarn—a 3-ply is a good average—and commence with fine needles on about 30 stitches, changing to one size larger every 10 rows. Knit in Stocking Stitch, and mark each change with a row of Purl, and cover some 8 to 10 different sizes in needles. This test will reveal many things. For instance, a yarn that is gauged too finely becomes bulky, and, when washed, board-like. On the other hand, if it is gauged too loosely it loses the character of the stitch and pattern. The ideal gauge produces a firm, soft and elastic fabric, one that will wash and retain its character and beauty.

Children's garments, especially undergarments, so often in the wash-tub, need a larger gauge than garments like jumpers and cardigans, which need infrequent washing. A large gauge produces an open, loose fabric, peculiarly hygienic and warm for underwear, bed-wraps, etc., and very warm when knitted in soft yarns.

TENSION

Good tension is acquired by allowing the yarn to run easily over the fingers when knitting, the control being even, neither strained nor slack, but masterly. The finger controlling the yarn is analogous to the tension control of a sewing or knitting machine, which never varies once the gauge is set for one particular **yarn** or the fabric will be irregular. Tension, then, must be complementary to the yarn in use, and should be slightly slackened with thicker yarn and tightened with finer yarns.

A new tension has to be learnt, or felt, with each yarn, and a new mental adjustment made. (*See also page* 35.) If the yarn is tensioned too tightly the knitting becomes tight, and the stitches will not move upon the needles. The yarn is also inclined to fray, and the knitter to become tired and weary.

In correctly tensioned knitting the stitches cling to the needles with sufficient elasticity to allow the needle to move, without allowing it to fall out of its own accord. (*See page* 22.)

Two people rarely work to the same tension, and a fabric commenced by one knitter cannot with success be finished by a second, as tension is something personal.

CORRECT TENSION

Hold the needles and yarn lightly, easily. Knitting is a pastime; there should be nothing grim about it. Pass the yarn over the needle and, once it has "clicked" past the crossed needles, do not strain, but take the loop through, and off the needle.

Insert the needle into the next loop, and here, if necessary, tighten the yarn a little before throwing it to form the next stitch.

Knitting which averages out too wide, while retaining the correct depth, is due to there being too much width between the stitches, and the extra adjustment before making the next stitch will correct this.

EXACT TENSION

This is "knitting to a given tension" or to written directions, where the gauge has been set by the author of the instructions (not the knitter), stating so many stitches and rows to the inch: needles —, yarn —.

Under these circumstances it is absolutely essential to knit up a square of fabric, using the needles and yarn quoted, to find if your tension produces the same gauge as the author's. It may or it may not. Your tension may be slacker or tighter than the gauge stated, in which case it is better to change the needles, using a size larger or smaller according to the result of the test, rather than try a deliberate control of tension by knitting tighter or slacker, as is sometimes advised. Tension is a personal thing and cannot thus be forced.

KNITTING TERMS

The following terms and abbreviations have been used throughout this book:

K.	Knit.
K.1.	Knit one stitch.
P.	Purl.
P.1.	Purl one stitch.
K.2 tog.	Knit 2 stitches together.
P.2 tog.	Purl 2 ,, ,,
K.2 tog. B.	Knit 2 stitches together through the back of the loops.
S.1.	Slip one stitch without knitting it.
S.1,K.1,p.s.s.o.	Slip one stitch knitwise. Knit the next and insert the needle into the slipped stitch, and pass it over the knitted stitch.
P.R.	Purl Reverse, or P.1. r.l.n. (return left needle). S.1., p.n.s.o. (pass next stitch over).
S.1, K.2 tog, p.s.s.o.	Double Increase Knit.
P.2 tog, S.1, p.s.s.o.	Double Increase Purl.
S.2,K.1,P.2,s.s.o.	(Pass 2 s.s. over.) Double Increase K.
P.R.D.	Purl Reverse Double.
M.1.	Make an invisible increase.
M.1 (B).	A made stitch by bar increase.
M.1 (L).	,, ,, ,, ,, lifted ,,
M.1 (R).	,, ,, ,, ,, raised ,,

M.2 (B).	Double Bar increase.
M.2 (L).	„ Lifted „
M.2 (R).	„ Raised „
O.	Over (yarn over needle). Visible increase.
O.2.	Yarn twice over needle.
O.1 (C).	Over, as on a Crossed Fabric.

KNIT MOVEMENTS,
STITCH AND FABRIC

THE POSITION of the hands in knitting varies with preference, custom, country and even district. In many countries the use of a knitting stick or pouch still prevails, and, where the custom has ceased, the habit of tucking the right needle under the arm has taken its place. The modern positions for the hands now generally accepted are shown in *Figs.* 29 to 32.

Figs. 29 and 30, in which the yarn is held in the RIGHT hand.

Figs. 31 and 32, in which the yarn is held in the LEFT hand.

Fig. 29.   Knit Position.   English

The former is customary in most English-speaking nations and known as English knitting; the latter is more prevalent on the Continent and in Eastern nations, and is often referred to as German knitting. Either produces a fabric of similar appearance, though in left-hand knitting the method of throwing the yarn and forming the stitch differs considerably in different parts of the world, as will be shown.

YARN IN RIGHT HAND

English Knitting

Fig. 29. Method of forming a Knit Stitch, when the yarn is held in the right hand. The yarn must pass easily over the fingers without hindrance, tension being

Fig. 30.   Purl Position.   English

sustained and controlled by the middle and third finger.

The needle is inserted from front to back of the stitch as shown, and the yarn thrown round the point of the needle and drawn through as a new stitch. The finger action in making the throw must be free and easy.

The position of the fingers in the diagram is exaggerated to show the placing of the yarn.

Fig. 30 shows the position of the hands in forming the Purl movement, the whole action of making the stitch being the reverse of that used in forming the Knit Stitch. The old name for Purl was Reverse Stitch.

YARN IN LEFT HAND.   *Continental Method*

Fig. 31 shows the method of forming the Knit Stitch when the yarn is held in the left hand. In this case tension is sustained

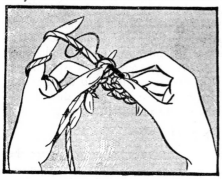

by the forefinger of the left hand, which releases the yarn with a downward shuttle-like movement with the formation of each stitch.

The right needle is inserted through the loop from front to back, the same as in *Fig.* 29, but, instead of the yarn being cast

Fig. 31.   Knit Position.   Continental

to encircle the needle in forming the stitch, the needle is manipulated to encircle the yarn (as shown by the movement of the arrow). In so doing it draws through the new loop or stitch. This manner of knitting demands a supple wrist movement as compared with the right-hand method, which needs a more nimble play of fingers.

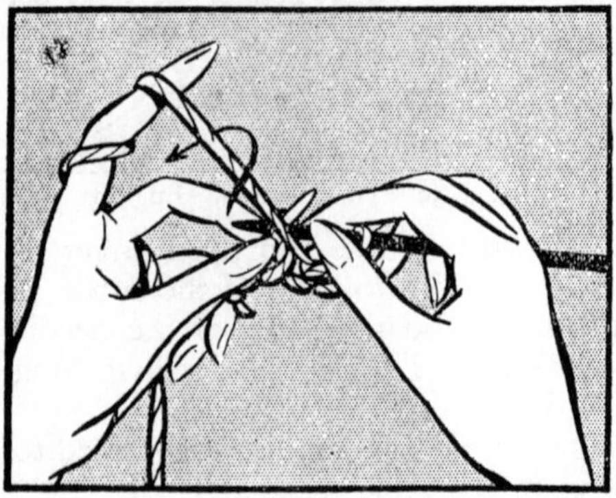

Fig. 32 shows the action of the Purl Stitch, which of necessity is the reverse of the Knit Stitch. The needle is inserted through the front of the stitch as in Fig. 30, and must then be brought forward and over the yarn as indicated by the arrow, thus again creating by the action of the needle a similar movement to that formed in the English method, by the throw of the yarn.

Fig. 32.   Purl Position.   Continental

The needles, for either movement, must be held very lightly with the thumb and middle finger. The first and third fingers merely control without grasping either. The distance between the needles and the forefinger of the left hand is exaggerated in the diagram in order to demonstrate the action. In reality this is close to the needle points, causing the journey of the needle over the yarn to be shorter than that made by the throw of the yarn in the right-hand method, so that greater speed can be attained once the movements are familiar. A Continental knitter will work at tremendous speed. In some districts the yarn is wound some fifty odd times round the left forefinger, as though it were a bobbin, though the double turn, shown in Figs. 31 and 32, is as now taught.

FLAT AND ROUND KNITTING

The hand positions shown in these four diagrams are the same in either Flat Knitting—worked on two knitting pins— or Round Knitting, worked on three or more knitting needles.

In Flat Knitting the fabric is built up in Rows, producing a single fabric, with four selvedges: base, top and two side selvedges. A new row is always formed on the right needle, the knitting advancing stitch by stitch until all the stitches on the left needle are exhausted. This completes one ROW.

Fig. 33.   Round Knitting, 4 Needles

In Round Knitting the fabric is built up in rounds or spirals, producing a tubular fabric open at both ends. Round Knitting has, therefore, only two selvedges: base and top.

A tubular fabric of this description can be knitted: (1) on two needles, using a third for knitting; (2) on three needles, using a fourth for knitting (*see Fig. 33*), or (3) on four needles, using a fifth for knitting (*see Fig. 34*). Large tubular fabrics are now usually constructed on a circular

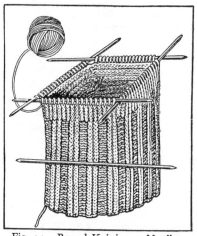

Fig. 34.   Round Knitting, 5 Needles

knitting needle, though in the old days as many as sixteen needles were used for the purpose, and in some districts this habit yet remains.

A round is completed when all the stitches on all the needles have been knitted, and the end of a round should coincide with the tag end of yarn left at the commencement when casting-on the first loop. This

FLAT FABRIC!

ROUND KNITTING

is an invaluable guide, as all rounds commence here, and, should a change of pattern or colour be necessary, it must commence from here, otherwise the commencement of the pattern will be uneven.

A tubular fabric can be produced on two knitting pins by Double Knitting, as described on *page 165*, but this will not be open at the base, and can only be open at the top by a special process of casting-off.

FABRIC CONSTRUCTION

Authorities differ in the number of stitches there are in knitting. Some say two—Knit and Purl—and some one, claiming that the Purl Stitch is merely a Knit Stitch reversed! Of the two, the Knit Stitch is the older. These two movements, Knit and Purl, are the foundation of ALL knitted fabrics, simple or elaborate.

The simplest use of these stitches in fabric construction is shown here, and can be knitted with the yarn in either the right or left hand—though in the majority of diagrams the working method given is right-hand knitting, this being more familiar. Both stitches have two forms of presentation: (1) UNCROSSED; (2) CROSSED, the former being that with which we are now familiar, though up to the Middle Ages the latter was the more popular.

KNIT STITCH—UNCROSSED

Knit Stitch, because of its great antiquity, is known by many names: Knit Stitch, Plain Stitch, Right Stitch, Open Stitch, White Stitch; the latter because in old knitting charts the Knit

A

1st Movement

Fig. 35
Knit Stitch
Uncrossed

B

2nd Movement

Stitches were always represented as white stitches in contrast to the Purl, which were black.

Knit stitch is familiar to all modern knitters. Hold the needle containing the cast-on loops in the left hand, and insert the right needle into the front of the loop as shown in *Fig. 35 A*. The yarn is then passed under the right needle and drawn through as a new loop (*Fig. 35 B*), and the old loop slipped off the left needle. Thus a new row of stitches is always being formed on the right needle. These same movements are repeated with the next and each successive stitch, until all the stitches on the left needle have been knitted off. The knitting needles then exchange hands, and the second row is worked in the same way. This is known as Plain Knit Stitch.

Fig. 36.   Plain Knitting
Garter Stitch

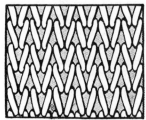

Fig. 37.   Stocking Stitch

Knit Stitch on Two Pins.   A fabric constructed thus on two knitting pins (Flat Knitting), using this one stitch only, is known as Plain Knitting or GARTER STITCH (*Fig. 36*). The surface of this fabric is "rough," as in one row the front of the stitches appear, but in turning the work, as is necessary in Flat Knitting, the back of the stitch must appear on the front of the fabric. This breaks the surface and forms little horizontal ridges, giving an impression of all Purl Knitting, and quite frequently this fabric is confusingly referred to as "Purl fabric" (*see Fig. 38*), whereas in reality it is the only existing fabric constructed entirely of Knit Stitches! Garter Stitch fabric is often referred to as Weft Knitting or Fabric.

PLAIN KNITTING

Knit Stitch on Four Needles. Quite a different fabric is produced when this same knit movement is worked on four needles or in Round Knitting, as the work is not turned at the end of a row, but continued round and round in successive spirals, so that the back of the stitch never shows, to disturb the smooth appearance of the surface. This is, then, technically known as STOCKING STITCH, Stockinette Stitch, or Smooth Fabric (*see Fig.* 37). The back of a Stocking Stitch Fabric is known as Purl Fabric (*see Fig.* 38 A).

In order to form Stocking Stitch on two knitting pins, every other row must be Purled or Reversed.

Stocking Stitch worked on two knitting pins has not the same regularity as Stocking Stitch worked in Round Knitting, because of this reverse movement in every other row, as in reversing the stitch the Purl throw is longer than the Knit throw. In measuring a tension gauge, this will be noticed, as there will be fewer rows in depth than there are rounds, even where the same yarn and needles have been used.

PURL STITCH—UNCROSSED

Other names for Purl Stitch are: Seam Stitch, Black Stitch, Ridge Stitch, Pearl Stitch, Back Stitch, Rib Stitch, Left Stitch, Raised Stitch, Rough Stitch, Wrong Stitch.

With the yarn to the front of the fabric, insert the right needle into the front of the loop as shown in *Fig.* 38 A and pass the yarn over and under the point of the needle, and draw both needles and yarn through the shaded stitch as in *Fig.*

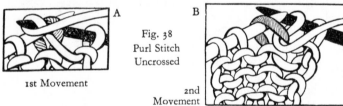

A

Fig. 38
Purl Stitch
Uncrossed

B

1st Movement

2nd
Movement

38 B. The new loop so formed is retained on the right needle as a new stitch, while the shaded loop is slipped off. The same process is repeated on each successive loop until all the stitches from the left needle have been knitted off.

KNIT STITCH—CROSSED. *Right over Left*

This is constructed by inserting the needle through the back of the loop instead of through the front, and so causing the loop of the stitch to cross right over left. In all other respects the movements remain the same. The yarn is to the back in forming the Knit movement (*Fig.* 39), and to the front in forming the Purl movement (*Fig.* 40). The fabric so constructed is known as CROSSED OR TWISTED STOCKING STITCH. When produced on two needles (Flat Knitting), the Purl as

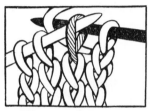

Fig. 39. Knit Stitch Crossed

Fig. 40. Purl Stitch. Crossed

well as the Knit Stitch must be made through the △ back of the loop, otherwise one row will be crossed and the other uncrossed and the fabric neither one thing nor the other.

The "crossed" journey of the yarn right over left can be easily followed in *Figs.* 39 and 40, and these should be compared with *Figs.* 43 and 44 where the stitch is crossed left over right, which is the old Eastern method.

Crossed Stocking Stitch is not so popular to-day as the Uncrossed variety, though it has a better elastic action, such as is needed on belts, garters, bandages, etc.

KNIT STITCH—UNCROSSED (Eastern)

This is formed by reversing both the movements of the yarn and the needles as worked by Western methods, so that the Plain or Uncrossed Knit Stitches are made through the *back* of the loop, while the Crossed Stitches (*Fig.* 43) are made through the front of the loop! The golden rule—yarn to the back for Knit Stitch and to the front for Purl—remains steadfast.

EASTERN
PURL
(Pearl)

Knit movement, *Fig.* 41. **Insert the** right needle into the △ back of the loop and throw the yarn △ over the needle, and draw the new loop through the shaded loop. Notice how the stitches sit upon the needle in the reverse way, the left side of the stitch being to the front instead of to the back, as in *Fig.* 35 B.

The Purl movement is shown in *Fig.* 42, where the right needle is again inserted through the back of the stitch, but the yarn thrown △ under the needle.

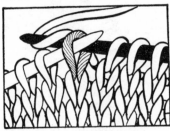

Fig. 41.   Knit Stitch
Uncrossed Eastern

Fig. 42.   Purl Stitch
Uncrossed Eastern

A comparison of the Eastern and Western fabrics reveals that, though these are derived by opposing movements of needle and yarn, the general appearance is much the same. In reality there is a subtle difference. The stitch is more square and the fabric closer, the difference being equal to about two sizes in knitting needles, and, should a very close, firm fabric be desired, such as for pram covers, bathing suits, gloves, etc., then this method of work will produce the desired effect.

KNIT STITCH—CROSSED (EASTERN). *Left over Right*

This is formed by Knitting and Purling into the *front* of the stitch, and throwing the yarn over the needle as in *Fig.* 43 for the Knit Stitch, and under the needle as in *Fig.* 44 to form the Purl Stitch. It should be noted that the resulting stitch is now crossed △ right over left, instead of left over right, as in *Fig.* 39. This method of crossing the stitch seems older, and in all probability this Eastern form of knitting was that practised when hooked knitting needles were in use, and felting (*see page* 3) so popular, since, the construction of the fabric being tighter and the resulting stitch more square, it would "felt" much more successfully. In the South of France, where knitted berets are still felted, this method of work, together with hooked needles (*see page* 16), is still used.

Fig. 43.   Knit Stitch
Crossed Eastern

Fig. 44.   Purl Stitch
Crossed Eastern

KNIT STITCH—UNCROSSED (Combined Method)

This method combines the Western (*Fig.* 39) with the Eastern movement (*Fig.* 44) in forming an uncrossed Knit Stitch, and in Russia and the neighbouring Balkan States this is the accepted mode of knitting.

The Knit Stitch, *Fig.* 45, is formed by inserting the needle through the *back* of the loop and drawing the needle and yarn through as indicated by the arrow, the yarn being held in the left hand.

The Purl Stitch (*Fig.* 46) is made by inserting the needle through the front of the loop, but taking the yarn $\triangle$ *beneath* the

Fig. 45.   Knit Stitch. Uncrossed
(Combined method)

Fig. 46.   Purl Stitch. Uncrossed
(Combined method)

point of the needle. The new stitch will be drawn through as indicated by the arrow.

By this method of work the yarn makes the shortest possible journey in forming either stitch, the distance being the same for either Knit or Purl throw. It is thus claimed, since both throws are of the same length, that this is the better way to work in Flat Knitting. The resulting fabric is more even and closer in construction, and, since knitted fabrics are also still felted in those districts, it felts more evenly. Stocking Stitch when constructed in silk or cotton, and on two pins, has a better appearance knitted by this method.

KNIT STITCH—PLAITED (REVERSE METHOD)

This is a most interesting stitch, formed by reversing the needle movements in *Figs.* 45 and 46. The Knit Stitch, *Fig.* 47, is made by inserting the needle through the front of the stitch as shown. In the first row this will produce ordinary uncrossed Knit Stitch, but the second or Purl movement, shown in *Fig.* 48, where the needle is shown inserted through the back of the stitch and the yarn cast △ *beneath* the point of the right needle, will cross the Knit Stitches below.

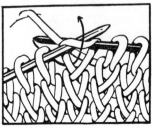

Fig. 47.   Knit Stitch.   Plaited
(Combined method)

Fig. 48.   Purl Stitch.   Plaited
(Combined method)

After this, the fabric will be crossed throughout, as in *Fig.* 47, the Knit Stitch crossing right over left and the Purl left over right, so that a PLAITED fabric is produced.

After washing a fabric knitted in this manner, the plait becomes much more evident, especially in a fairly thick yarn, and many ancient examples of knitting seen in museums are constructed in this way. This method of knitting is sometimes used as a basis of Bead Knitting.

COMPARISONS

WESTERN STOCKING
STITCH

Fig. 49 is an analytical chart, comparing the construction of Stocking Stitch according to the different methods as explained.

Western Method. A. Knit Stitch uncrossed, with *right* side of loop to front on needle. B. Knit Stitch crossed left over right, and left side of loop to the front, on the needle.

Eastern Method. C. Knit Stitch uncrossed, with left side of loop to front on needle. D. Knit Stitch crossed right over left, right side of loop to the front on needle.

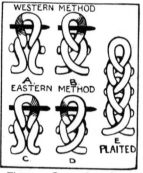

Fig. 49.   Comparison Chart

Combined. By uniting the Western Open Knit Stitch (*Fig.* 35 A) with the Eastern Purl Stitch (*Fig.* 42) a Plaited Fabric, as shown at E, is derived.

The carefully drawn diagrams shown here will clear up many queries that have arisen on the subject of Knit movements. Methods both ancient and modern are given, and, though both Continental and Eastern Knit movements are made with the yarn in the left hand, the latter is different in action and older, though yet to be found in many parts of Europe, Asia and northern Africa.

SELVEDGES

CASTING-ON, CASTING-OFF OR BINDING, AND EDGE STITCHES

ALL SELVEDGE EDGES in knitting are automatically formed as the work proceeds.

In Round Knitting there are two selvedge edges: (1) The foundation or Cast-on edge; (2) The finishing or Cast-off edge.

In Flat Knitting there are four selvedge edges: (1) The foundation or Cast-on edge; (2) and (3) The right and left side edges of the fabric; (4) The final or Cast-off edge.

Each of these selvedges will vary with the purpose for which the fabric is constructed, and must be chosen with care beforehand to get the best effect.

FOUNDATION SELVEDGES

No one method of Casting-on will serve every purpose. Some garments need a light elastic base, others a strong elastic base. Some fabrics need a fancy foundation, and others must be so constructed that the base line differs in no way from the rest of the fabric, and is to all intents and purposes not there. Invisible! The right base selvedge used in the right place makes all the difference to the success of the knitted article, giving strength where necessary, decoration when needed, invisibility when no definite bulky edge is wanted.

All methods of Casting-on must be tensioned to the same elasticity as the knitted fabric and not tightened up, which is so often the case.

For this purpose a larger needle is often selected, or the stitches can be laid over two needles, which is the Continental method.

FINISHING SELVEDGES

This same regard to tension is just as necessary when Binding or Casting-off, for which purpose the old workers used the hook end of their knitting needle, and a crochet hook is still often preferred.

SIDE SELVEDGES

Edge stitches, forming the selvedge sides, in Flat Knitting are important, and must vary with purpose, being "chained" or decorative on an exposed edge, but firm on an edge which will be later joined as a seam.

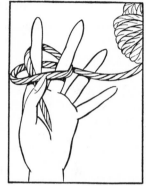

Fig. 50 A. Making the first loop

CASTING-ON OR LAYING-ON

The First Loop. *Figs.* 50 A to C show the first loop which should be used in preference to a knot, as it draws more freely.

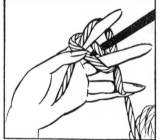

Fig. 50 B. Making the first loop

The yarn is wound twice round the first two fingers (*Fig.* 50 A) and the needle inserted through the back loop as in *Fig.* 50 B, and drawn through as a loop or first stitch, *Fig.* 50 C.

The first loop accomplished, cast on the required number of stitches, choosing the appropriate method, according to requirements.

ENGLISH AND CONTINENTAL METHODS

Both the right-hand (English) and left-hand (Continental) methods of forming a Single and a Double Cast-on selvedge are given. The actions are different, as the methods of knitting differ (*see pages* 47, 48), but the resulting selvedge is identical in both cases.

Fig. 50 C
Making the first loop

METHOD 1. SINGLE CAST-ON

Using one needle and one end of yarn (*Fig.* 51 A).

English Working Method. The yarn is laid round the thumb or
the left hand from right
to left, as in A, *Fig.* 51 A,
and the needle inserted
upwards through this
loop, and slipped off on
to the needle. This same
movement is then re-
peated again, and until
the required number of
stitches have been
formed. An alternative
action at B, *Fig.* 51 A,
shows the yarn looped

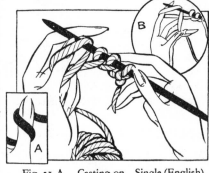

Fig. 51 A.   Casting-on.   Single (English)

round the forefinger.   Either is correct, as both will produce
the same result.

This simple method of Casting-on was very popular among
the old knitters, and is still popular on the Continent, and is
that usually first taught to the young knitter.

Continental Working Method. Fig. 51 B.   Two needles, instead of

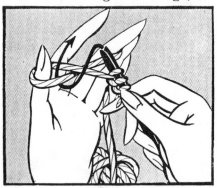

one, are used, and held
together in the right
hand. This opens the
loops considerably,
and makes the knit-
ting of the first row
much easier and the
edge more elastic. The
second needle is with-
drawn when the Cast-
on is completed. The
yarn is looped round
the thumb and third

Fig. 51 B.   Casting-on.   Single (Continental)   finger as shown, and

the stitches are added by inserting the needles upwards through
the loop on the thumb, as indicated by the arrow.

Fig. 51 C shows resulting selvedge by either method. The knitting pin is shown as transferred to the left hand ready for knitting the first row, which is worked through the △ *front* of the loop, knitting and not slipping the first stitch of the first row.

Fig. 51 C. Selvedge. Single

Uses. Single Casting-on is excellent for undergarments, especially children's, as it is light and will not mark a delicate skin.

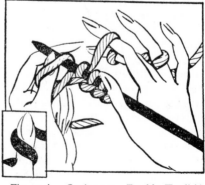

It is also used in making buttonholes and button-stands (*see Fig.* 170, *page* 169) when of necessity the three or four new stitches must be accomplished by the use of a single yarn and one needle. Used when new stitches need to be added to the end of a knitted row, also in forming certain knitting patterns. Can be transformed into a very loose edge by Casting-on twice the required number of stitches and reducing them in the first row to the correct number, by knitting off every other stitch and dropping the one in between.

METHOD 2. DOUBLE CAST-ON

English Working Method. One needle and two ends of yarn, *Fig.* 52 A. Make the first loop as in *Fig.* 50, but some distance from the end of the yarn, the length varying according to the required number of stitches to be made. The shorter length is then passed round the left thumb, as in Single Cast-on, but, instead of merely slipping the loop off as before, it is △ "knitted off" from the ball end of

Fig. 52 A. Casting-on. Double (English)

the yarn. The shorter end is then pulled tight and one **new** completed stitch formed. This process is repeated until the required number of stitches have been Cast-on. The first row is knitted into the △ *front* of the stitch, in plain or pattern as required. When working in Stocking Stitch, this first row is often Purled, by which means the "head" of the stitch is kept uniform and to the back of the work.

Continental Working Method. Fig. 52 B. Two needles are cus-

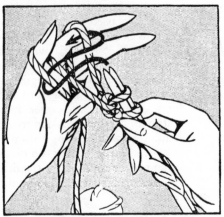

tomary. Take both needles together in the right hand and form a loop (*Fig.* 50), making this, as before, some distance from the end of the yarn, according to the number of stitches required. Now take both ends of the yarn and hold them together in the palm of the left hand, dividing them apart with the

Fig. 52 B. Casting-on. Double (Continental) thumb and forefinger as shown in *Fig.* 52 B, the ball end being looped over the forefinger and the shorter end round the thumb.

The needles then follow the journey of the arrow in forming the stitches, travelling *under* the first loop on the thumb, and over and down through the back loop on the forefinger. The thumb loop is then released and the stitch tightened on the needles with an upward movement of the right hand, without releasing either end of the yarn, held in the palm of the hand. The same process is repeated until the required number of stitches have been made, when the second needle is withdrawn and that carrying the stitches transferred to the left hand ready for the first row of knitting, which is worked through the △ front of the stitches. With a little practice, speed is quickly attained, and those accustomed to left-hand knitting accomplish this Cast-on with considerable speed.

In actual working, the space between the needle points and the thumb will be much reduced, though for instructional purposes this space enables the method to be clearly followed.

Fig. 52 C shows the selvedge construction of Double Cast-on as pro-duced by either method of work. The short end of yarn is shown in black

Fig. 52 C. Selvedge. Double

and the ball end in white for sake of analysis, though in reality they are both of the same colour. The stitches have also been loosened in order that the journey of the yarn may be followed.

Uses. Double Cast-on forms a strong yet elastic edge, and is one preferred by professional knitters. Particularly successful as a jumper selvedge, when a strong yet elastic edge is neces-sary. Should the knitting be in two contrasting colours, then both can be utilised in this method of work, by joining the two together at the first loop, and using a different colour in each hand. For special effects the short end carried by the left hand can be increased to any thickness, using the yarn 2 or

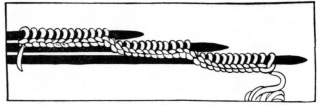

Fig. 52 D.   Arrangement of Stitches in Round Knitting

3-fold, and even substituting a contrasting and thicker yarn, cord or cotton should a particularly bold edge be required for any purpose.

Fig. 52 D shows the method of Casting-on for Round Knit-ting by either method.

METHOD 3.   KNITTING-ON

Two needles and one end of yarn (*Fig.* 53).

First make a loop (*Fig.* 50), and into this insert the second

needle with the right hand (*Fig.* 53 A). Cast the yarn round the point of the right needle as for knitting, and draw a new

loop through the first (*Fig.* 53 B). This new loop is then transferred to the left needle, as in *Fig.* 53 C, thus forming a second stitch, and through this a third loop will be knitted and drawn as before, and so on, until the required number of stitches have been formed. (The loop at 53 C has just been set in its correct position upon the white needle, at which point the black needle will be withdrawn and inserted again as in *Fig.* 53 A, ready to form the next stitch.)

Fig. 53.   Knitting-on

This method of knitting-on stitches is greatly affected by the way in which the loops are knitted off in the first row, and, when the necessary number of stitches are constructed, it is wise to consider the type of selvedge desired.

Should a loose loopy selvedge be desired, then the loops should be knitted off through the *front*, as in *Fig.* 53 D, knitting, and not slipping, the first stitch. This diagram shows three completed stitches on the black needle and a fourth about to be made.   Notice the open and untwisted journey of the yarn in *Fig.* 53 D and compare it with that in *Fig.* 53 E, where the same Cast-on has been knitted off through the *back* of the loops. Here it will be seen that the construction of the four completed loops on the black needle is quite different, as the loops below encircle the neck of the stitch on the needle and the whole fabric is tightened up, and, while very firm, is almost devoid of elasticity.

Uses. The loose selvedge, as in *Fig.* 53 D, can be used for underclothing, picot hems, and edges to be attached to another edge, and for soft edges in pattern and lace fabrics. The selvedge derived by knitting through the back of the loop is better not used on garments where elasticity of edge is essential to wear, since, after several washings, the strain on the loops causes the yarn to break. When knitting with yarns devoid of elasticity this method is often preferred. All yarns are not elastic, and a selvedge must be tensioned in sympathy with the spinning tension of the yarn.

Fig. 53 D. Selvedge Treatment
Knitting through the front of the stitch

Note. Knitting-on is peculiar to English knitting, as a similar selvedge required by Continental workers will be derived by the use of a *crochet hook*. Form a chain, and then run the knitting needle through the loops of

Fig. 53 E. Selvedge Treatment
Knitting through the back of the stitch

the chain and build the knitted fabric on this base. Providing the loops have been picked up correctly, i.e. the △ outside of the loop every time, the first row of knitting will react as in *Figs*. 53 D or 53 E.

METHOD 4. CABLE CAST-ON

The working method is very similar to Knitting-on shown

Fig. 54. Casting-on. Cable

in *Figs*. 53 A to C. The first loop is made as in *Fig*. 50, and the second as in *Fig*. 53 C, but the third and each succeeding loop is made as shown in *Fig*. 54. The needle is inserted *between* the stitches, and a new loop knitted and added to the needle in this manner. The first row is knitted through the front of the stitch, and the effect is a decorative rope-like edge, strong and fairly elastic.

Uses. Inclined to extend the edge, and so effective on glove gauntlets, cuffs, etc. Can be constructed in a thicker or double yarn for bold effect.

METHOD 5. CASTING-ON (INVISIBLE)

The object of this method is rather different from that of any other, since it is to *avoid* and not create a definite selvedge edge. This is accomplished by *"laying"* the yarn round the needles and a foundation yarn, which can be part of the ball end, or of an independent nature. (*See Fig. 55.*)

First leave a long end or cut a separate length of yarn, △ more than sufficient to hold the required number of stitches. With the ball end, make the first loop (*Fig. 50*), and slip this over two knitting needles. Hold these firmly in the right hand, and proceed to wind the yarn forward, under the needles and the foundation yarn, and back over the needles and forward again, this time missing the foundation yarn, but going beneath and round it on the next journey over the needles. The movements can be followed quite clearly from the diagram. Finish as shown, and then withdraw one needle and proceed to knit in the ordinary way, knitting through the △ front of the loops for the first row. After this the knitting proceeds as usual.

Fig. 55. Casting-on. Invisible

Uses. This is a valuable method of laying foundation stitches, as it leaves the selvedge free for any purpose. If the foundation yarn or cord is removed, a row of loops is exposed, which can be picked up and knitted in the opposite direction. In joining together a knitted lace border, these loops would be used for grafting to the opposite end, and so avoid any join. For silk evening scarves, the removal of the foundation cord allows these stitches to be decorated with a looped-in fringe. The opposite end would be finished in similar manner.

This selvedge is particularly successful when knitting in cotton, as it permits of any extension. Often used on knitted cotton curtains or bedspreads, where it is essential that the base of the work should stretch to the dimensions that the weight of the fabric demands. An extra long foundation thread is necessary for such purpose, and the edge is then finished with fringe or knitted lace, leaving the base thread for security on a heavy fabric, and removing it (at preference) on one of lighter nature. The opposite or Cast-off edge should be made to pair by merely drawing the yarn through the knitting loops of the last row, looping a fringe through the stitches in the same way (*See page* 70).

METHOD 6. PICOT CAST-ON

Two knitting needles are necessary. First make a loop (*Fig.* 50) and knit-on one stitch. With these two foundation stitches

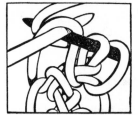

A   B

Fig. 56
Casting-on. Picot

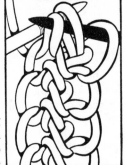

upon the needle, proceed to knit a long strip in the following manner. Yarn forward to make an edge stitch. Slip the first stitch purlwise and knit the second as shown by the black needle in *Fig.* 56 A. Now lift the slipped stitch over the knitted stitch as in *Fig.* 56 B. Turn the work and repeat the process (forward, S.1, purlwise, K.1) until the number of picot loops so formed along the edge of the strip would be equal in number to the requisite stitches desired. These loops are then picked up on a needle and knitted off as ordinary stitches, the effect being a dainty picot selvedge.

The trick to remember in working this particular Cast-on is that you must △ not allow the "made" stitch to cross over the slipped stitch, so that in knitting the second stitch the thumb of the left hand must hold the loop extended, while the stitch is being knitted. The slipped stitch is then drawn over the knitted stitch, as explained, and the picot loops are kept even, and well fanned out.

Uses. This forms an elaborate selvedge and looks effective knitted in fine yarns, silks or cottons, and used for glove gauntlets, cuffs, etc.

CASTING-OFF OR BINDING-OFF

The last row or selvedge edge of a knitted fabric must be constructed differently in order to prevent the stitches unravelling. The process is known as Binding or Casting-off, and must be worked to the same tension as the knitting, otherwise the selvedge becomes contracted, and in wear will break and allow the work to unravel.

There exist several different methods of Casting-off, all of which should be tried, and that most suitable adopted. A needle two sizes larger can be used as a precaution against Casting-off too tightly.

TOO TIGHT!

METHOD 1. HOOK CAST-OFF

The oldest method of Casting-off was done with a crochet hook, and originally, no doubt, with the hook end of the knitting needle. Take the hook and draw a new loop through the first knitted stitch on the needle. Do the same through the second, and then draw the second loop through the first. This is then retained on the needle and a new loop drawn through the third stitch, which is then in turn drawn through the second, and so on, until all the stitches have been crocheted off in this manner. Finally the yarn is cut and the end drawn through the last loop. This manner of Casting-off was, and still is, preferred when the knitting fabric is in cotton or silk, as these yarns, being less elastic, are inclined to tighten up at this final selvedge edge when the stitches are knitted, whereas in

CAST-OFF!

crochet the length of the hooked loop can be perfectly controlled and contractions avoided. The method needs a little practice to acquire regular and dexterous handling of the hook.

METHOD 2. BINDING-OFF

Knit Row. Knit the first two stitches and draw the first stitch over the second, and off the needle, *Fig.* 57. Knit a third and draw the second knitted stitch over this, and so on until the last stitch has been reached. Here the yarn is cut about a finger in length and the end drawn through the last stitch, and so finally secured. Though this is the most

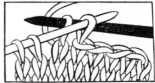

Fig. 57. Casting-off. Binding

popular and best known method of Casting-off, it is one most likely to tighten in the process, and the suggestion shown in *Fig.* 57 of △ using one large needle in the right hand as a precautionary safeguard against tightening will be found very helpful. A difference of two sizes is usual.

Purl Row. Casting-off in Purl, or on the wrong side of the work, the stitches will be purled instead of knitted. In such case it is easier to lift the second stitch over the first by inserting the left or white needle through the loop from the △ back instead of from the front.

Ribbed patterns should be Cast-off in pattern, i.e. knitwise over the Knit Stitches, and purlwise over the Purl Stitches.

METHOD 3. SUSPENDED CAST-OFF

This, as its name suggests, has a suspended or slowed-up action, as a check to tightening. The working process is the same up to the point where the first stitch (black) (*Fig.* 58 A) is drawn over the second. From

CASTING-OFF
SUSPENDED!

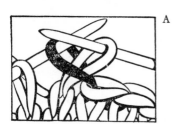
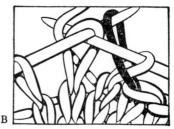

Fig. 58. Casting-off. Suspended

here the difference occurs, as this (the black stitch) is retained on the point of the left needle while the third or next stitch is knitted, as in *Fig.* 58 B, when both the black stitch and the new stitch are slipped off together in one movement. This will leave two stitches on the right needle, the first of which is then drawn over the second and retained on the left needle as before, and so on, until the last two stitches, which are knitted together and the yarn cut and drawn through as before.

This Cast-off is almost proof against contraction, as the suspended action to the black stitch controls the working yarn and checks the tendency to draw this too tight in working.

METHOD 4. INVISIBLE CAST-OFF

In cases where the construction of a definite selvedge edge is not required as a finish, the yarn is merely strung or drawn through the loops of the last row in a straight length and the fabric allowed to stretch free and unhampered to its full extent. The end is finally tied through the last loop. This method is mainly used on flat knitted objects, such as cot covers, bed-spreads, scarves, etc., and then finished with a fringe or knitted lace. It is also used where the knitting is to be drawn together, such as the ends of scarves to be decorated with a single tassel. The opposite complement to this selvedge is given in *Fig.* 55, Invisible cast-on.

METHOD 5. DIAGONAL

A diagonal selvedge must be specially formed by "turning" (*see Fig.* 186, *page* 187). When the fabric is formed to the required angle, the stitches can then be Cast-off, by any method, as in a straight row.   This ensures a clean angular selvedge.

SIDE SELVEDGES

Having considered the base and final selvedges of a knitted fabric, there now only remain the side selvedges. These of necessity must be either "open" or "close"—"open" on such articles as scarves, where both side selvedges must show (unless the knitting be circular), and "close" on selvedges which are to be seamed together, such as those on different parts of a garment.

METHOD 1. CLOSED

Selvedge. Close or Seam. A seam selvedge when completed is meant to join to another seam selvedge, as in *Fig.* 59. This edge, therefore, must be firm and strong, so △ ALL stitches are knitted—knitted on the Knit row and purled on the Purl row. By this means a row of little loops or "heads" are formed along the edge which can be conveniently picked up when seaming (*see Fig.* 185, *page* 185).

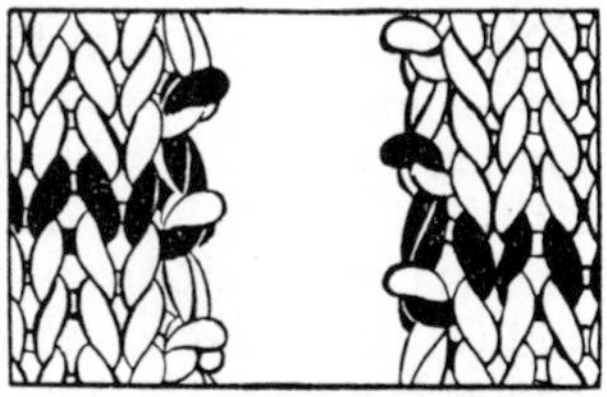

METHOD 2. FANCY

Selvedge. Fancy Side. Mainly used on a fabric of Open or Lace Stitch.

Knit Row. Yarn forward to Make 1, K.2 tog. (*See Fig.* 68 A, *page* 81.) Continue in pattern.

Purl Row. Yarn to back of needle to Make 1, P.2 tog. (*See Fig.* 68 B, *page* 81.) Continue in pattern.

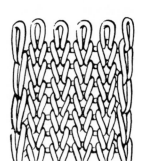

Fig. 59.   Seam Selvedge

METHOD 3. OPEN

Selvedge. Open. Chain Edge. When the side edges of knitting are open and meant to show, they are more decorative and tidy when finished with a chain edge, as in *Fig.* 60.

Knit Row. Slip the first and last stitch of every row, knitwise.

Purl Row. Purl all stitches.

Fig. 60.   Chain Edge

On a fabric in Garter Stitch, slip the first stitch of every row purlwise, with the yarn forward, taking it to the back after slipping the stitch.

Curled Edges. To prevent the edges of a fabric in Flat Knitting from curling when worked in Stocking Stitch, purl the second and penultimate stitches in the Knit row only. The Purl row will not change. Men's ties are usually worked in Round Knitting to obviate this roll, while narrow strips in Flat Knitting will not roll if worked in Garter or Moss Stitch.

SHAPE: INCREASING AND DECREASING

By Increasing or Decreasing the number of stitches contained in a row or round of knitting, the width of a knitted fabric is "widened" or "narrowed" in size. Both units (increasing and decreasing) have a double purpose of use; (1) practical; as they control shape in garment-making, and (2) decorative as used in the construction of all Lace and Fancy Fabrics. The old name for increasing was Widening, and that for decreasing, Narrowing; and these terms are still occasionally found in knitting literature.

The same working methods apply to both forms of knitting, Flat or Round, and the units should be paired left and right, in order to make the addition or reduction of stitches as decorative as possible.

INCREASING

In fashioning or shaping garments, angles, side seams, etc., the Increase or Decrease should be worked on the front of the fabric, and preferably not on the first or last stitch in a row, as this would disturb the appearance of the selvedge and cause an irregular seam when joined. The best position (pattern permitting) is the third or fourth stitch from the beginning or end of the row, and in Round Knitting the third or fourth stitch either side of the Seam Stitch. Whichever stitch is chosen must remain relatively the same in each row, when forming any one angle; or the shape will be distorted.

The positions for Increasing or Decreasing in garment-making should coincide with the position of darts, gussets and seam angles which in ordinary dressmaking would be made by cutting. The number of rows knitted between each Increase or Decrease will vary with tension, fabric and angle desired.

In forming an acute triangle (*see Figs.* 61 A and 65) only

one row of knitting divides the shaping, but in forming a side seam, where the angle is more gentle, the Increases would average every 4th, 6th or 10th row, according to fabric and tension. The exact slope of a garment can always be checked against a foundation pattern (*Fig.* 156) and knitted to shape.

The value of pairing the units (Increasing or Decreasing) right and left will be appreciated from the following diagrams, which reveal the methods as a decoration in themselves. Also, when correctly paired, the pull to the fabric is even and in accord with the angle of the seam, and so less likely to break.

Note. All diagrams here show these units applied to un-crossed fabrics, i.e. knitted through the front of the stitch in the usual manner, but the same methods apply to Crossed Fabric (*see page* 53) by reversing the actions, i.e. when increasing, knit first into the back of the stitch and then into the front, which would be the reverse of *Fig.* 61 B. Where any special differences occur, these are noted and illustrated, since in some cases the two are interchangeable, while in others the methods have become mixed and need re-sorting.

INCREASING. INVISIBLE AND VISIBLE

There are two methods of increasing: (1) Invisible; (2) Visible. The first is used mainly for garments and achieved by "Made" stitches. The second in constructing Lace and Fancy Fabrics, and formed by an "Over." △ The two methods should not be confused, as their purposes and uses are very different.

Invisible. A "Made" stitch (Make 1 or M.1) is, as its name implies, one extra stitch "made" direct upon the needle by forming two stitches out of one. The extra stitch Made thus is practically invisible, and the general appearance of the fabric remains undisturbed and void of gaps. There are three different ways of forming "Made" stitches, as shown.

Visible. An "Over" (Over 1, O.1 or O.) provides a △ foundation upon which a new stitch will be formed in the *next* row. Thus, unlike the "Made" stitch, it leaves a gap in its own row, but becomes a stitch in the next.

An Increase can be Single (one extra stitch) or Double (two

extra stitches), and, in Doubling, the Increasing Unit can be either invisible or visible, as required.

INVISIBLE

"MADE" STITCHES.   SINGLE INCREASES
METHOD 1.   BAR INCREASE.   (*M.1.B.*)

Fig. 61 A. shows the most popular method of Increasing in garment-making, as it produces a small bar across the front of the fabric. This is of great value when counting the number of Increases made on a given angle of any length, such as side or sleeve seams. In pairing it is irregular, as the bar succeeds the "Made" stitch, and, to ensure its position being the same on the left as on the right, the Increase must be knitted one stitch earlier, as shown in *Fig.* 61 A, where it is

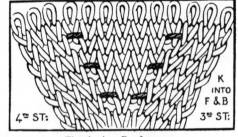

Fig. 61 A.   Bar Increase

Fig. 61 B
Bar Increase.   Knit

Fig. 61 C
Bar Increase.   Purl

made on the third stitch from the beginning of the row (right) but on the fourth stitch from the end of the row (left). An alternative method is to avoid the increase at the end of the row, and form it on the third stitch at the beginning of the Purl row, which will give the same effect, but on different rows. This is a question of design.

Working Method. Fig. 61 B.   Knit first into the front of the stitch and form one loop as shown, and then knit again into the back of the same stitch to form a second, as in *Fig.* 61 B. Both loops are then slipped off together and the extra stitch is MADE. On the next (Purl) row this stitch will be purled

BAR INCREASE

as an ordinary stitch.

Purl Row. Fig. 61 C. Purl first into the front of the stitch and then into the back of the same stitch, as shown by the black needle. Then slip both loops off the left needle together. The bar thus formed will appear on the front of the fabric.

METHOD 2. LIFTED INCREASE (*M.1.L.*)

To Increase by Lifting and knitting into the head of the stitch below, either before or after knitting the true stitch on the needle. The "Made" stitch so formed will have no bar, as shown in Fig. 62 A, and is practically invisible, so that, divided by several rows of knitting, its position is difficult to locate. This is often desirable, as bars are not always required.

Lifting will cause a slight contraction of the fabric in persistent vertical repetition, an effect more noticeable on cotton fabrics and mixtures, but which, with this warning, can be corrected by the tension of the "Made" stitch. This makes a useful Horizontal Increase, where three or four extra stitches are needed for fullness, as the method can be repeated on consecutive stitches,

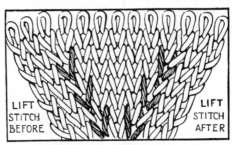

Fig. 62 A. Lifted Increase

Fig. 62 B
Lifted Increase. Knit

Fig. 62 C
Lifted Increase. Purl

providing the tension be slightly slackened. It is often used in the construction of Fancy Fabrics, because of its invisibility.

Working Method. Fig. 62 B. Insert the black needle from front to back through the head of the stitch below that on the needle, as shown, lifting it out of the row. Knit a new stitch through this loop. Afterwards knit the true stitch upon the needle in the ordinary way. This method should be used in shaping the left side of a triangle, as in *Fig.* 62 A. To shape the right side, lift the stitch below △ after first knitting the stitch upon the needle. The lifted stitch will now be the second stitch below, as the right needle contains the stitches of a new row.

Purl Row. The right or black needle is inserted from back to front through the head of the stitch below (*Fig.* 62 C), and a new stitch Made: afterwards the stitch on the needle will in turn be purled.

METHOD 3. RAISED INCREASE. (*M.*1.R.)

Fig. 63 A. This Increase is formed by Raising and knitting up the running thread between two stitches.

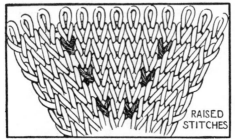

Fig. 63 A.   Raised Increase.   Invisible

There are two methods of work, Invisible and Visible. The running thread in each case is picked up in the same way. The difference occurs in the manner of knitting it, and the results are very different. The same working methods are used left and right, as shown in *Fig.* 63 A. (Should the return row be knitted, as in Garter Stitch, then

Fig. 63 B. Raised Increase. Working Method

Fig. 63 C. Raised Increase. Working Method

Increasing method *Fig.* 67 C is an alternative.) This Increase is very popular on the Continent, where it is preferred to any other, and is particularly successful in glove knitting, or in forming a vertical Increase either side of a central stitch.

Working Method. (1) *Invisible.* Pick up the running thread between the stitches with the left needle, inserting it from front to back as in *Fig.* 63 B to form a loose strand over the left needle. Insert the right needle through the *back* of this, as shown in *Fig.* 63 C, where the black needle is about to knit off the new stitch.

Purl Row. Same. Pick up thread from front to back, and Purl through back.

Fig. 64

Raised Increase. Visible

Working Method. (2) *Visible.* Pick up the running thread as before, but knit into the front as shown in *Fig.* 64. This Increase should only be used as a shaping on Fancy or Lace Fabrics, as the result is an open space beneath the made stitch. In Fancy Fabric construction the method is particularly valuable.

INVISIBLE.
DOUBLE INCREASES.

To Increase two stitches instead of one is known as a Double Increase. There are two principles of work.

Method 1. Create two extra stitches out of one, i.e. knit, purl and knit into the front of the same stitch before slipping it off the needle. This method is better used in fabric construction.

Method 2. By Doubling the unit as in *Fig.* 65, i.e. making two Single Increases in immediate succession, pairing them right and left as in *Figs.* 61 A, 62 A, and 63 A.

DOUBLE INCREASE

Either unit, Bar, Lifted or Raised, can be used and doubled. In

Fig. 65, Bar Increase is shown repeated in vertical formation to make a DART shape. Pairing the Increases in this way is the most decorative method of forming a CENTRAL INCREASE.

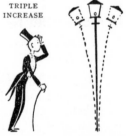

Fig. 65
Double Increase. Bar

Double Increase, Bar. Fig. 65. On an uneven number of stitches, M.2. Bar, the first Increase being made in the stitch preceding the central stitch, and the second in the central stitch itself. This will produce a central chain with a bar either side, as in *Fig. 65.*

Double Increase, Lifted. (M.2.L.) On an even number, make a left and right Lifted Increase on the two central stitches. On an uneven number of stitches, combine the units, and knit into the same Lifted stitch before and after knitting the middle stitch. Repeated in vertical order this will leave a tiny perforation down the centre, which may or may not be desired. To avoid this space, knit into the back of the central stitch.

Double Increase, Raised. (M.2.R.) Knit into the running thread before and after the central stitch.

TRIPLE
INCREASE

VISIBLE INCREASES
OVERS. (Single Units)

Overs are used as a means of creating extra stitches in Lace or Fancy patterns, and are not generally regarded as a means of shaping. (*See excepting Fig. 67 C.*) The correct way to throw an "Over" (O.1 or O.) on a Knit or Purl Row is shown in *Figs. 66 A and 66 B.* Written directions sometimes refer to this movement as "Wool Forward, Knit," or "Wool Round Needle," but "Over," the original term, is shorter and more descriptive of the action, as the yarn is brought forward and taken △ over the needle, and is thus used throughout this book. Overs as used on both Uncrossed and Crossed Fabrics are shown.

OVERS. UNCROSSED FABRICS (O.1.)

Knit Row, Over. Fig. 66 A. Yarn forward, as though to purl. Take this Over the needle and knit the next stitch. On the return row the Over is treated as a stitch and purled through the front, in common with the other stitches.

Purl Row. Over. Fig. 66 B. Yarn over and round needle to the front again, purl the next stitch. On the return row, knit into the front of the Over as though it were a complete stitch.

Fig. 66 A. Over (Knit)   Fig. 66 B. Over (Purl)

To form an Over after a Knit Stitch and before a Purl, bring the yarn forward and once round needle. To form an Over after a Purl and before a Knit Stitch, the yarn is already in position to the front, and the next stitch is knitted.

Notice the same cypher "O" is used for either a Knit or Purl Over, no other being necessary, as an Over on a Knit row can only be made as in *Fig.* 66 A, and in a Purl row as in *Fig.* 66 B.

Should, for some special effect, a change be needed, and an Over as for a Crossed Fabric be required, then it is specially stated in written instructions by the designer.

OVERS. CROSSED FABRICS (O.1.C.)

The method of throwing the yarn to form an "Over on a Crossed Fabric" (*see page* 53) is shown in *Figs.* 67 A and B. The movements are reversed on both Knit and Purl rows in common with the method of knitting.

Knit Row, Over. Fig. 67 A. Yarn over and completely round the needle. Insert the needle through the back of the stitch and knit. The yarn is shown in this position in *Fig.* 67 A. On the return row, purl the Over through the back in common with the other stitches. When this Over is used off its own fabric it must be described as Over 1 Crossed, or O.1 C.

Purl Row, Over. Fig. 67 B. Take the yarn back and over the needle as shown, purling the stitch through the back. On

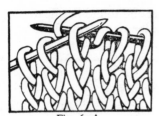

Fig. 67 A
Over. Crossed Fabric. Knit

Fig. 67 B
Over. Crossed Fabric. Purl

the return row the Over is also purled through the back. (Described as Over 1 C. when used off fabric.)

Fig. 67 C shows an interesting combination of methods, as the Over is thrown as for a Crossed Fabric (O.1 C.), while the fabric itself is an ordinary uncrossed Garter Stitch, worked through the front of the stitch, as in the usual manner. On the return row the Over will be knitted through the front in common with the other stitches, and the result will be an invisible increase, and not a hole!

Fig. 67 C
Over. Garter Increase

This method of increasing is of particular value on a Garter Stitch Fabric, as it allows the new stitch to spring from an independent base, twin to neither neighbour, and so entirely free from any restriction. As such it is used by the Shetland knitters, who specialise in Garter Stitch, when forming successive Increases on a triangular shawl, where the fabric must be continually extended by means of Increasing and yet show no source of origin.

Many uses of combining these two methods of throwing the yarn in Fancy Fabric construction exist and will be illustrated in a later book. Some knitters unconsciously combine the two methods, finding the Purl throw, *Fig.* 67 B, more pleasing than *Fig.* 66 B, but in doing so it should be △ remembered that the Over is "off fabric," and to ensure a hole or open space, the method of knitting on arrival at the Over should be reversed, i.e. knit through the *back* of the Over if its origin is Crossed, and through the front if its origin is Uncrossed.

OVERS. SELVEDGE

Fig. 68 A shows how to form an Over on the first stitch in a Knit row. Yarn forward, insert the needle knitwise into the

first stitch, throw the yarn over the needle and knit. *Fig.* 68 B shows the working method at the commencement of a Purl row. Yarn back inserted needle, purlwise, to purl the first stitch. When completed, in each case there will be two stitches

Fig. 68 A
Over, Edge. Knit

Fig. 68 B
Over, Edge. Purl

instead of one on the right needle. A Side Over can be used as an increase, or to form little picots along the edge of knitted lace, and is usually followed by K.2 tog.

OVERS. LACE FABRICS

In Lace and Fancy Fabrics an Over is often followed or

preceded by a Decrease, but this does not change the formation of the Over in any way. A single example is given in *Fig.* 69, "Over, S.1, K.1, p.s.s.o." The action can be clearly seen in the diagram.

OVERS. MULTIPLE

Expediency is the only limit to the number of Overs used in succession, as the throws or turns can be increased to three, four or five in Lace Fabrics, according to requirements. On the return row each Over must be knitted or purled off as a

Fig. 69. Over. Lace Action

stitch. A series of Overs must be knitted and purled off alternately, arranging the order so that the *last* Over is knitted on a Purl row, and purled on a Knit row. Example:

Over Double (O.2)
Knit Row. Yarn forward, as in Fig. 66 A, and once completely round the needle. Knit the next stitch. On the return row (Purl), purl the first Over and knit the second.

DECREASING

Over Triple (O.3)
Knit Row. Yarn forward, as in *Fig.* 66 A, and twice round needle. On the return or Purl row, knit, purl and knit into the three Overs.

Over Double (O.2)
Purl Row. Yarn as in *Fig.* 66 B, only twice round needle. Purl next stitch. On the return or Knit row, knit the first Over and purl the second.

Over Triple (O.3)
Purl Row. Yarn round needle as in Fig. 66 B, but making three turns. On the return or Knit row, purl, knit, purl into the three Overs.

At one time, when garments were mainly constructed in Round Knitting, Overs were a means of dividing a tubular fabric. Ten or twelve Overs would be made, and dropped on the next row. When completed, these bars would be cut and folded back and the edges finished with crochet.

DECREASING OR NARROWING

In Decreasing, or reducing the number of stitches in a row or round of knitting, the subject of pairing is even more important, as the angle formed by the lie of the top stitch is more apparent, and, if pulling in the opposite direction to the angle it is forming, the stitch is more likely to break. In fabric construction, pairing becomes a matter of design.

What is meant by the angle of the top stitch will be seen in

Single

	Right	Left	
K.2 tog.			S.1, K.1, p.s.s.o.
P.2 tog.			P.1, ret. to L.N., p.n.s.o.

Double

S.1, K.1, p.s.s.o., ret. to L.N., p.n.s.o.			S.1, K.2 tog., p.s.s.o.
S.1, P.1, ret. to L.N., p.n.s.o., ret. to R.N., p.s.s.o.			P.2 tog., ret. to L.N., p.n.s.o. (P.2 R.)
			S2. K1. P.2 s.s.o.

Fig. 70.   Signals.   Pairing Decreases

Fig. 71 A, which reveals that the Decrease formed on the right, S.1, K.1, p.s.s.o., produces a left slope, while that on the left, K.2 tog., a right slope. Used thus, they form a pair, and a perfect decreasing line, left and right, both Decreases sloping with the angle of the fabric. By exchanging this order the selvedge line is broken.

Signals. For immediate reference, the angle formed by the top or Decreased stitch is shown by a little signal drawing in the corner of each diagram, so that its effect is quickly recognised. These are assembled for brief reference in *Fig.* 70. A solid black signal line indicates the angle of the upper stitch, in a Knit row. When the signal is lined, it indicates a Decrease made on the Purl row, though the signal indicates its appearance on the △ front of the fabric.

Arrows (p.s.s.o.). In order to abbreviate the written instructions on the diagrams, the letters p.s.s.o. (pass slipped stitch over) are indicated by an arrow, pointing the direction in which the slipped stitch will be passed. On Double Decreases there are two arrows. The text gives the instruction in full, but the arrows will serve later as a quick reminder.

SLIP PRINCIPLE △

In slipping a stitch to form a Decrease on a Knit row, it should always be slipped knitwise; if slipped purlwise, it will be crossed when it is drawn over the succeeding stitch. On the Purl row, slip purlwise.

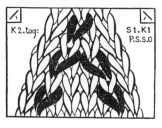

Fig. 71 A

Decreasing.   Left and Right Knit

WORKING METHODS
KNIT DECREASE (*Single*)

Fig. 71 B
Decreasing. Right
Angle. Knit

Knit or K.2 tog. Fig. 71 B. Insert the needle knitwise through two stitches and knit them together as one stitch (right angle).

*S.*1, *K.*1, *p.s.s.o. Fig.* 71 C. Slip one stitch and insert the needle knitwise through the next, as shown at A, and knit it. Now insert the left needle through the stitch previously slipped, as at B, and draw this over the knitted stitch, as indicated by the arrow. *Figs.* 71 B and C are a pair, left and right, as shown by the signals.

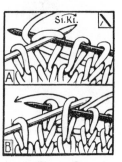

Fig. 71 C
Decreasing. Left
Angle. Knit

*K.*2 *tog.* B. *Fig.* 72. Knit two stitches together through the back of the stitches. The signal mark indicates the upper stitch to lie in a similar direction to that in *Fig.* 71 C. It is—and this method is often given as—an alternative to *Fig.* 70 C, though in knitting through the back of the loops the stitches are crossed, which weakens the yarn in close repetition, when used as a shaping Decrease. Strictly speaking, this Decrease should be used only on Crossed Fabric, or for special design effects.

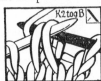

Fig. 72. Decreasing
Crossed. Knit

Fig. 73. Decreasing
Mixed. Knit

*S.*1 (*p.*), *K.*1. *Fig.* 73. Insert the needle purlwise into one stitch and knitwise into the next and knit the two together, drawing the yarn through between the loops as shown. This results in one crossed stitch and one uncrossed stitch, and the signal sign also indicates a left angle. This Decrease is used mainly in fabric construction, where effects require a Purl and Knit Stitch for a Decrease, also for decreasing a stitch and an Over.

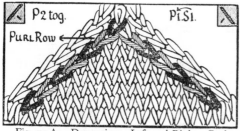

Fig. 74 B. Decreasing
Right Angle. Purl

Fig. 74 A. Decreasing. Left and Right. Purl

CHAINED DECREASE

A Knit Decrease can be used on every round in Round Knitting and so form a chain, as in *Fig.* 74 A, but, in order to decrease thus in Flat Knitting, a Purl Decrease must be used on the Purl rows. The solid black stitches show the Decreases made on the Knit rows, which are the same as in *Fig.* 71 A. The Decreases made on the Purl rows are lined. These have

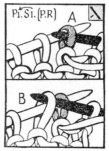

Fig. 74 C. Decreasing
Left Angle. Purl

been carefully paired, so that there is no apparent difference between the Decreases on either row. Notice the new signal mark which indicates a Purl Decrease, $\triangle$ as seen on the front of the fabric. The angle on a Purl fabric can be seen in the working diagram, *Fig.* 74 C.

PURL DECREASE (*Single*)

Purl or P.2 tog. Fig. 74 B. Insert the needle purlwise through two stitches and Purl them both together as though they were one stitch. Right angle on front of fabric. Remarkably effective used on front of fabric as decrease on knit rows.

P.1, S.1, p.n.s.o., or P.R. (Purl Reverse). Fig. 74 C. The arrow indicates p.s.s.o. Purl the first stitch and return again to the left needle as shown at A. Insert the right needle into the stitch beyond and draw this over the purled stitch as at B, and afterwards restore the original stitch (black) to the right needle. This Decrease is often referred to as Purl Reverse. The signal indicates a left angle on the $\triangle$ front of the fabric.

DOUBLE DECREASES

A Double Decrease will reduce three stitches to one, and can be formed: (1) by doubling the decreasing unit, i.e. using

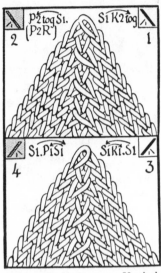

Fig. 75. Double Decrease. Vertical

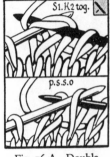

Fig. 76 A. Double Decrease. Left. Knit

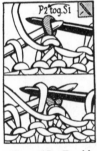

Fig. 76 B. Double Decrease. Left. Purl

two Single Decreases, as just explained, in succession, pairing them strictly right and left as explained; (2) by Decreasing two or three stitches in various ways so that the angle of the top stitch slopes either to the right, left or vertical, giving the angle of decoration required. Such arrangements can be used as required in fabric construction, and make fascinating CENTRAL DECREASES, pure or mixed, in Chevron Knitting, as in *Fig. 75.*

DOUBLE DECREASE

WORKING METHODS

Knit Decrease (S.1, K.2 tog., p.s.s.o.). Left. Fig. 76 A. Slip one stitch and knit the next two stitches together.

Then insert the left needle through the slipped stitch and draw this over the knitted stitch as demonstrated. The signal drawing indicates a left angle. The repetition of this Decrease is shown in central formation at the top of *Fig.* 75.

Purl Row (P.2 tog., S.1, p.s.s.o.). This will produce the same angle on the front of fabric (*see Fig.* 75). Purl two stitches together, and put the resulting stitch back on the left needle as in *Fig.* 76 B. Insert the right needle into the stitch beyond and lift this over the middle stitch and return the stitch again to right needle. The Purl signal indicates the angle.

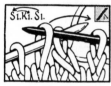

Fig. 77
Double Decrease
Right. Knit

Knit Decrease (S.1, K.1, p.s.s.o., ret. L.N., p.n.s.o.). This action is shown in *Fig.* 77. Slip one stitch and knit the next. Then pass the slipped stitch over. Transfer the resulting stitch to the left needle and draw the stitch beyond over this, as indicated by the arrow. The signal indicates a right angle, and the knitted effect in central formation is shown at the bottom (3), *Fig.* 75. *Figs.* 76 A and 77 are a pair. (*See Fig.* 70.)

Purl Row (S.1, P.1, S.1, p.s.s.o.). Slip one stitch and purl the next. Now slip the stitch beyond on the left needle purlwise and return it to left needle again. This is to turn it the reverse way. Transfer the purled stitch to left needle, draw the △ turned stitch over it. Return this stitch to right needle and then pass the first slipped stitch over it. This brings both the right and left stitches over the central stitch in the correct order, and will produce the same effect on the front of the fabric as the Knit (*Fig.* 77). This Decrease is often called Double Purl Reverse. (D.P.R.)

CHAIN DECREASE (*see Fig.* 78)

Working Method (S.2, K.1, p.2 s.s.o.). (Pass two slipped stitches over.) Insert the needle knitwise into two stitches as though to knit them together, but, instead of knitting them, slip them both off

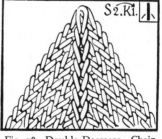

Fig. 78. Double Decrease. Chain

together. Knit the next stitch beyond, and then lift the two slipped stitches over this knitted stitch. This makes a remarkably attractive vertical Decrease, with an unbroken chain running up the centre, as in *Fig.* 78. The signal mark indicates the action of the stitch, the heavy black line denoting the upper stitch.

TRIANGULAR SHAPES

Increasing and Decreasing is, as noted before, the means of controlling shape, a few examples of which are given in *Fig.* 79. (1) Is a left-angle triangle or left slope. Cast on the required number of stitches and decrease (K.2 tog.) at the beginning of every knit row. (2) To form a right-angle triangle, begin with two stitches and increase (M.1) at the end of every knit row. (3) This is a double triangle with Double central increase (M.2, Bar) on the central stitches. This method △ fans the rows of knitting out from the centre as indicated by the dotted lines. (4) Another triangle, but this time the rows run horizontally. Such effect is derived by M.1 on the second stitch at the beginning of every knit and purl row. (5) Supposing the triangle be required the other way up, then just reverse the methods. Cast on the required number of stitches for the width, and decrease on the second stitch at the beginning of every row.

These are primary shapes and angles, all of which can be applied to practical effect in garment-making.

MITRE

A mitre is formed by an angle of 45° as shown by the lines AA and A'A' in *Fig.* 80. The shaping is always done on the △ angled edge; this leaves the opposite edge undisturbed and free to develop in pattern as required, as on a lace border this would probably be scalloped.

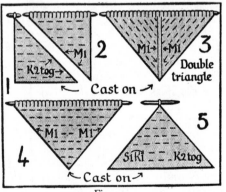

Fig. 79
Triangular Formation

To build outwards as at AA, increase on
the Purl row. This leaves the Knit or pattern
row better scope for development.

Cast on 2 stitches.

Row 1. Knit.

Row 2. Purl. M.1 on last stitch.

Continue as shown in diagram until the
desired width is obtained.

To decrease to a point as at A'A', K.2 tog.
at the beginning of every Knit row.

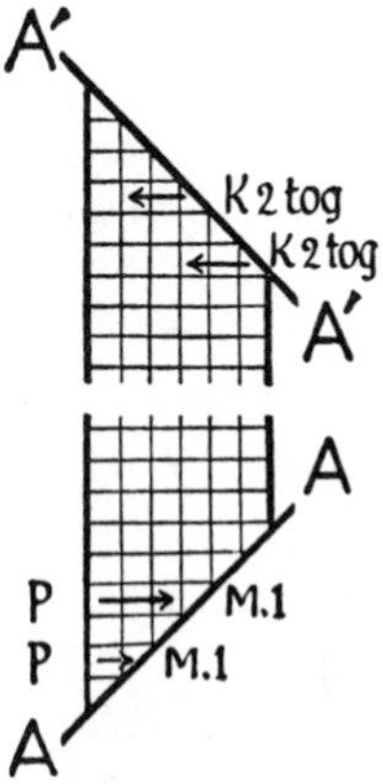

DIAGONAL OR BIAS KNITTING

There are two methods of work: (1), in
which the stitches of the fabric slope to the
right, as at A, and (2), in which they slope
to the left, as at B. This is merely a matter of arranging
the Increasing and Decreasing units. At A, the Decrease
(K.2 tog.) is made at the △ beginning of the row, this lost
stitch being made good at the end of the row by Increasing

Fig. 80.   Forming
a Mitre

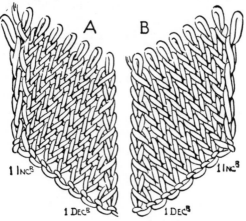

Fig. 81.   Diagonal Knitting

(M.1) (Raising). At B, the order of the units is reversed, the
Increasing unit (Raising) being formed at the △ beginning of
the row, and the Decreasing (K.2 tog.) at the end of the row.

Any other Increasing or Decreasing units arranged in this way will produce similar effects. The fabric can be in any stitch or colour. Bands of colour, 10 or 12 rows in each, are most effective as they appear to be on the bias. Knitted as a scarf, the fabric should be broad, as it stretches considerably, and Garter or Moss Stitch is preferable, Stocking Stitch being inclined to curl.

CHEVRON KNITTING

CHEVRON KNITTING

This is derived by joining A and B in *Fig.* 81 together as one fabric, uniting them with one Double Decrease, or two Single Decreases, in the middle of the row, and increasing at the beginning and the end of the row, as before, as follows: Knit Row, M.1 at commencement of row. Knit (pattern or Stocking Stitch) to the middle of the row. Here make a Double Decrease. Knit to last stitch but one, and M.1 (Raising). Knit last stitch.

The order can be reversed, making the middle and Doubling unit the Increase as follows:

K.2 tog. Knit to the middle of the row and here make a Double Increase (*see Fig.* 65). Knit to last two stitches. K.2 tog.

The resulting fabric will thus △ fan out from the centre, as shown on the jumper, instead of converging to the centre, as by the previous method.

COLOUR KNITTING

OLOUR appears to have been the first means of varying the appearance of a knitted fabric, an early example of this being a child's sock of the 5th or 6th centuries A.D. found on the site of the ancient Coptic town of Antinoe, and now at the Leicester Museum. This has bands of colour rather like a modern football jersey, comprising five rounds of knitting for each colour, green, red, purple, yellow and blue. The sock is knitted in Crossed Stocking Stitch and has no seam stitch, while the colours appear to have been introduced with little concern to the termination of a round—perhaps on the second needle, or on the third, so that the rings are irregular in their beginnings and endings.

The magnificent example of Arabian colour knitting of the 7th to 9th centuries (*Fig.* 82) is as astonishing in technique as it is beautiful in design. It was found in Egypt at Fostat.[1] The fabric is silk, with 36 stitches to the inch, the pattern being in a deep red maroon on a ground of gold silk, and knitted in Crossed Stocking Stitch (Eastern, *Fig.* 43). The silk yarn is

By courtesy of Dr. Fritz Iklé

Fig. 82.   Arabian Knitting 7th to 9th centuries

stranded from colour to colour on the back as in *Fig.* 88, and in this particular fragment the design has been knitted upside down, as the stitches are all going in that direction, but since it is the technique of knitting with which this book is concerned, the fabric (*Fig.* 82) is shown as it is constructed. No finer example of silk stranded knitting has been found: it remains supreme until this day.

[1] Fostat = an ancient city on the site of Cairo.

BROCADE KNITTING

Fig. 83. Sleeved Waistcoat, Italian knitted in silk and gold threads,
17th century. (Back view)

The 17th-century example of Brocade Knitting in *Fig.* 83 reveals a change of fabric with a change of colour by introducing the Purl stitch as a means of high relief, as in a velvet brocade, and no doubt the colour knitting of this period was inspired to such effects by the beautiful brocaded velvets of the Renaissance.

This was knitting in the grand manner, when the beaux of the period wore their waistcoats and capes knitted in silk and metal threads and patterned in the most marvellous and intricate all-over floral designs.

The waistcoat (back view, *Fig.* 83) with sleeves is knitted in terra cotta silk, the background being in Stocking Stitch, while the all-over brocade pattern is of gold, and in purl stitches. The floral outline of the pattern is further emphasised in blue silk, added when the knitting was finished, after the manner of Swiss Darning. The garment, when completed, was finished with a lining of linen. The basket pattern shown at

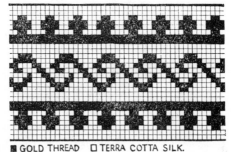

■ GOLD THREAD □ TERRA COTTA SILK.

Fig. 84.   Detail of Waistcoat Border (Chart)

hem and cuffs (probably covered by sash and other cuffs) represents a popular finish, as found on many knitted garments of this century. The colour knitting of this period has never since been surpassed, nor are such intricate designs now attempted, though the little borders running

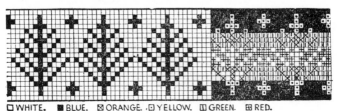

□ WHITE.   ■ BLUE.   ⊠ ORANGE.   ⊡ YELLOW.   ⊞ GREEN.   ⊞ RED.

Fig. 85 A.   Tree of Life (Chart).   Fair Isle

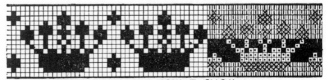

☐ WHITE. ■ BLUE. ⊠ ORANGE. ▥ GREEN. ▣ YELLOW.

Fig. 85 B. Crown of Glory (Chart). Fair Isle

Fig. 86
Albanian
Design
for sock
top
(Chart)

■ BLACK. ☐ WHITE. ⊠ RED. ⫴⫴⫴ TWISTED BAND (WHITE)
▨ YELLOW (SEWN OVER KNITTING).

■ BLACK. ☐ WHITE. ⊠ RED.

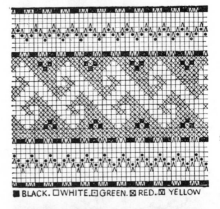

Fig. 87
Bulgarian
Design
for sock top
(Chart)

■ BLACK. ☐ WHITE. ▣ GREEN. ⊠ RED. ▨ YELLOW

■ BLACK. ☐ WHITE. ⊠ RED.

across the shoulders and at the cuffs and hems are familiar, and often used in similar manner as decoration to-day. This border is shown, in diagram form, in *Fig.* 84.

The best known examples of such knitting come from Fair Isle, Scandinavia, Spain and the Balkan States. *Figs.* 85A to 87 show examples of different popular designs collected from various European centres, some of which have a religious or national significance such as the Tree of Life (*Fig.* 85 A), the Crown of Glory (*Fig.* 85 B), etc., each country boasting of its own particular design and rarely repeating those of any other. The peasant form of this knitting is generally done in the natural colours of the wool.

In the commercialised versions the introduction of colour other than the natural shades of the wool played many curious tricks with certain traditional designs, one in particular from Fair Isle being transformed from the united crosses of St. Andrew and St. Patrick first into a flower, and later into the form of letters suggesting OXOX!

Traditional Fair Isle designs rarely contain more than two different colours in any one line of knitting, both being usually varied in the next line or round, but designs from the Continent often carry three or four different colours in any one line. Colour knitting in spite of its long and glorious past has become almost universally known as Fair Isle, and even appears under that name in the programmes of the French *couturiers*. Tradition has it that the Fair Islanders learnt the art from the shipwrecked sailors of the Spanish Armada, and to substantiate this story we yet find the same form of fabric, and in similar patterns, among the Basques of northern Spain.

FAIR ISLE

Colour knitting of this description necessitates a special technique, the unused colour in any line being carried from pattern to pattern on the back of the work by a process of "Stranding" or "Weaving."

Small patterns are stranded. Large are better woven, unless the fabric is to be lined.

DESIGNS

These are worked out on graph paper, each square representing a stitch. Different colours are represented by different symbols. Most Cross Stitch and Canvas designs as prepared for embroidery can be used as charts. Also crochet charts. Simple patterns usually allow of two different colours only in any one given row, and diagonal lines are better, as the colours encroach in the succeeding rows (*see Fig.* 87). Examples of charts are given in *Figs.* 84 to 87. In knitting, the chart is read from △ right to left for the knit row and from △ left to right for the purl, and commences at the bottom right-hand corner.

MATERIALS

Wool, silk or mixtures of both can be used, but all yarns must be of the same ply or size in any one piece of work.

TENSION

This is of paramount importance in either Stranding or Weaving, as, should the floating yarn be held too tightly, the knitting will appear distorted on the front and the pattern warped. If correctly tensioned, the fabric should have the same elasticity as an ordinary knitted fabric.

STRANDING

What is understood by Stranding is shown in *Fig.* 88, which shows the back of the work and the yarn "Stranding"

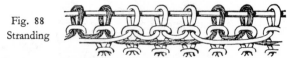

Fig. 88
Stranding

from colour to colour in loose floating threads. Two colours only are used, which permits of the work being carried out by the expedient method of knitting simultaneously with the left and right hand, combining the English and Continental methods of knitting. (*See Figs.* 29 and 31.)

The knitting pattern should be studied anew at the commencement of each line, as, for the convenience of the knitter, the dominant colour of the line is more easily controlled if carried by the right hand. This in most cases is the background colour. The position of the hands as demonstrating

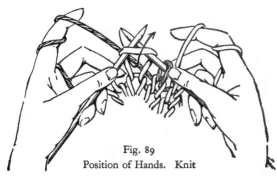

Fig. 89
Position of Hands.   Knit

the combined actions of knitting is shown in *Figs.* 89 and 90. *Fig.* 89 shows the Knit Stitch and *Fig.* 90 the Purl Stitch. The direction of the arrows in both diagrams shows the movement of the right needle in forming a Knit or Purl Stitch in the Continental manner.

A casual glance at these drawings would suggest a work

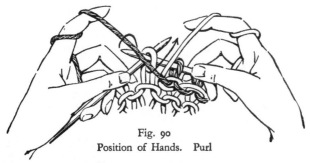

Fig. 90
Position of Hands.   Purl

wrought with difficulties, but such is not the case, as, once a simple border knitted thus in two colours is completed, ordinary knitting in its turn will seem strange.

In Stranded Knitting there are four movements to be

memorised, two Knit movements (right hand and left hand), and two Purl movements (right hand and left hand).

KNIT MOVEMENTS—STRANDING

Fig. 91 shows the method of knitting with the right hand (white stitches) while "Stranding" with the left, the right hand

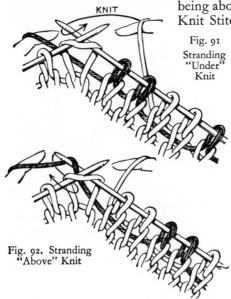

KNIT

Fig. 91
Stranding
"Under"
Knit

Fig. 92. Stranding
"Above" Knit

being about to make an ordinary Knit Stitch as indicated by the arrow, while the left hand carries the "Stranded" yarn (shown black) along the back. This same right-hand movement is repeated so long as the "white" stitches forming the background are required. The left hand will at the same time continue "Stranding," but with particular care to tension, keeping the yarn △ BELOW and away from interference with the knitting action.

Fig. 92 shows a change in pattern where the black yarn, held in the left hand, is about to form the pattern stitch; while that held in the right is to be stranded. The movement of the needle is indicated by the arrow, and special care must be paid to the tension of the yarn held in the right hand lest it become tightened and strain the loop, △ and so cause an unevenness to the surface of the pattern.

These two knit movements as here explained are sufficient when the fabric is being constructed in Round Knitting, but in Flat Knitting the movements of the Purl row are necessary.

PURL MOVEMENT—STRANDING

The Purl movement of the right hand is shown on *Fig.* 93, where the needle is about to make a white Purl Stitch in the usual way, while the left hand is Stranding the left or black yarn. The diagram shows an actual change of pattern and movement from black to white stitches. *Fig.* 94 shows a change of pattern wherein the black yarn, held in the left hand, must form the stitches, while the yarn to be Stranded is carried in the right hand. Here it will be seen that the left hand is about to make a "left-hand" Purl Stitch, while the right hand is Stranding the white yarn. The position of the right hand remains thus so long as black stitches are required to form the pattern.

Fig. 93. Stranding "Under" Purl

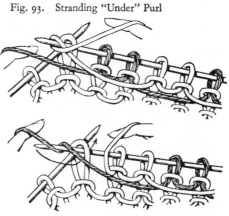

Fig. 94. Stranding "Above" Purl

Fig. 95 shows the appearance of the Stranded yarns on the

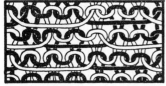

Fig. 95. Stranding back of fabric

back of the fabric, where it will be noted how easily they "float" from pattern to pattern without any impediment, and in strict accordance with the movements just described.

Stranding is better used for small patterns, where the floating yarn is only carried behind three or four stitches.

Corrugated Fabrics. Obtained by knitting 3 stitches white and 3 black, and keeping these colours vertically above each other, as stripes. The stranded yarn is tensioned very tightly, so that the front of the fabric appears hooped. Also known as Cartridge pleating. Can be self-colour by using two match-ing yarns.

GLOVES IN STRANDED KNITTING

WEAVING

The difference between "Stranding" and "Weaving" is shown in *Fig.* 96, and should be compared with *Fig.* 88, as the difference is very considerable, though only on the back of the fabric. The front of the fabric should be identical. "Weaving" as applied to knitting is a process of "Unders" and "Overs," or, more correctly interpreted, "Aboves" and "Belows," just as in loom weaving. A study of *Fig.* 96 will

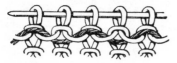

Fig. 96.   Weaving.   Correct

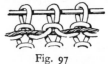

Fig. 97

Weaving.   Wrong

reveal the journey of the woven thread, first "Above" and then "Below" each alternate stitch on the needle. This is true Weaving. Weaving is particularly practical in large patterns as it secures in position the travelling yarn on the back, which might otherwise catch and drag the fabric.

Weaving needs a little practice in order to realise just how to throw the yarn ABOVE or BELOW, as desired, especially in complicated patterns, and for this purpose systematic diagrams have been prepared, which, if followed with yarn and needles in hand, will explain the whole process, and, once this is understood, the method can be easily memorised.

TENSION

Particular regard must be paid to the tension of the yarn in Weaving, just as in Stranding, △ otherwise the woven thread will be drawn straight, as in *Fig.* 97, which is wrong, and very different from the easy-flowing, undulating line shown in *Fig.* 96, which is correct. In one the knitting will be so tight that it will have no elasticity, in the other the fabric will be as supple and pliable as in ordinary knitting. △ Tight Weaving will also thicken and spoil the effect of the pattern. Tension, therefore, is of extreme importance, for both practical and general appearance of the fabric and pattern.

"ABOVE" OR "BELOW"

What is understood by ABOVE and BELOW in Weaving is shown in *Fig.* 98 A and B. In *Fig.* 98 A the yarn is "Above" and in *Fig.* 98 B "Below." The combination of the two is shown in *Fig.* 96. In *Fig.* 98 C the stitches of the knit row have been drawn, but very open, so that the regular journey of the woven thread alternately "Above" and "Below" each stitch can be appreciated. In reality this woven thread will not be seen at all on the front of the work.

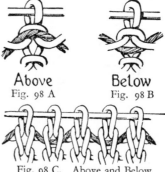

Above
Fig. 98 A

Below
Fig. 98 B

The position of the hands in Weaving is the same as that shown for Stranding in *Figs.* 89 and 90, and the right hand carries the dominant colour of

Fig. 98 C. Above and Below

the line. There are FOUR different movements to master in BOTH the Knit and Purl rows (8 altogether) when considering regular "Above" and "Below" weaving, viz.:

Movement 1. Weaving the left yarn ABOVE, while knitting or purling a stitch with the right hand. (Knit and Purl rows.)
Movement 2. Weaving the left yarn BELOW, while knitting or purling a stitch with the right hand. (Knit and Purl rows.)
Movement 3. Weaving the right yarn ABOVE, while knitting or purling a stitch with the left hand. (Knit and Purl rows.)
Movement 4. Weaving the right yarn BELOW, while knitting or purling a stitch with the left hand. (Knit and Purl rows.)

WEAVING
KNIT ROWS
Weaving Left-Hand Yarn.
Movements 1 and 2.

Fig. 99 A. How to knit a stitch with the right hand and at the same time weave the left yarn ABOVE. This is easy to remember, as the left yarn is placed *above* the needle as shown, while the right hand will knit a stitch as indicated

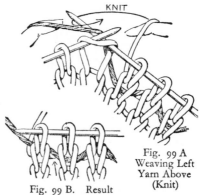

KNIT

Fig. 99 A
Weaving Left
Yarn Above
(Knit)

Fig. 99 B. Result

by the arrow. The result is shown in *Fig.* 99 B, the arrow pointing out the "Above" weave just formed. *Fig.* 100 A

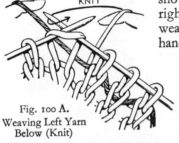

shows how to knit a stitch with the right hand and at the same time weave in the yarn held in the left hand BELOW. In this case the

Fig. 100 A.
Weaving Left Yarn
Below (Knit)

Fig. 100 B. Result

movement is also simple, as the left-hand yarn is below the needle as shown, while the right hand will knit as indicated by the arrow. *Fig.* 100 B shows the result. These two movements, "Above" and "Below," must be alternated on each stitch △ so long as the yarn held in the LEFT hand is being woven "Above" and "Below," as shown in *Fig.* 98 C.

Weaving Right-Hand Yarn. Movements 3 and 4.
Fig. 101 A. How to knit a stitch with the left hand, see arrow, while holding the yarn in the right hand, so that it will lie ABOVE this same knitted stitch when completed. Result in *Fig.* 101 B, where the right-hand yarn (white) is about to lie, as indicated by the arrow *above* the newly knitted black stitch.

Fig. 101 A. Weaving Right Yarn Above (Knit)   Fig. 101 B. Result

Figs. 102 A to C show how to knit a stitch with the left hand and at the same time weave in the yarn held in the right hand. The movement is a little more complicated, and is shown in slow motion over three diagrams, with arrows and letters to indicate the process.

Fig. 102 A. Make a knit movement with the right hand (*a*) and then lay the left yarn over the point of the needle (*b*). These two movements are shown completed in *Fig.* 102 B,

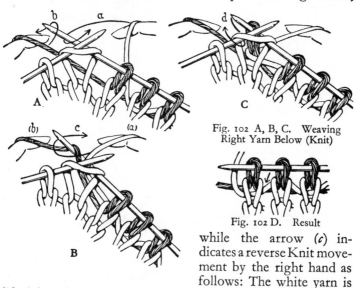

Fig. 102 A, B, C.   Weaving
Right Yarn Below (Knit)

Fig. 102 D.   Result

while the arrow (*c*) in-
dicates a reverse Knit movement by the right hand as
follows: The white yarn is
lifted from its knit position and taken round and beneath the
right needle point, at the same time drawing the black yarn into
a loop (*Fig.* 102 C). This forms a black stitch which will finally
be taken through by the right needle, as directed by the arrow
(*d*). The result is shown in *Fig.* 102 D, with the newly made
black stitch upon the needle, and the white or right yarn
woven in below.

These two movements as shown in *Figs.* 101 and 102 must
be alternated so long as it is necessary to weave in the RIGHT
yarn above and below and △ while knitting stitches are being
formed with the left hand. These FOUR movements complete
Weaving as applied to the KNIT row.

PURL ROWS

Weaving in Left-Hand Yarn. Movements 1 and 2.
Fig. 103 A.   How to purl a stitch with the right hand, while
weaving in the left yarn *above*. The purl stitch will be completed

as indicated by the arrow. The result (Above) is shown in *Fig.* 103 B.

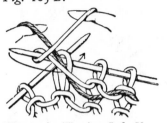

Fig. 103 B.   Result

Fig. 103 A. Weaving Left Yarn Above (Purl)

Fig. 104 A shows how to purl a stitch with the right hand while weaving in the left-hand yarn *below*, the result being shown in *Fig.* 104 B. These two movements are easily memorised as in weaving "Above," △ the yarn to be woven is held

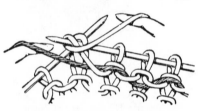

Fig. 104 B.   Result

Fig. 104 A.   Weaving Left Yarn Below (Purl)

above the needle, and in weaving "Below," △ it is held *below* the needle.

These two movements, like the two Knit movements, are alternated so long as the left-hand yarn is the one to be woven.

Weaving in Right-Hand Yarn. Movements 3 and 4.

Fig. 105 A.   How to purl a stitch with the left hand while weaving in the right yarn "Above." The yarn is held *above*, and the purl stitch will be completed as directed by arrow.

Fig. 105 B.   Result

Fig. 105 A.   Weaving Right Yarn Above (Purl)

Result in *Fig.* 105 B, where the white yarn is about to take its "Above" position.

Figs. 106 A and B show the more complicated method necessary in order to throw the right yarn "Below" when forming a Purl Stitch with the left hand. Insert the right needle purlwise into stitch (*Fig.* 106 A), and take △ right or white yarn upwards between the needles as shown in (*a*). Now place the black or left yarn over the needle point (*b*) and reverse the movement just made with the white yarn, as indicated by the arrow (*c*). This will draw the left yarn into a loop as shown in *Fig.* 106 B, which is then taken through the stitch upon the needle, as indicated by the arrow (*d*). The result is shown in

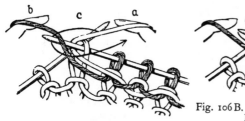

Fig. 106 B. Weaving Right Yarn Below (Purl)

Fig. 106 A. Weaving Right Yarn Below (Purl)

Fig. 106 C, where the white yarn is now below the newly made black stitch upon the needle.

These two movements as shown in *Figs.* 105 and 106 must alternate so

Fig. 106 C. Result

long as it is desirable to weave in the right-hand yarn. This completes the FOUR Purl movements, equivalent to the four Knit movements previously explained. The next consideration is to apply these movements when knitting in pattern.

PATTERN WEAVING—TECHNIQUE

All patterns which are to be woven and knitted on two pins (Flat Knitting) must contain an △ *uneven* number of stitches, but in Round Knitting they must have an △ *even* number of stitches. Before commencing any design, count the number of stitches contained in the pattern. If these are of an even number, △ and the knitting is Flat, then add one extra stitch at the end of the row, and treat this as an edge stitch. Make a △ similar adjustment if the knitting is Round, adding a stitch to make the number even. This edge stitch must be knitted and not slipped. In reading the pattern, remember that this extra edge stitch △ must be ignored as a pattern stitch, otherwise the design will knit up disjointedly.

By casting-on an uneven number of stitches for Flat Knitting, an even tension and weave is assured, as in *Fig.* 107. The first

A. B. A. B. A. B. A.

Fig. 107. Regular Weaving

stitch must △ always commence on an "Above," as this automatically weaves in both yarns and causes each successive "Above" to be over another "Above," and each "Below" over another "Below," as in *Fig.* 107. Here the "Aboves" and "Belows" are indicated by the letters A and B respectively.

Before △ commencing any row, the two yarns should be separated, as they will be found twisted from the previous row, and an "Above" made with the yarns still twisted will be clumsy.

The weaving shown in *Fig.* 107 should be practised before attempting any particular pattern, as, once the rhythm has been acquired, the changes necessitated by pattern become far easier to make. In *Fig.* 107, the left-hand yarn has been woven on both Knit and Purl rows. Weaving of this description is often used to strengthen the heels and toes of stockings.

Pattern weaving proper necessitates the automatic change from colour to colour (black to white) without in any way disturbing the sequence of the "Above" and "Below" order of the weaving on the back of the work. The following diagrams show how such changes are best accomplished.

REGULAR CHANGES
KNIT ROWS

Changing from Left to Right.
Fig. 108 shows simple pattern weaving in two colours.

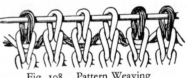

Fig. 108. Pattern Weaving

Fig. 109 A. Change to white stitches, or change from left- to right-hand yarn. The white yarn has just formed a "Below" and is now about to knit a stitch as shown by the arrow, so that the next "Above" will be made with the left or black yarn. By this means the "Above" and "Below" movement will still continue, with little interruption. Pattern permitting, then, △ always change to a right-hand Knit Stitch on an "Above." The convenience and neatness of such a change can be appreciated by the result shown in *Fig.* 109 B.

Fig. 109 A. Change from Left to Right Above (Knit)

Fig. 110 A. Change from Right to Left Below (Knit).

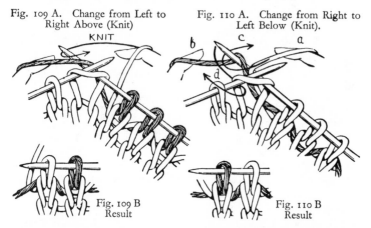

Fig. 109 B Result

Fig. 110 B Result

Change from Right to Left. Fig. 110 A. Changing from white to black (or from right- to left-hand knitting). It will be seen that the black yarn which has been woven up to now has just formed an "Above," so the white yarn must continue the journey "Below" by the movement shown by the arrows in *Fig.* 110 A, or as detailed in *Figs.* 102 A to C. The result of this change is shown in *Fig.* 110 B.

Figs. 109 and 110 illustrate a △ REGULAR change, and can be easily remembered by the formula, △ "Change to right hand on an 'Above' (right—above), or to left hand on a 'Below' (left—below)."

REGULAR CHANGE PURL ROWS

Change from Left to Right. The same rules which govern the Knit rows apply also to the Purl rows. *Fig.* 111 A shows a change from black to white in pattern. The right hand is about to purl a white stitch, while the left yarn is being woven as an "Above," and in consequence is held above the needle while the Purl Stitch is being formed. The result of the change-over is shown in *Fig.* 111 B.

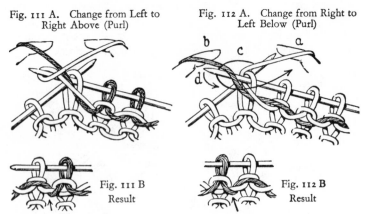

Fig. 111 A.   Change from Left to Right Above (Purl)

Fig. 112 A.   Change from Right to Left Below (Purl)

Fig. 111 B
Result

Fig. 112 B
Result

Change from Right to Left. Fig. 112 A shows a change in pattern from white to black. (This movement is shown in detail in *Figs.* 109 A and B.) The weaving ends on an *Above,* so that the white yarn must continue the journey *below,* and the result, as shown in *Fig.* 112 B, reveals how neatly this is accomplished.

These rules—△ change to a right-hand Purl Stitch on an "Above," and to a left-hand Purl Stitch on a "Below"—hold good on the Purl row as on the Knit, and in all patterns which permit of this Regular method of changing, the movement will be accomplished on a half-stitch, as shown in *Fig.* 113. This illustrates a line of knitting in a pattern of black and white as it would appear from the back, when the changes have been Regular, and made by the Knit and Purl movements just described. The unbroken rhythm of the weave as indicated by the letters A and B should be noted, with the change effected on a half-stitch.

IRREGULAR
      CHANGE

Some patterns demand an Irregu-lar change; that is, changing on the opposite movements **to**

Fig. 113.   Regular Changing

those just described, a right stitch being changed on a "Below," and a left on an "Above" weave, with the result as shown in *Fig.* 114. Such changes cannot be avoided, but if this contrary action is recognised when such a change occurs, and the "Above" and "Below" movement still followed, the change-

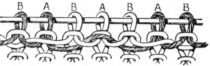

Fig. 114. Irregular Changing

over will be effected in a stitch and a half, and the general rhythm resumed again immediately. The journey of the yarn "Above" and "Below," though apparently Irregular, is still maintained as shown by the letters A (Above), B (Below) in *Fig.* 114.

Irregular patterns need careful tension, otherwise the change is apt to distort the front of the work.

WOVEN KNITTING

In Woven Knitting, *Fig.* 115, the woven side of the fabric becomes the front and the knitting stitches are to the back. This type of fabric was used in early Victorian days for making knitted waistcoats for men, and was also known as Waistcoat Knitting.

The Weaving is carried out by the principles just described, using the two right-hand Knit movements "Above" and "Below," as

Fig. 115. Woven Knitting

shown in *Figs.* 99 A and 100 A, and the two Purl movements shown in *Figs.* 103 A and 104 A, the woven yarn being carried by the left hand on both rows.

The yarns should be of a bold character and of different ply, as the woven yarn is usually a little thicker. The knitting is worked on two knitting pins, and the pattern shown in *Fig.* 115 is achieved by △ casting-on an *even* number of stitches, and commencing every row on an "Above" weave. (Compare this with *Fig.* 107, where the same weaving principles are used, but with an *uneven* number of stitches.)

The woven yarn (left hand) must be tensioned rather lightly and maintained the same throughout. Two colours only, black and white, have been used in *Fig.* 115, but the work permits of other colours in alternating rows, as experiments will prove.

Knitted waistcoats of this description were often enriched with silk embroidery stitches, Cross Stitch, Bullion Knot, or even two Back Stitches being worked to link the woven yarns together at the places of contact. Knitted in delicate shades, the fabric is effective for pram covers, bed jackets or slippers.

GEOMETRIC KNITTING

Colour knitting patterns of a geometric nature are neither Stranded nor Woven. The colours are changed as the

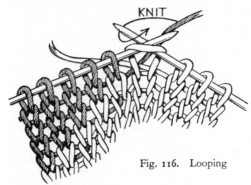

Fig. 116.   Looping

pattern demands by merely △ looping the two yarns, to avoid gaps, as shown in *Fig.* 116. In forming a diagonal line to the *right*, as in *Fig.* 116, the △ right yarn is crossed in front of the left on the Knit row and left

here; on the return Purl row crossing is not necessary as the purl stitch will encroach in pattern, and the yarns automatically be looped. When forming a left diagonal as in *Fig.* 117, △ the cross is made on the Purl row but not on the Knit.

Vertical bands of colour must be looped △ every row, as there will be no encroaching stitch to form a natural link in either direction. Separate balls of yarn are needed for every change of colour, and a simple diagonal line, such as shown in *Fig.* 117, would demand the

KNITTING IN
SEVERAL COLOURS

use of three separate balls, two of white and one of black. A Harlequin design such as shown in *Fig.* 118 would necessitate the use of seven different balls in every line of knitting, and even more if the pattern were extended beyond that shown in the diagram.

Fig. 117. Simple Geometric

Fig. 118. Advanced Geometric

The knitting is only conveniently done on two knitting pins, as the different yarns being left at the end of each pattern would, in Round Knitting, $\bigwedge$ be discovered on the opposite side of the colour to be knitted.

TARTAN PATTERNS

Tartan socks worn by the Highland regiments are knitted in this way. These demand the simultaneous use of many different balls and colours, sometimes twenty, since each diamond and diagonal line must have its own particular ball, and each, in changing, $\bigwedge$ is looped to its neighbour, as shown in *Fig.* 116. Tartan socks are knitted flat on two knitting pins, and seamed down the back when completed. They can be done in Round Knitting providing after each round the knitting is turned, i.e. after completing a round, knit to the seam stitch, knit this turn, slip it and purl back in pattern.

FESTIVE KNITTING

Fig. 119 shows a unique piece of colour knitting as worked by the peasants on the Dalmatian coast. The socks are worn on festive occasions, at weddings, religious feasts, etc., and in the house without shoes, so that the pattern is seen. The motif consists of roses, green leaves and yellow gorse, and the knitting is worked on five needles (round), while the pattern is worked at the same time, but backwards and forwards across the front only. The pattern is carried on the instep needle, and the pattern stitches in each alternate round are slipped and $\bigwedge$ the background stitches of black only are knitted. When this needle is completed, leave the black yarn and purl back on this same instep needle, only this time knit with the colour pattern wools only, knitting the stitches which were previously slipped, and slipping those which were previously knitted. By this means, the different

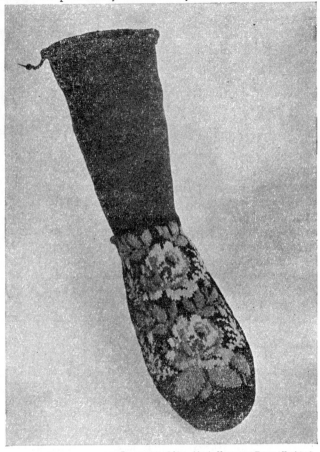

Fig. 119.   Festive Sock from the Dalmatian Coast

yarns used for the pattern are taken back again to their correct position. The round with the black yarn is then completed, and on the next round the knitting will proceed in the usual way, using the different colours as needed. In turning there will be no space, because of the stranded black yarn beneath. This rose motif is on the front of the sock only, the sole, toe and the spaces between the motif being knitted in black.

There is a certain amount of stranding from colour to colour, but of no distance, so well is the motif planned and balanced. The roses are shaded, pink, red and blue in each flower, and the leaves are veined with brown.

FESTIVE KNITTING

A pattern of this description could be worked on a Stocking Frame (*see page* 116) with ease, and quite probably this peculiar technique originated from this source.

JAZZ KNITTING

This is knitting worked in any solid fabric—Stocking Stitch, Moss Stitch, etc.—and in every conceivable colour that happens to be left over in the wool bag. There must be some system in the colour arrangement, otherwise the result is chaos, and the best way is to collect all the colours together and use the ball of largest dimensions for the background colour. This should be repeated after every or every other change of colour.

Method. Knit right across the fabric, varying the number of rows with the different colours so that the horizontal strips are of different widths. A waved stripe of this description is quite successful, in the following pattern:

Row 1: K.2, * M.1, M.1, K.3, K.2 tog., S.1, K.1, p.s.s.o. K.3. *

Row 2: Purl.

Repeat these two rows.

Use extra fine needles, as this makes the fabric very solid, and useful for hot-water-bottle covers, etc.

COLOURED KNITTING

To intercept the fabric with a wide band of Purl is most effective. Purl fabric is the reverse side of Stocking Stitch, and is knitted in the same way.

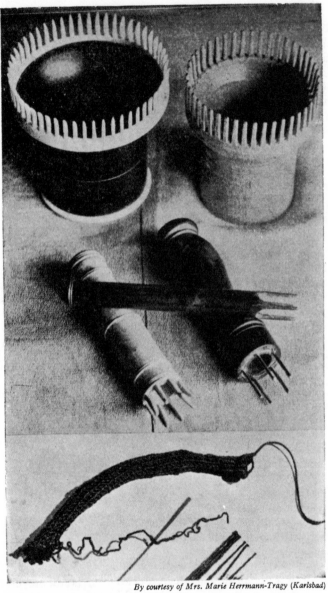

By courtesy of Mrs. Marie Herrmann-Tragy (Karlsbad)

Fig. 120. Circular Knitting Frames, 18th century, of ivory and wood,
together with Tubular knitting in silk

FRAME OR RAKE KNITTING

RAME, OR RAKE KNITTING, has been known by many different names, such as Ring, Box, Bung, Spool, Reel and French knitting. In France we find that the great tasselled caps worn by the Revolutionaries were knitted this way on ring or circular frames, while shawls, petticoats, blankets, stockings, bags, purses, sacks, nets, hammocks and even curtains were made on Ring or Straight knitting frames in France, Britain, Germany and other parts of middle Europe.

The fabric could be plain or patterned (*see* Festive Knitting, *page* 113). The great knitted carpets (*see Fig.* 1) could have been constructed in this way on long straight frames, stranding the colours from peg to peg, with ease.

But history has left little record, either written or pictorial, of Frame knitting, yet it was a quick and easy way of making large fabrics, straight or shaped, and its use for this purpose survived up to the middle of the 19th century. From thence it

REINS FOR CHILDREN

dwindled to a kindergarten occupation, but later enjoyed an unexpected wave of popularity during the World War of 1914–18, when it served as a congenial occupation for the blind and wounded. The technique of frame knitting is the same as that practised by children in making whipcords and reins on cotton-spools, and, though rarely worked to-day, it has contributed throughout the ages its quota to the general development of knitting; and must, for this reason, be recognised in any book dealing with the subject.

An interesting collection of 18th-century knitting frames, of the luxury type, is shown in *Fig.* 120. There are four different shapes, the larger circular model being 3″ in height, and made of ivory, mounted on horn. This has 54 pegs. The smaller is made of wood, and contains 44 pegs. The three smallest frames, made long for convenient use in the hands, have pegs of varying number. The largest has 8, being made of wood; the next, also of wood, has 5 steel pegs, while the smallest, with 4 pegs, is cut out in horn. Animals' horns were often used thus for small frames. Each frame is open both ends so that the increasing knitting can fall through. The larger frames would be used for stocking making. The small knitted silk cord, shown below, was worked on the 8-peg frame in

the year 1804 by the grandmother of the present owner. It is as fine as a silk stocking. In medieval days the soft woollen or flax girdles worn by certain monks were also knitted upon frames of this type.

FRAMES

The old knitting frames, and the modern ones too for that matter, were either straight or circular in shape. The straight frames were used for making single fabrics and the circular for tubular articles, the principle being the same now used in modern knitting machinery. Straight frames would measure anything from 12″ to 60″, and Cap or Ring frames from 6″ to 14″ in diameter. The old workers kept sets of ring frames in different sizes graded in much the same way as cake tins.

Both types of frames were fitted with wooden, steel or bone pegs, regular in height and distances apart, those set close together producing finer fabrics. For coarse work, such as hammocks, sacks, etc., the pegs would be 2″ apart, or wound on every other peg of a smaller frame.

To Make a Frame. Strong, well-seasoned timber, about 1″ thick, must be chosen, otherwise the frame will warp, and the knitting become uneven. The old straight frames were often constructed

Fig. 121
Straight Frame

of wood 4″ to 6″ thick (*see Fig.* 121), and supported on wooden trestles. Such frames would be fitted with 70 to 200 pegs. One peg equals one knitting stitch; thus articles up to a width of 200 loops could be made on such a frame.

The centre opening varies in width from $\frac{1}{4}''$ to $\frac{3}{4}''$, the pegs being placed about $\frac{1}{4}''$ to $\frac{1}{2}''$ from the edge of the opening. The closer these are together, the nearer they must approach the edge of the opening.

The average distance is about $\frac{1}{2}''$ apart, and $\frac{1}{4}''$ in from the opening. Height, $\frac{1}{2}''$. Those used by the blind are usually $1''$ in height, and for kindergarten work they are about $1''$ apart and $\frac{5}{8}''$ from the edge. On straight frames the pegs can fall immediately opposite or alternate with those on the opposite side.

HOOKS

The knitting loops are lifted over the pegs with the fingers, or with an instrument curved at the point like a string needle or nut-pick, either of which make a good substitute for the old frame hooks, which were shaped like a bent nail, attached to a wooden handle.

MATERIALS

All kinds of yarns, wool, flax, hemp, string or cotton can be used: garments, stockings, etc., in wool, curtains in cotton, and bags in macramé string. The thicker the yarn the larger in proportion will be the fabric.

Double string should be used for strong shopping bags and hammocks. Rainbow wool for kindergarten work.

STRING BAG

WORKING METHODS

Tubular fabrics such as scarves, caps, stockings, mittens, etc., are better made on circular frames, but both straight or tubular fabrics can be made on straight frames.

Straight fabric can be made on a circular frame by missing a peg, and working backwards and forwards instead of in circular rotation. Small articles can be made on large frames, but not vice versa.

CASTING-ON

The stitches, or loops, are "wound" or "cast-on" the pegs as shown in *Fig*. 122, and this represents the fundamental winding for all patterns on either straight or circular frames.

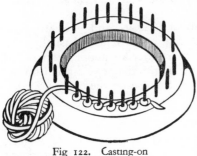

Fig 122.   Casting-on

The yarn is first knotted to one of the pegs or made firm in a slit on the edge of a frame (*see Fig*. 123). From here the yarn is wound round each peg as in *Fig*. 122, until the starting point is again reached. Two windings are necessary before the work can commence. When the cast-on is completed, the loops should be pushed well down to the base of the peg to make room for the second winding. This applies to the knitting throughout, as it keeps the tension even and the work from becoming too tight. The second winding is shown in *Fig*. 123, but on a straight frame, though the method is the same on either shape.

SECOND WINDINGS

The manner in which the second winding is made determines the stitch or pattern in which the fabric will be made. There are only two fundamental second windings, one where the yarn is laid along outside the pegs, as in *Fig*. 123, and the second where it is looped round the peg, as in *Fig*. 124. The first produces a much closer knitted fabric than the second and is known as Plain or Close Stitch. The second, a more open and crossed fabric, is known as Raised Crossed Stitch. The former is a fabric similar to ordinary stocking stitch, and the latter one to Crossed Stocking Stitch.

The term "Crossed" is more often used to explain the windings, which "cross" the middle opening, than to explain the appearance of the fabric. In working straight fabrics, a spare peg will occur at the end of each alternate row, having only one wind. This is correct, and equivalent to slipping a stitch in ordinary knitting.

PLAIN OR CLOSE STITCH

Make the second windings as in *Fig.* 123. The yarn is laid round the outside of the pegs, and held in position through the slit at one end. The cast-on loops are then lifted over the yarn, and off the peg, one completed loop being shown at A, and a second in the process of being lifted off at B. The loops

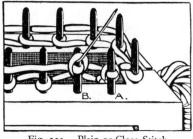

Fig. 123. Plain or Close Stitch

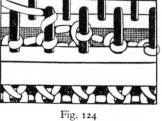

Fig. 124
Raised Crossed Stitch

can be lifted thus, one at a time, or both hands can operate simultaneously on the two sides of the frame, and, once the first stitch has been lifted, the tension becomes very slackened, and this double operation is more simple.

When all the loops have been lifted, a third winding the same as the second is made, and the loops again lifted over and off the pegs, and so on until the length of fabric required is constructed.

RAISED CROSSED STITCH

The second winding in *Fig.* 124 is identical with the original cast-on shown in *Fig.* 122, and is the same on a straight or circular frame. As an example of variety possible on a knitting frame, this stitch is shown here worked on one side only of a straight frame, and as a single fabric. This method of working from right to left, and left to right, will plait the stitch, as in *Fig.* 47. Were this winding made in one complete and circular journey, a Crossed Stocking Stitch, as in *Fig.* 39, would result.

RIB IN CLOSE STITCH

Ribbing (*Fig.* 125) introduces the use of Purl or "Back" Stitches, these being worked on the back row of pegs.

To cast-on, wind as in *Fig.* 122; only to and fro across the opening of a straight frame as in *Fig.* 125 A. This being a "close" pattern, the second and each subsequent winding should be as in *Fig.* 125 B, winding first to the right, as shown, and back, covering the pegs in the same order, and the stitches then lifted over. This will produce a 1 and 1 rib, similar to that made in ordinary knitting.

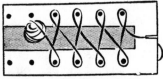

A.   1st Winding (1 & 1)

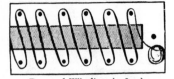

B.   2nd Winding (1 & 1)

Fig. 125.   Ribbing.   Close Stitch

RIB IN RAISED CROSSED STITCH

A 1 and 1 crossed rib is produced by making the first and each successive winding following the same crossed journey as that made by the cast-on loops. *Fig.* 126 shows this, and the commencement of the second winding. Note the odd peg at the back, which is missed each alternate row, to form a slip or chain edge.

TWO AND TWO RIB IN CLOSE DOUBLE CROSSED STITCH

This necessitates the grouping of two pegs in the front row and two pegs in the back row, and the cast-on follows this order as shown in *Fig.* 127. This being a Close ribbing, the first winding follows the same journey, but without encircling the peg.

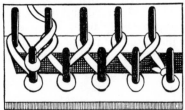
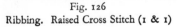

Fig. 126
Ribbing.   Raised Cross Stitch (1 & 1)

Fig. 127.   Ribbing (2 & 2)

To make a plaited 2 and 2 rib, the first and each subsequent winding should follow the identical journey of the cast-on loops. All ribbed patterns, even or uneven, are worked on this principle.

IN TWO COLOURS

Vertical and horizontal stripes can be introduced as follows:

Vertical Stripes. Colour scheme, black and white. To cast-on, wind each alternate peg in black, and on the return journey cast-on over the vacant pegs with white. Continue the subsequent windings in this way, keeping the black loops over the black and the white over the white.

Horizontal Stripes. Cast-on with black, and make the first winding as in *Fig.* 124, also in black. Before lifting the loops, make a third winding in white; thus three loops will be formed on each peg, two in black and one in white. Take the bottom loop over the two upper, and leave two loops on the peg. Wind again with black, and the next time wind with white, always lifting the bottom loop over the two above it.

This treble winding considerably strengthens the knitting, and the method was often used in one colour only when strong articles such as shopping-bags, etc., were being made.

OPEN PATTERNS

These are made by missing one or more pegs at regular or irregular intervals, such as K.2, miss one, repeat; or, in greater elaboration, K.2, miss one, K.3, miss 2, K.4, miss 3, K.5, miss 4, K.4, miss 3, K.3, miss 2, K.2, miss 1, K.2.

Such a pattern would be used in curtain making, and resembles an ordinary drop-stitch pattern. In casting-on, the vacant pegs forming the pattern are missed by passing the yarn along on the inner side of the peg, and winding the others. The second and each successive winding will follow this same procedure.

Open squares and oblongs are formed by knitting on four pegs and missing four pegs. After three or more rounds,

alternate the process. Border patterns are formed by introducing several rows of plain knitting in varying widths between
the open parts. Ribbon can be threaded into these spaces.

CASTING-OFF

The method as shown in *Fig.* 128 applies to either straight
or circular knitting. Knit a stitch on peg B. Transfer this to
peg A as shown, and lift the bottom loop over and off the peg.
The remaining loop is then returned
to peg B, and the process repeated
with the next loop on peg C, and
so on until all the loops have been
passed off.

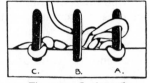

Fig. 128. Casting-off

On a straight frame the yarn is
cut at the last loop and the end
drawn through, as in ordinary knitting. The last loop on
a circular frame should be slipped through the first cast-off
loop, and the cut end of yarn drawn through this loop.

Rib patterns are cast off in the same manner following the
journey of the loops to and fro over the opening. This will
cast-off in pattern, or the knitting can be taken off the pegs and
rearranged in a straight row. In this case the cast-off will not
be in pattern.

Tubular knitting may be finished by threading a length of
yarn through the loops, tying them into a bunch, and decorating with a tassel. Tubular articles may also be joined together
as bags when casting off. To do this, lift the loops from the
back row on to those of the front, making two loops on each
peg. Cast-off as before, only two loops are picked up and
transferred instead of one. This working will make a loose
edge, which can be tightened by just slipping the bottom loop
over the top, and then casting-off. Fringing is another finish.
Take the knitting off the frame and knot the fringe straight
into the loops, either double or single.

FINISHING THE CAST-ON EDGES

The cast-on edge of all frame knitting is always loose and
unsatisfactory without some further finish, so pick up the
loops and return them again to the frame, and cast them off as

just described. The fabric can be made double by joining the two together in this process. Another method is to finish with crochet.

INCREASING AND DECREASING

To Increase. (1) Wind in an extra peg at the beginning or end of the row. (2) Pick up the running thread between the stitches and put it on the peg. This necessitates a rearrangement of the other stitches. (3) Change to a thicker wool. (4) Change a Close stitch to a Raised stitch.

To Decrease. Circular articles made on round frames can be decreased by transferring the work to a straight frame, and reducing the number of stitches by transferring two loops to one peg and knitting them off as one. Rearrange the loops. Decreasing such as this should be made every third round. Straight knitting is usually decreased at either end by knitting off two loops together.

Decreasing can also be accomplished by changing a Raised stitch (*Fig.* 126) into a Close stitch, which method reduces the knitting by about half the width, and was one used in shaping the old long stocking caps. If the knitting is already in Close stitch, then the same result can be obtained by changing to a thinner yarn. On a Ring frame the fabric can also be reduced in width by transferring the work to a smaller ring frame.

CORDS AND GIRDLES

Both are made on small frames containing anything from four to eight pegs (*see Fig.* 120), the most common cord being made by children on a cotton-spool, into which four wire nails have been driven.

An ancient knitting spool carrying four pegs one end and five the other is shown in *Fig.* 129.

A handsome cord can be worked on five pegs in either of the stitches, Close or Raised, and, in macramé or ordinary string, is solid and strong.

Fig. 129
Ancient Spool

Monks' girdles were made on frames of eight or ten pegs, and in flax. This

COTTON-
REEL
KNITTING

would form a casing, which was filled by drawing through
the aperture more flax or soft cotton cord (candle-wick)
The cord should be cut twice the required length and
drawn through double, and two or three lengths may be
necessary to acquire the right thickness. Quite a useful
cord can be knitted on an ordinary straight or circular frame
using two pegs only, as shown in *Fig.* 130. Should a very
thick cord be needed, then
leave a spare peg between.

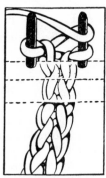

Fig. 130.   Cord

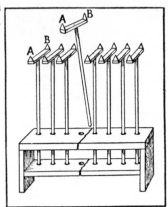

Fig. 131 A.   Loop Knitting Frame

LOOP KNITTING

Yet another but less familiar kind of knitting frame is shown
in *Fig.* 131 A. This is about 14″ in height. Little is known
of its origin, this sketch being made from an old 18th-century
model in the Leicester School of Technology, and is still used
by the students there in creating new knitting patterns adapt-
able to machinery. The frame consists of upright rods about
12″ high, which are square at the base, and carry a crossway
piece, A/B, at the top. These rods are removable as in
working, the loops or stitches collect around them, and,
when a certain length of fabric has been created, rods
must be removed, as shown in *Fig.* 131 A, and the fabric released so that the work may continue. Knitting patterns of
great elaboration can be created, and the frame can be
extended to any width by inserting a spare section in the
middle.

WORKING INSTRUCTIONS

To cast-on, wrap the yarn over the front arm (A), forward two, and back under one, or forward three and back under two. Stocking Stitch. For the second and subsequent rows, the yarn is merely laid along the top of the arm, as in *Fig.* 131 B, and the loops lifted over and off.

Purl stitches are made by lifting the loop over back of cross pieces (B). For Garter Stitch, alternate rows are front and back, i.e. one row lifted over from front cross piece (A) and next row over back cross piece (B). For Rib (1 and 1) one loop front, one loop back. The size of stitch is regulated by position of yarn on cross piece. Near front for small stitches, further back for large.

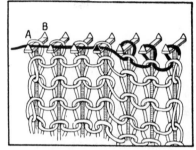

Fig. 131 B.   Working Method

PEG KNITTING

This form of knitting was done by the old Red Indian tribes of America, and is similar in technique to Frame Knitting. The pegs are wound as shown, and wherever three stitches appear in a wind, the bottom one is lifted over and off the peg. The same sort of knitting can be done on the four fingers of the hand, and some think the first knitted loop ever made originated this way! (*See Fig.* 132.)

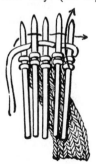

Fig. 132

LOOPED KNITTING

$\mathcal{L}$OOPED KNITTING is shown in *Fig.* 133 A and is formed by looping the yarn round the needle and finger as shown in *Fig.* 133 B. Use needle a little thicker than the yarn, and cast on the required number of stitches. Knit one row.

Fig. 133 A. Looped Knitting

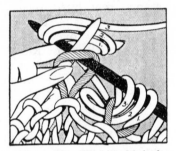

Fig. 133 B. Working Method

Second Row. Knit the first and last stitches in this row, and commence the looping on the second stitch. Pass the yarn twice round the forefinger of the left hand and then round the needle, and knit through the loops so formed, as one stitch. This process is repeated in every stitch, and, when the row is completed, the empty needle should be run through the loops to straighten them out.

Third Row. Knit, knitting the groups of stitches as one stitch. △ When finished, pull each loop smartly into shape.

This will complete a single row or single fringe, but if a wide border of loops is required, then repeat the second and third rows as many times as needed. Repeated thus, without interval, the loops will cover the complete surface as for a rug. If this is not desired, it is better to lengthen the space between the looped rows by introducing three rows of Plain

Knitting, which will permit of sufficient space for the loops to lie flat.

The loops can be graded in depth by winding certain loops round two fingers instead of one. Looped knitting is generally used as borders to pram covers, cot covers, bedroom slippers, and to form fringes of varying length.

LOOPED
KNITTING

LOOPS GAUGED

This ensures strict regularity by working over a gauge or ruler.

First Row. Holding the gauge against the △ right needle, slip the first stitch and insert the needle knitwise into the second. Bring the yarn between the needles as though to knit, and then round over the needle and the ruler two or three times as required, and finally between the needles again, knit off all the loops so formed as one stitch. Repeat on every stitch, except the last, which knit.

Second Row. Knit, △ still keeping the ruler in position through the loops, until the row is completed and then withdraw. Repeat these two rows consecutively or at intervals as required.

TWO COLOURS

Loops of contrasting colours can be added by working two yarns simultaneously one in either hand. Hold the yarn forming the loops in the left hand and loop this round two fingers of the left hand. △ Knit using the second yarn first through the loops so formed, and then through the stitch on the needle, and then draw the first stitch over the second. Repeat.

LOOP EDGE UNRAVELLED

The side selvedge of any knitting, plain or fancy, can be unravelled, when the knitting is completed, to form a loop edge as follows. Cast-off in the usual way, finishing △ one before the last stitch. Drop this, and unravel from top to bottom of the work. This will form a row of loops along one side of the fabric. By dropping two stitches a wider edge will be formed. This can be left so, or further decorated with a knotted-in fringe.

KNITTED FRINGE

A Knitted Fringe can be knitted in any yarn, wool, silk or cotton. This can be used doubled, trebled, or quadrupled, according to the yarn used, and the weight of fringe desired. A cotton fringe is better quadrupled, which necessitates the simultaneous use of four balls of cotton, △ the four strands being held together and knitted as one.

Cast-on a number of stitches divisible by three. Nine stitches will make quite a deep fringe when unravelled, six a medium fringe.

Row 1. * K.1, O.1, K.2 tog. * Repeat.

Row 2, and △ each succeeding row is the same.

Knit sufficient length to decorate article required, and then cast-off as follows:

With six stitches on the needle, △ cast-off three only, and finish. Unravel the remaining three stitches, unravelling the entire length of the knitted strip, until one side presents a fringe of even loops, while the opposite side has the appearance of a knitted braid. This is then attached to the fabric with an overcast stitch. Another way is to attach the fringe row by row as it is being knitted, picking up a loop at a time and knitting this together with the last stitch in the strip. A variation to the braided side of the knitting is obtained by working: * O., K.1, K.2 tog.* △ Knit each succeeding row the same. To straighten the fringe, damp it, and allow it to hang straight, and dry.

MOSS KNITTING

Fig. 134
Moss Knitting

If a knitted fringe as just described is damped △ before it is unravelled, and then ironed to dry it, or put in the oven and baked, it will, when unravelled, have a permanent kink. This is the principle of Moss Knit-ting, so called because it was always knitted in green, and, being permanently crinkled,

looked like moss. Moreover, it was used to make birds'
nests, baskets, etc., which were then filled with flowers or
eggs, and used as a decoration on a table or sideboard (*see
Fig.* 134). The baskets were first covered with flannel, and
to this foundation the rows of baked green knitting were
sewn. Such knitted strips could be worked in any stitch,
preferably Garter Stitch, using about
six stitches and casting-off only three
and unravelling the remainder.

A modern use of Moss Knitting is
for wigs. These are suitable for amateur
theatricals, fancy dress, etc. By
combining Moss and Looped Knitting
(using very large loops), quite a good
imitation of an 18th-century powdered
wig can be achieved, especially in white rayon yarns.

KNITTED WIG

RUG KNITTING

Another form of Looped Knitting, sometimes known as
Oriental Knitting, is used for knitting rugs. This is worked
on the weaving principle, using two separate yarns, as shown
in *Figs.* 99 A and 100 A, *pages* 101 *and* 102 (weaving in the left-
hand yarn "Above" and "Below"). Instead, however, of the
yarn being woven △ straight across the back as shown, it is
looped round the fingers of the left hand in the "Above"
weaving action, i.e. every other stitch.

The work progresses:

Row 1. K.1.* *Above weave,* loop woven yarn under finger and
over needle. Knit. *Below weave,* yarn below, knit next stitch.*
Repeat from * to *, alternating these two movements. At the
end of the row, the woven yarn is cut.

Row 2. Knit.

Row 3. As Row 1, commencing to weave on the first stitch.
Use rug wool for the looping, but, for economy, the second
yarn can be in coarse dish-cloth cotton. If the work appears
thin and open, through knitting too loosely, weave in two
strands occasionally, instead of one.

Patterns of any description, and in any number of colours,
can be "woven" on this principle. After two or three rows

of weaving are completed, the loops should be cut, and when the rug is completed, the pile is evened by trimming it in the same way, as the pile of a knotted rug. Use: car rugs, floor rugs, etc.

Alternative Method. Short ends of cut rug wool can be woven in on the same principle, using an "Above" and "Below" weave to attach each short length, i.e. △ two stitches are necessary to attach each piece.

BEADED AND BEAD
KNITTING

HIS FORM OF KNITTING enjoyed the height of its popularity throughout the 18th and the beginning of the 19th
century, culminating in work so fine, and patterns so realistic
in colour, as to resemble miniature paintings. The subjects
depicted romantic scenery, figures, flowers and hunting scenes,
as clear in outline as a scene on porcelain. The finest
examples of this period were the bead bags made in Vienna;
and the fancy to cover ordinary bottles with Bead Knitting,
and use them for perfume containers, has left us other beautiful
specimens. Some of these still exist in private collections and
museums.

The work had a universal vogue. Bonnets, scarves, dresses,
mittens and lace were all fashionable in Bead and Beaded
Knitting, and the custom of beaded insertions has remained
in many European countries, as part of the festive national
costume. Children's fashions of this period were invariably
beaded.

The exquisite bonnet in *Fig.* 135, worked in the famous star
pattern, the sections of which are a mass of tiny opalescent beads,
shows the high standard of Bead Knitting in England during
the early 18th century. The little coat beneath is an interesting
example of Bead and Beaded Knitting from Germany of the
early 19th century. The band of colour across the centre of
the coat is a solid mass of beads, in various shades of pink and
red. The coat itself is knitted in white, with intermittent
groups of three beads arranged across the diagonal stripes.

Our ancestors revelled in such knitting not only for clothes,
but accessories, and the many little bags, purses, wristlets
and belts displayed in various National Museums tell an
eloquent story of its once immense popularity. The smaller
knitted purses of this age were gems, both in colour and
design.

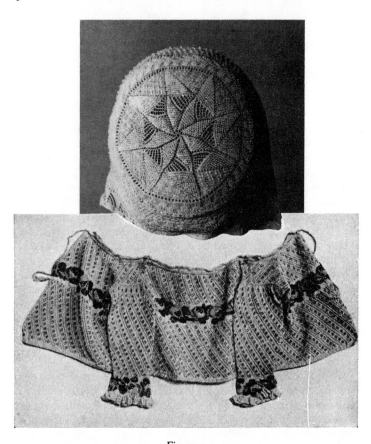

Fig. 135

Bonnet in Bead Knitting — *By kind permission of the Victoria and Albert Museum*
Coat in Bead and Beaded Knitting — *By kind permission of Siegfried Lämmle, Munich*

Beaded cuffs and mittens were a fancy of Victorian days, knitted in silk and spot designs of steel or gold beads. "Stocking" purses were decorated in the same way, one end with gold beads for golden coins, and the other end with steel beads for silver coins; the significance of these two colours on one small purse being often lost on a modern generation which has never enjoyed the use of gold currency!

BEADED AND BEAD KNITTING

There are two methods of work.

The first, BEADED KNITTING, where the beads are knitted in on certain rows at regular or irregular intervals to enrich the appearance of the knitted fabric. This is the simpler form, and often found on little beaded cuffs and shown on the little coat in *Fig.* 135.

The second, BEAD KNIT- TING, is sometimes known as PURSE KNITTING, a name descriptive of its use, since it immediately conjures up a vision

STOCKING PURSE

of bead fabric, whereon the beads are packed so closely to- gether that the knitting stitches are obliterated. See the insertion border of the little coat in *Fig.* 135, also the more familiar bead handbags. Bead Knitting is more complicated than Beaded Knitting, and needs practice to acquire the knack of settling the beads with precision and regularity.

BEADED KNITTING

Designs. The object of Beaded Knitting is to repeat a bead at regular intervals for the purpose of decorating a knitted fabric, and, if worked in parallel rows or in rectangular shapes, the design needs little planning, beyond the regular and pleasing spacing of the beads. A pattern such as that in *Fig.* 139 is a simple matter to plan and knit, but should a diamond design, as in *Fig.* 140, be required in all-over effect on a knitted gar- ment, then the whole design should be planned out on graph paper in order to obtain a good balance and repeat.

Almost any knitted pattern can be beaded, and beads can be added to open lace-like fabrics, just as easily as to solid fabrics. A favourite idea was to add a bead at each junction of an open lattice design. In fact, given proper consideration as to design, colour and effect, a bead can be added to many Lace and Fancy patterns with pleasing results.

Materials. In Beaded Knitting the beads can be of any size and shape provided a proper relationship is maintained between the yarn or thread used for knitting, the size of which should

BEADED!

about fill the hole of the bead. If very large beads are required (such as might be used on a curtain border), then wooden beads are better, as they are lighter in weight. The beads should be symmetrical in shape and size, and can be bought loose or in strings or bunches. The needles must be of a size to form a loop smaller than the bead, otherwise it will slip through to the back. For certain open effects, very large needles can be used, and then the bead will swing between the stitches, clear of any loop, and so add colour to an open fabric. A bead needle approximate to the hole of the bead should be used for threading.

Uses. Beaded Knitting can be used on jumpers, caps, berets, bags, belts, children's clothes and bathing suits, and was at one time used to decorate knitted lace curtains.

THREADING

Commence by threading the beads upon the knitting yarn (wool, silk or cotton), and since, in Beaded Knitting, the beads are usually all of one colour, the simplest method is to transfer them straight from the hank to the knitting yarn, in the manner shown in *Fig.* 136. (If loose beads are used, they must be threaded separately.)

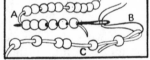

Fig. 136.   Transferring the Beads

The original thread from the hank in *Fig.* 136 is marked A, and the knitting yarn C, and the beads are transferred from

THREADING

the hank A, to the yarn C, via B, which is a fine cotton, threaded double into the eye of a needle, as shown, to permit the easy passage of the bead. This method of transference must of necessity be used when the knitting yarn is rather thick, but in the case of silk or fine cotton it is possible to dispense with both the needle and the thread marked B by piercing A (i.e. the thread of the hank) about 2″ from the end and threading C (the knitting yarn) through the aperture, as though it were the eye of a needle. The beads can then be transferred as required, △ but with care, or the hank thread, which is never too strong, is easily broken.

WORKING METHODS

In Beaded Knitting the beads are added on the second and each alternate row as shown in *Figs.* 137 and 138. △ The second, and all even rows in Flat Knitting being those worked from the back of the fabric (*Fig.* 137). Simple all-over beaded

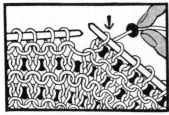 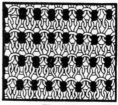

Fig. 137	Fig. 138
Beaded Knitting. Working Method	Beaded Garter Stitch Fabric

designs are in Garter Stitch. The first stitch in the row may be slipped or knitted, and each bead is pushed up to the △ front of the work (*see Fig.* 137) in the direction of the arrow (quite close to the needle), and the next stitch is then knitted. This same process is repeated after each stitch all along the row or as required. Beads added too near the edge incline the work to curl.

It will be noticed that the beads swing between two stitches, and that the hole through the head of the bead lies △ parallel with the needles. This is a distinctive feature of Beaded Knitting. A firm tension is necessary in order to keep the beads in position, and on the right side of the work, otherwise they slip through to the back.

All the diagrams show the knitting loose and open, but this is for instructional purposes only, and to allow the position of the beads and knitting stitches to be better studied. In reality the fabric is as ordinary knitting. Exception can, of course, be made when a light, open mesh is needed. Then a stout knitting cotton can be used, and fairly large needles

(No. 8), also large beads, when the open stitches intersected with beads (they can be of different colours) produce a remarkably pretty effect.

Some of the old samples of Beaded Knitting show several beads—as many as six or eight—pushed up between each stitch. These then form little loops all over the fabric, an idea very prevalent for decorating cuffs and bags in Victorian days.

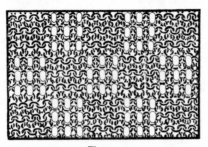

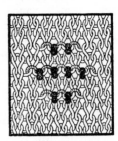

Fig. 139
Beaded Knitting, Checks

Fig. 140
Beaded Knitting on
Stocking Stitch Fabric

After the beaded row is completed, △ the succeeding row is knitted plain and without beads, and then the next bead row is worked as before. Consecutive bead rows are not practical in Beaded Knitting, as they incline the work to curl. The appearance of *Fig.* 137 as seen from the front side of the work is shown in *Fig.* 138.

Fig. 139 shows an all-over check pattern in white beads on a Garter Stitch ground, and from this hint it will be found an easy matter to invent other simple geometrical patterns, such as alternating squares and oblongs, stripes, diamonds, hexagons, etc.

OTHER FABRICS

Fig. 140 shows a Beaded Stocking Stitch fabric, and here the principle of working is slightly different. The beads are added on the second row, as before, △ but in this case on a Purl row. The beads are pushed up as shown in *Fig.* 137, but the stitch △ before and after each bead must be knitted, not purled, in order to throw the bead to the front of the fabric. These Knit Stitches will have the effect of Purl Stitches on the right side of the fabric. See shaded stitches, *Fig.* 140. This principle applies to all fabrics other than Garter Stitch. On a fabric of Stocking Stitch worked in Round Knitting the yarn would be brought forward to purl and the beads would be pushed up on the front of the work in the same way.

The point to watch is that the stitch △ preceding and that succeeding the bead is of kindred kind, i.e. two Purl or two Knit Stitches, as a bead will only swing evenly between two of similar character.

BEAD OR PURSE KNITTING

Bead or Purse Knitting differs considerably from Beaded Knitting, both in appearance and preparation. The pattern is △ formed by the different colours of the beads and is prepared in the threading process, the knitting being merely a means of securing the beads in position, and not intended to show at all on the front of the work.

MATERIALS

Use fine but strong thread, sufficient to fill the hole of the bead yet not so thick as to prevent easy movement; otherwise the beads will fray and break the thread. Fine steel needles are necessary—Nos. 16 to 20, larger if beads and thread permit.

DESIGNS

Bead designs must be planned and charted on graph paper, as shown in *Fig.* 141. This is a very simple little mosaic pattern, copied from an old English purse of the 19th century, and would serve as a first piece of work; but whether the design be simple or complicated matters not, the method is the same, △ a chart must be used as a guide, in order to obtain a clear and regular bead picture.

THREADING △

This is the most important part of the work. After the chart is prepared, the pattern is threaded up as shown in *Fig.* 142, commencing from the top left-hand corner of the chart, marked A, *Fig.* 141, and finishing at B. △ All patterns must finish at B, as all knitting charts are read from right to left and commence at the bottom right corner. The last bead threaded will, therefore, be the first to be knitted

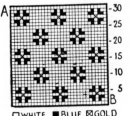

OWHITE ■BLUE ⊠GOLD

□WHITE ■BLUE ⊠GOLD

Fig. 141

Chart for Bead Knitting

off. To make certain of this, the number of squares forming the pattern must be counted vertically. The chart in *Fig.* 141 contains thirty-one rows —an odd number—so, to ensure that the last bead will be B on the right, the threading must commence at A on the left. Had the pattern contained only thirty rows, then the threading would have commenced at the top right-hand side in order to finish at B. The rule is: △ odd rows commence threading from the left, even rows commence right.

The entire pattern is threaded bead by bead in this way. In *Fig.* 142 the four top rows only have been threaded, and these compare to the four top rows of the chart. The fifth row would be a repeat of the third, and

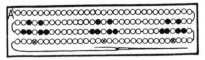

Fig. 142.   Threading a Bead Pattern

the sixth would be a repeat of the second. This would complete the first line of motifs, and the seventh row, which is a plain row, would then be threaded, and so on.

△ The beads must be threaded strictly in pattern, as one bead more or one less than the chart demands in any one row will disjoint the entire design. In threading, avoid all cracked and uneven beads, and those with small holes likely to crack in threading. A small hole will also fray the thread.

To assist in counting the rows, thread in a short piece of wool, about an inch long, at the end of each row. A large pattern can be threaded in sections, beginning at Row 10, and threading to Row 1. For the second threading, begin at Row 20 and thread to Row 11, and so on. △ Be careful to begin the correct end of the row, and to remember that the last bead threaded will be the first to be knitted. Should it be necessary at any time to transfer the beads on to another thread because of fraying, then the method of transferring shown in *Fig.* 136 should be adopted, △ taking care not to reverse their order.

WORKING METHODS

△ Bead Knitting can only be joined at the beginning of a

row, and on the extreme edge, and must be joined with a knot. Two edge stitches are made at the beginning and end of each row, before the bead stitches are commenced, as beads on the

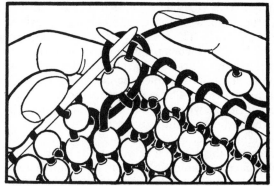

Fig. 143. Bead Knitting, Knit Stitch

extreme edge of the fabric are difficult to manage. In the case of Round Knitting, this difficulty will not occur.

Bead Knitting is worked in Crossed or Twisted Stocking Stitch (*see Fig.* 39, *page* 53), and the beads are knitted in with every stitch on △ both the Knit and Purl rows. On the Knit row the bead is passed through the loop to the front of the work with the left forefinger, as shown in *Fig.* 143, while the needles are still inserted in the loop, after which the left needle is withdrawn. The stitch on the needle should be well opened so that the bead can pass through quite easily, as, once the stitch is off the needles, it closes up

Fig. 144. Bead Knitting, Purl Stitch

automatically because of its crossed formation. The tension should be kept firm, without being immovably tight, otherwise the beads slip through to the back of the work. In working the Purl row, the back of the knitting will be towards the worker and the beads will therefore be pushed through the loops from the back to the front of the work (*see Fig.* 144). The needle is inserted through the back of the loop and the stitch must be opened with the needles and the new bead brought up to the place where the needles cross, and then passed through the loop with the thumb, simultaneously with the making of the stitch. The arrow in the diagram shows where the thumb will be placed when pushing the bead through the loop.

In working this Purl movement, keep the right hand well over the needles. This enables the bead to be helped through the loop more easily. The right needle should be held firmly and the left needle withdrawn from the loop (stitch) in preference to the ordinary Knit movement of slipping the loop off with the right needle.

The secret of this knitting is to keep the left hand active. In most other forms of knitting, done in the English way, the left hand is passive and the work done by the right hand.

COMPARISON

It will be noted that, in Bead Knitting, $\triangle$ the beads are actually on the stitches, and not between them, as in Beaded

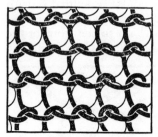

Fig. 145. Back of Bead Knitting

Knitting. This causes the bead to lie at a tilt, almost upright, as the hole through the bead will run almost vertical, as shown in *Fig.* 145. This is the back of the work. In Beaded Knitting it will be remembered that the hole lies horizontally, and by this distinction the two methods of knitting can be recognised. A Crossed Knit Stitch, i.e. one knitted through the back of the loop, can, if desired, be used for Beaded Knitting; and for isolated beads, introduced as a high light in pattern knitting, beads are better added in this manner; as the one crossed stitch is sufficient to keep each bead in position. In old knitting directions this would be called a "Bead Stitch," and the crossing be understood. The Beaded parts of the bonnet in *Fig.* 135 are worked this way. There are several ways of crossing a Knit Stitch, as explained, and the Plaited method, given in *Fig.* 47, is sometimes used as a basis of Bead Knitting.

EMBROIDERED KNITTING

URING THE 18TH CENTURY, when needlepoint lace was the coveted possession of every beau and belle, fine cotton knitting, delicate and lace-like in pattern, was created and embroidered with lace stitches to serve as a less expensive imitation of this beautiful but expensive lace. An example of this kind is shown in *Fig.* 146, a small bonnet, where it will be seen that all the solid parts of the pattern have been made the foundation for embroidery stitches. These consist of long Bullion Knots arranged as leaves either side of a centre vein. They cover a solid six-pointed star, while others are grouped as flower petals upon the smaller diamond shapes. The embroidery stitches have been beautifully worked, and the knitting is extremely lace-like and typical of the exquisite perfection to which cotton knitting of this century aspired.

Embroidery stitches of this kind, but in coarse thread and on coarser knitting, were used on bedspreads created well on into the 19th century.

LACE STITCHES

Most embroidery stitches of an embossed character such as Bullion Knot, used in *Fig.* 146, will blend quite pleasingly with cotton knitted fabrics, when of a lace-like character.

SWISS DARNING

What is known as Swiss Darning is the most popular form of embroidery to use on solid fabrics such as Stocking Stitch, etc. The

SWISS DARNING

working method is shown in *Fig.* 147, where it will be seen that the second yarn, shown black, is merely covering a row of knitting stitches. The black yarn is shown as finer

Fig. 146. Bonnet. 18th Century Embroidered Knitting

than the background, so that its journey can be traced, but in
reality the same ply must be used or the embroidery stitches
will not cover properly. The large, blunt-pointed needle in
Fig. 147 shows the position for the next stitch, and the arrow
the position for the succeeding stitch.

Fig. 148 shows the method of working a pattern in Swiss
Darning, the pattern being carried over several lines of knitting
to form a block of colour. This same method can be applied to
blocks or forms of any shape or
dimension.

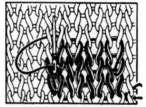

Fig. 147.   Swiss Darning
Knit

Fig. 148.   Swiss Darning
Pattern Formation

To begin, tie the yarn to one of the stitches as at arrow,
and cover the required number of stitches as in *Fig.* 148. In
mounting to the row above, insert the needle as shown beneath

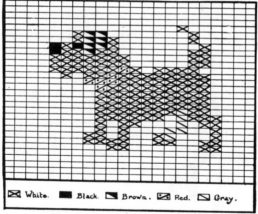

⊠ White.   ■ Black.   ◣ Brown.   ⊠ Red.   ◳ Gray.

Fig. 149 A.   Swiss Darning.   Chart

the head of the stitch, and continue in the reverse direction to
cover the stitches of the succeeding row. To do this the
knitting can be turned upside down, as a moment's study of

this diagram will reveal that knitting stitches are in reality the same from either aspect, and, once the rhythm of the darning has been acquired, there will be no mistaking the journey of "ins" and "outs" which the needle must make. The knitting stitches are purposely extended in *Fig.* 148 so that the method can be accurately followed, and the turns at the end of the rows correctly made. △ The tension must be strictly in accord with the knitting or the effect is lost.

CHARTS

Swiss Darning patterns of this nature can be worked in one or many colours, and all sorts of little motifs, animal, bird or

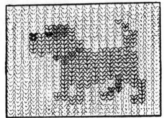

Fig. 149 B
Swiss Darning. Dog

Fig. 150
Swiss Darning. Initials

flower, can be created by working from a chart as shown in *Fig.* 149 A. Here five different colours are used, represented by five different symbols.

The chart shows oblong spaces and not squares, as knitting

stitches take an oblong shape. This is rather important, as to work in Swiss Darning from a chart especially prepared for embroidery, such as Cross Stitch patterns, where each stitch is square and not oblong, the resulting effect would look somewhat queer. A dog similar to this one would come out long and narrow like a dachshund, and not as he is shown completed in *Fig.* 149 B.

where he looks exactly like the chart. △ When working from charts not specially prepared for knitting, make a tension measurement, and add extra rows of darning to the height as necessary.

Swiss Darning is often used to add an extra bright stitch of colour to a Woven or Stranded knitted pattern worked in Colour Knitting. It is also used to outline an all-over pattern, similar to that in *Fig.* 82, *page* 92. In *Fig.* 150 it is used to form an initial for marking purposes. All stockings were at one time marked this way, and knitting samplers of letters and numbers kept. In Switzerland and Austria, Swiss Darning is often used for creating bizarre patterns on ski gloves in preference to Weaving or Stranding, as it is claimed to be softer, more porous and so warmer. *Fig.* 151 shows the method of working when the fabric is ribbed. The needle shows the upward movement for making the Purl Stitch, and the arrow the downward movement.

Fig. 151. Swiss Darning. Purl

CROSS STITCH

Cross Stitch embroidery is quite effective on a coarse knitted fabric. The method of work is shown in *Fig.* 152 A and here the position of the needle is important, as this is the best way of forming the cross so that it is not dragged out of shape by the elasticity of the fabric. Tie the yarn to the head of a stitch and bring the needle out at A. Take the needle across the stitch and insert it at B, and bring it out as arrow

Fig. 152 A. Cross Stitch
Working Method

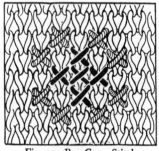

Fig. 152 B. Cross Stitch
Pattern

to form the next stitch, as in the diagram at C, and so on. These movements are useful in forming individual Cross

Stitches, but for a long row of Cross Stitches it is a simpler matter to make a line of half-crosses in one direction, and, on the return, fill in the other half-cross. A simple pattern in Cross Stitch, using two different colours, is shown in *Fig.* 152 B.

HONEYCOMBING

Honeycombing has always been a favourite method of decorating a knitted ribbed fabric, and the work is immensely simplified on a knitted fabric, as the vertical ribs form a guide, and the stitches can be easily counted and the work kept perfectly straight (*see Fig.* 153 A).

Honeycombing owes its origin to being a legitimate method of controlling fullness on a linen fabric, and on a knitted

HONEYCOMBING

fabric it has the same effect, so extra fullness must be allowed when any knitted garment is to be decorated with Honeycombing. On a linen fabric, the extra width necessary is three times that of the finished Honeycomb pattern. On a knitted fabric this would be far too much, and only about half as much again should be allowed.

The ribbing should not be too wide; a 3 and 1 rib as in *Fig.* 154 A makes an effective background. The wider the ribs are apart, the more the contraction and the greater the fullness, which is not always too comely on a knitted garment.

WORKING METHODS

There are two forms of Honeycombing, and both are effective on knitted fabrics. The form shown in *Fig.* 153 A and B is the more popular, and is worked from △ left to right, with the embroidery thread taken from group to group of stitches beneath the fabric. Commence on the left at A, and bring the needle out at B, and make a stitch as shown. Three back stitches are made thus as at C. The needle then travels again behind the fabric, and emerges to make another group of three as at D, and so on. These stitches in

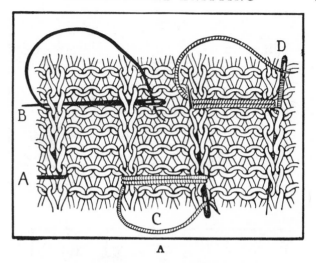

A

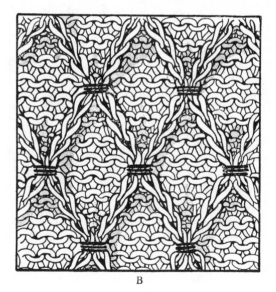

B

Fig. 153. Honeycombing. Method 1

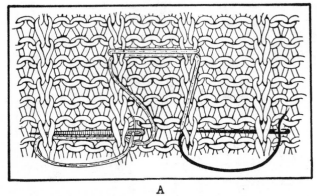

A

B

Fig. 154. Honeycombing. Method 2

Fig. 153 A are left spread open so that the work can be followed, but in reality each group of three are drawn together (not tightly, as they are in linen) to produce the decoration shown in *Fig.* 153 B.

The second working method is shown in *Figs.* 154 A and B, and is worked from △ right to left (*see Fig.* 154 A). The procedure is the same, only the linking thread travels from one group of stitches to another over the surface of the fabric, as shown by the little arrows, and this forms a zigzag line of contrasting colour to the pattern, as shown in *Fig.* 154 B.

LADDER HEMSTITCHING

An effective method of decorating a Ladder Drop Stitch pattern is shown in *Fig.* 155. Insert the needle downwards under two bars and over two, and twist as directed by the arrows. This pattern is most effective worked in a yarn the same colour as the fabric.

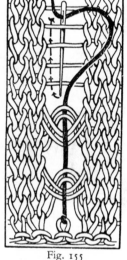

Fig. 155
Ladder Hemstitching

APPLIQUÉ

Motifs are often applied to knitting, though this fabric is not one that takes kindly to Appliqué, unless the applied motifs happen also to be knitted. By this means the golden rule of applying one similar fabric to another similar fabric is retained and with successful results, as both, being of the same nature, will wash. The favourite motifs for Appliqué are small nursery animals of angora wool, brushed and applied to pram covers.

In applying these animals, △ see that the direction of the knitting is the same, and that the stitches of the applied object run parallel to those beneath, otherwise the pull of the fabrics will be different, and the knitting become distorted when washed.

GARMENTS

ALL THE TECHNIQUE of knitting, Casting-on, Casting-off, Increasing, Decreasing, Turning, Grafting, etc., etc., are put to practical use in garment-making, and to understand all of these is to ensure success in the undertaking.

A knitted fabric has a natural elasticity because of its construction, but this should not be abused by leaving the question of fit to its accommodating nature, △ otherwise the figure will fit the garment instead of the garment fitting the figure! This is quite another matter, and often the case why knitwear is taboo to the full figure.

Fit in a knitted garment is obtained in the same way as fit in a garment of any other fabric: by knowing individual measurements and working to them. The growing tendency is to knit from paper patterns, but these, being constructed for other fabrics, seldom have the simplicity of outline necessary for one of knitted fabric.

The simplest possible outline of any paper pattern is the body shape known as a Block or Foundation Pattern. Upon this any design can be constructed and measured with certainty, as on the body of the person herself.

The outline is simple, as knitted garments should be simple. Their beauty is not complication, but fabric, which can be varied at will to form any effect desired. If done with reason, all the effects obtained in dressmaking by cutting, insetting, gathering, seaming, etc., can be obtained by a change of fabric, and by Increasing and Decreasing, according to the effect desired.

MEASUREMENTS

The Block Pattern in *Fig.* 156 is specially designed and simplified for knitting requirements. The method of construction is also simple, and can be followed by anyone. The necessary measurements are few, but must be accurate and are better made by a second person and written down as made.

(*Note.* A sheet of brown paper, scissors, ruler, inch tape or measure, pencil and rubber will be required. Cutting paper, squared with inch measurements, is useful, as the lines provide a guide for the position of shaping, Increasing, Decreasing, etc. These can, of course, be ruled in on ordinary brown paper):

BODY MEASUREMENTS

    1. Bust Measurement   ? inches.
    2. Back Length   ? inches.
    3. Back Width   ? inches.
    4. Waist   ? inches.

SLEEVE MEASUREMENTS

    1. Inner Arm Seam   ? inches.
    2. Elbow   ? inches.
    3. Wrist   ? inches.

BUST MEASUREMENT

This must be taken round the fullest part of the figure, adjusting the tape across the front, under the arms, and across the back. Do not strain. Take the measurement easy, and write down the exact figure and △ decimal recorded.

BACK LENGTH

Take a piece of string and tie round the waist. Push this well down to the hips and the small of the back. Measure the back, from the nape bone of the neck △ to the string. This position of string gives position for waist measurement.

BACK WIDTH

This is measured across the widest part of the back, i.e. across the shoulder-blades, but △ not across the shoulders. This is a back measurement, not a shoulder measurement.

WAIST

Round body at depression above hips.

INNER ARM SEAM

Measured from the armpit to the wrist-bone.

ELBOW

Measured round the elbow-bone, with the arm bent.

WRIST

Open the hand, with the thumb to the side, and encircle the hand and thumb with the tape, and take the measurement.

EXAMPLE

The pattern shown in *Fig.* 156 is drafted to the following measurements:

Bust	36 inches.
Back Length	15 inches.
Back Width	13 inches.
Waist	30 inches.
Armhole of Pattern	16 inches.
Inner Arm Seam	18 inches.
Elbow	12 inches.
Wrist	8 inches.

MEASURING!

NO TURNINGS

No turnings are allowed in cutting a Block Pattern, as it is constructed to represent the body and form a basis of measurement. No turnings are necessary in knitting, since all edges have a natural selvedge and are overcast together; therefore a knitted garment, unlike one of any other fabric, can be constructed direct from a Foundation Pattern without any additions.

BLOCK PATTERN

This represents half the front and half the back of the body, so the two width measurements, i.e. bust and width of back, must be halved. To avoid decimal divisions, locate the measurement on the tape and fold it in half.

Any measurement made upon this pattern amounts to the same as being made on the person, as it is the body shape in paper opened out flat.

"BLOCK" PATTERN

CONSTRUCTIONAL LINES (*Fig.* 156)

AA′ = Half total bust measurement.

AB = Total length of garment required + 1″ (measurement must finish below the waist-line. The length given would suit short cardigan).

AC = 1″.

CD = Back length to waist level.

E = Midway CD.

F = Midway CE. Rule these measurements as shown in dotted lines.

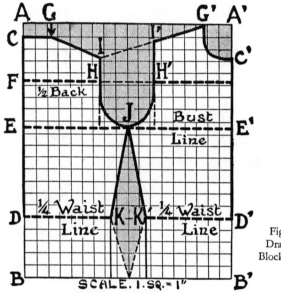

Fig. 156
Drafting a
Block Pattern

PATTERN LINES

FH = Half back width. Rule a perpendicular line.

CG = One-third half back width.

HI = CG measured on perpendicular line. Rule in back shoulder GI.

A′G′ = CG. Rule a dotted line from G′ to I.

A′C′ = A′G′ + $\frac{1}{2}$″.

G′I′ = GI. (Both shoulder measurements equal.)
        Drop a vertical line from I′.

J = A point midway armhole.
Drop a vertical dotted line from J. Repress each side dotted line surplus measurement until DK and D'K' each equal quarter waist measurement. Continue straight to basque line, or as suggested by dotted lines for fitted basque.

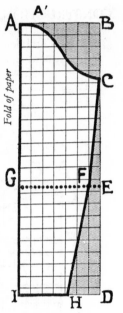

Fig. 157 A
Drafting a Sleeve Pattern

When knitting, make JK' (front) longer than KJ (back) by knitting in extra rows as follows:

For a bust measurement less than 36″, add rows to equal $\frac{1}{4}$″. For a bust measurement of 36″, add extra rows equal to $\frac{1}{2}$″. For bust measurement of 40″ and more, add rows equal to 2″. These extra rows can be made in dart formation by turning, or knitted across and eased in either side when joining the side seams in a space of 2″, finishing 1″ before J. (*See* heavy line on *Fig.* 158.)

The measurement AB = total length required, can be any length *below* the waist, the depth being adjustable to the garment required. Body lines never vary, only garment lines.

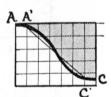

Scale. 1 sq. = 1″

Fig. 157 B. Sleeve Top

SLEEVE (*Fig.* 157)

AB = Half armhole measurement, minus 1″. (This measurement can only be made after the front and back of pattern are cut, as it is made as directed by the arrows in *Fig.* 158, round the armhole of the paper pattern.)

BC = Quarter armhole measurement, plus $\frac{1}{2}$″.
CD = Inner seam length.
E = Mid-way CD.
FG = Half elbow width.

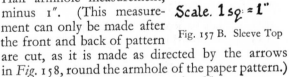

HI = Half wrist width.

AA′ = 1″.

CC′ = 1″. Draw in armhole.

> *Note.* Top of sleeve when it is cut measures 1″ to 2″ more in circumference than the armhole of the pattern. This to be eased in on fronts between I′ and H′.

NOTE. The letters are given in the order in which the lines should be drawn and the pattern constructed.

Bodice. The neck and the base of the armhole must be drawn in freehand; all the other lines can be ruled.

Sleeve. The line between C and H is not a straight line, but drawn in two sections, one from C to F, the second from F to H.

The curve to the crown of the sleeve is a freehand line, like an elongated letter S, as shown in *Fig.* 157 B. Mark the points A′ and C′. Lower A′ ⅛″, and higher C′ ⅛″. Rule a straight line from these two points and draw an S shape as shown by black line. Cut the sleeve pattern. Note that this must be cut to the fold of the paper. Only the half block, as given, is necessary for the body, as both sides in knitting are shaped alike. If the full pattern is desired, just cut the block as explained and then place centre back and front to fold of paper and cut a working pattern, △ but do not cut the block.

WAIST AND HIPS

Fig. 158 shows waist adjustments, KK′ fitted waist, MM′ loose waist, L straight, no waist at all. This is rarely advisable, as a slight indication of waist always ensures a better fit. When the hips are larger than the bust, take the hip measurement, quarter this and measure as on line XX′ (*Fig.* 158) from B′. Rule a line from X to J as shown by arrow. This will be the half front section. Take the same measurement for the back from B. Cut out the pattern.

EXPERIMENT

It is advisable to draft *Figs.* 156 and 157 in miniature on squared paper, making one ¼″ square to equal one inch, as the method will be more easily grasped and better applied to a full-size pattern.

The most important measurements are the back length and the bust measurements, as on these the whole of the pattern is constructed. △ Be most accurate in making these.

TO FIT THE PATTERN

As there are no turnings, the pattern cannot be overlapped and pinned together in the ordinary way, but must be pinned over separate strip of paper about 1″ wide, cut to the necessary length. This is laid under the edges of pattern to be joined (the side seams and the shoulders) and pinned on both edges. Make certain that the edges of the back portion and the front portion touch without overlapping. Pin the inner seam of the sleeve and armhole together in the same way. If the measurements have been taken correctly, there should be no alteration.

KNITTING INSTRUCTIONS

The necessary number of stitches to cast-on will be ascertained by a tension gauge (*see page* 41).

If the yarn and the stitch are of the type that must be pressed (*see page* 237), then press the tension square and count the stitches afterwards. △ Do not over-press or stretch. Count before and after pressing and note the difference.

The width to be increased at the sides of a garment is ascertained by erecting the vertical lines K′, K, *Fig.* 158. This shows a measurement of $1\frac{1}{2}″$ either side, or 3″ on the front and 3″ on the back. The shaping for the armhole is derived by erecting the vertical lines O, O′, *Fig.* 158. The necessary shaping for the sleeve is ascertained in the same way, by erecting a vertical line from H. (*See Fig.* 158.)

DESIGNING

How to design on a block pattern is shown in *Fig.* 159. Do not cut or design on the original Block Pattern, but place this over another piece of paper and cut a second and design on this. If more convenient, design to scale in miniature on graph paper.

Decide on the style required and draw in the necessary lines. *Fig.* 159 shows a jumper in Stocking Stitch fabric with turnover collar, fastening with button-stand. Vest effect in open contrasting fabric, outlined with another contrast of fabric (Moss Stitch), finished with basque and cuffs of ribbed fabric, four different fabrics being used to get this effect. To

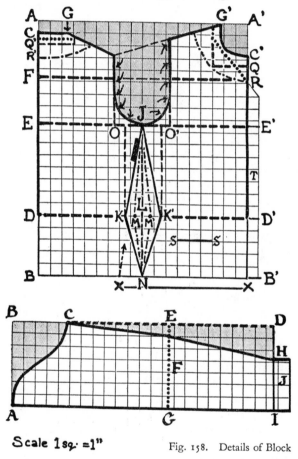

Scale 1 sq. = 1"   Fig. 158.   Details of Block

ascertain the depth of vest, take a measurement on self and mark-off same on pattern. Also, do same for width measurements.

A garment can begin by casting-on the base selvedge and

constructing upwards, or it can commence at point J (arm-hole) and be knitted across the figure.

It is generally constructed from the bottom upwards. So all shaping—increasing and decreasing—must be considered from this aspect. Skilfully used, a garment or

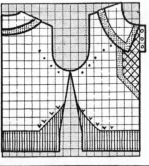

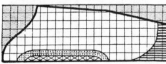

section of a garment can take any shape required, but every detail must be planned out beforehand, as shown in *Fig.* 159. Make all necessary measurements on yourself, and transfer these to the pattern. It is quite simple, as the fundamental shape already exists. Check the fabric as it grows continually on the pattern. Accuracy depends on the gauge. Make a first experiment on a simple shape and stitch, and allow such designs as shown in *Fig.* 159 to be a later effort.

Fig. 159.   Jumper Design

Cardigan. To make a cardigan from Block Pattern, measure the necessary depth below waist-line. Lower the armhole ½″. Make the under-arm seam straight from J to L, or slightly shaped if required. Add a button-stand to both fronts about 1″ wide as shown at T, *Fig.* 158. Position for pocket about 2″ below waist-line.

STYLE AND FABRIC

Style lines in knitting are usually confined to a change of neck-line or length of sleeve, as very little variety exists in shape. Variety of fabric, however, is the charm of knitting, and since the world of fabric is literally at the finger-tips, change can be made when desired.

The old knitters provided themselves with a sampler of knitting stitches (*see Fig.* 4, *page* 11), and chose their fabrics with knowledge, and

PATTERN
LINES

there is still no better way than to emulate this example.

△ In changing stitch thus, gauge all patterns beforehand, as some "take up" more than others.

NECK-LINES

The neck line on block pattern is throat high. The ribbing of a round neck often finishes at this level, with perhaps a back opening of 2" fastening with a button-stand. The depth of the ribbing must be marked within this line, as shown at dotted line R, *Fig.* 158, and a vertical line dropped from the shoulder, at this point, will give the width of stitches contained in the curve.

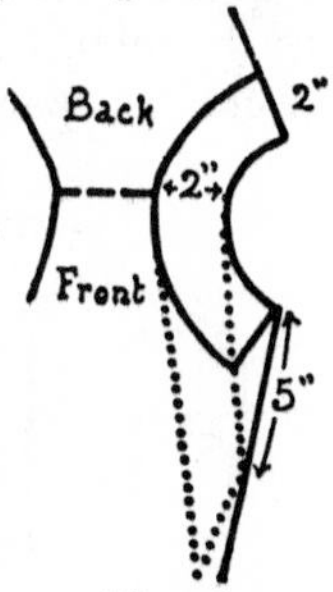

To lower the neck all round, measure 1" or as required down from C and C', and 1" along the shoulder from G and G'. Draw in the new neck-line, making other inch measurements at intervals to assist in keeping the curve at a regular distance. All measurements should be first made on yourself and then transferred to the block.

Fig. 160
Separate Collars

Square Neck, Fig. 158. This is lower in the front than the back. Allow a depth of 1" (or as required) for front and $\frac{1}{2}$" at shoulders and back. Depth of ribbing beyond this measurement.

V-shaped Neck. Measure the required depth for the front first on yourself and then on the block, and rule in as shown in *Fig.* 158.

Separate roll-over Round collar as in *Fig.* 160 is obtained by placing the shoulder seams together and measuring as directed 2" all round, or required depth. For a turnover V shape rule in as shown by the dotted lines. Make the front depth 5" or to suit your figure. A deeper V is more imposing on a fuller figure. Also greater depth to collar in either shape.

SLEEVES

To form a puff sleeve, *see Fig.* 161. Outline block top of sleeve on sheet of paper. Measure length 5" (or as required) down from armhole and draw horizontal line. Add curve of ¾" to base. Divide sleeve as shown and cut, separating the divisions 1" or 2" apart as required. Redraw and then recut sleeve.

The extra width will be allowed when casting-on, and a double decrease will be made in the middle of each dart, decreasing to A where the sleeve will be the original width. Supposing each dart to be a width of 2" and the gauge 6 stitches to the inch, 12 stitches will be decreased. This means 6 double decreases spaced over the required distance for each dart.

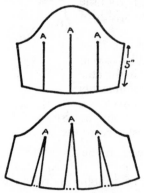

Fig. 161.   Puff Sleeve

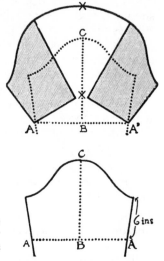

Fig. 162.   Square Sleeve

To extend the top of sleeve, adjust pattern as in *Fig.* 162. Outline top of sleeve on paper. Line AA' is 6" down from armhole. Rule this, also central line BC, and cut. Open out the pattern as shown. Redraw and recut sleeve. The additional height CX = BX.

Square Shoulder. This can be made by darts, increasing an inch in depth, to the top of the sleeve. The principle would be similar to inverting the arrangement shown in *Fig.* 161.

Cuff. A turned-back cuff is added to length of sleeve as at J in *Fig.* 157 A.

SKIRTS

Measurements
  1. Waist.
  2. Hips.
  3. Length.

The hip measurement is made round the widest part of the figure. The length is regulated by the distance from the ground.

The Skirt Draft shown in *Fig.* 163 is constructed to the following measurements:

  Waist, 28″.
  Hips, 38″.
  Length, 30″.
  Hem 54″
  Hip 9″ below waist.

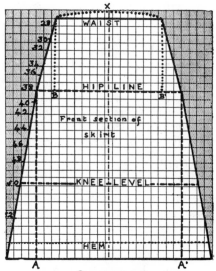

One square = 1″

Fig. 163. Skirt Draft

Knee level, 9½″ above bottom of skirt.

The front section only is shown, the back being the same as the front, with the exception of extra inch added to back waist in curve as shown. To obtain this, cast-off across front. With 6 stitches to the inch this will leave 84 stitches on the needle. Knit another inch (8 rows), casting-off 9 stitches at the beginning of each row. Then cast-off the remainder.

NEEDLES

Skirts are usually constructed on circular needles and in Round Knitting. If in Flat Knitting, they are made in sections and joined.

FABRICS

Skirt fabrics are usually of solid design. If knitted in Stocking Stitch, a 2″ hem should be first knitted in Garter or Moss Stitch, otherwise the fabric will curl under and need to be finished with a sewn hem.

TO FIT THE PATTERN

A skirt can be given an impression of panels by introducing stripes of two or more Purl stitches at regular intervals. When knitting in a fancy stitch or pattern, this is the better way, as the decreasing can be regulated either side of the stripe, and the repeat of the pattern stitch better controlled.

Decreasing. The first decreasing Round is about 5″ above the base line of hem just below knee bend. Here about 8 or 12 stitches are decreased at intervals, in one round. The interval between each decreasing round will vary according to gauge and number of rounds to the inch.

GAUGE

Knit a tension square and count the number of stitches to the inch and the number of rows before and after pressing. A knitted skirt is apt to drop from 1″ to 2″ in wear. Pressing gives some idea of the drop likely to occur. Take this into consideration when arranging length.

The dotted lines erected at A and A′ show the amount of decreasing between the hem and hip—16″. The dotted lines erected at B and B′ show the amount of decreasing between the hip and the waist—10″. (*See Fig.* 163.)

PLAIN SKIRT

Gauge, 7⅓ stitches to inch. Width, 54″.

$54 \times 7\frac{1}{3} = 400$.

Cast-on 400 stitches.

Knit hem to depth of 2″ in Garter Stitch. Change to Stocking Stitch and knit another 3″.

1st Decrease: * K.48, K.2 tog. *. Repeat to end of round, finishing with K.2 tog. Knit another 2″ in depth.

2nd Decrease: * K.47, K.2 tog. *. Repeat. Knit another 2″.

The next decreasing round will be: K.46, K.2 tog., and continue knitting and decreasing thus until hip width. Then knit straight to hip, and from here decrease to waist width.

PANEL SKIRT

A six-panel skirt, constructed to the dimensions given in *Fig.* 163, is made as follows:

Gauge: 6 stitches to inch. Width, 54″.

54 × 6 = 324 stitches.

Cast-on 324 stitches.

Knit hem to depth of 2″ in Moss Stitch.

Pattern Round 1.   * K.52, P.2. *.   Repeat 5 times. Knit another 3″ and then decrease.

1st Decrease: * S.1, K.1, p.s.s.o., K.48, K.2 tog., P.2. *. Repeat.

This decreases 12 stitches in one round, or 2″, as shown in Fig. 163. The skirt width is now reduced to 52″.

2nd Decrease: This is made after knitting another 4″. * S.1, K.1, p.s.s.o., K.46, K.2 tog., P.2.*. Repeat. Continue decreasing as shown in Fig. 163.

DETAILS OF GARMENTS

Alphabetical Order

SMART DETAIL, such as well-finished pockets, evenly united shoulders, neatly formed neck-lines and well-joined seams, all add to the groomed appearance of a knitted garment.

ARMHOLE

In shaping an armhole, the same number of decreases must be made on both sides of the garment. Knit to the position for the armhole, and lay the knitting on the block pattern, when the number of stitches to be cast-off will be seen at a glance. Gauge and yarn will each affect the following decreases.

Small. For slim figures the usual number to cast-off is three at the beginning of armhole, two on next decreasing row, and one at end of every other row as necessary.

Large. For fuller figures, the number is graded over several rows (*see Fig.* 164). For shaping the back, cast-off five and knit to end of row. Cast-off five at beginning of next row and purl to end of row. Turn and cast-off four, knit row. Cast-off four at beginning of next row and purl back. Cast-off three, knit row. Cast-off three at beginning of next row and purl back. Turn and cast-off two, knit row. Cast-off two at beginning of next row and purl back. Turn and decrease one each end, and continue thus on each alternate row, or according to pattern, until the required shape is attained. △ Always check against pattern. The fronts will be shaped in the same manner.

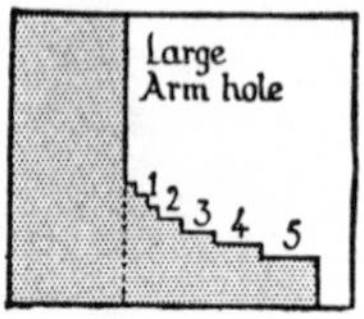

Fig. 164
Shoulder Shaping

For a medium armhole, or if a thicker yarn is used, the ratio would be 4, 3, 2, 1, instead of 5, 4, 3, 2.

BEADING OR RIBBON HOLES

A row of evenly spaced holes through which ribbon or cord can be passed is made in *Fig.* 165. K.2, * Over, K.2 tog. Repeat from * to end of row.

Row 2: Purl each Over as a stitch.

This will produce a very close beading, but the holes can be spaced any distance evenly, or grouped in twos as required, by increasing the number of knitted stitches between each hole.

Fig. 165
Beading
or
Ribbon
Holes

A deeper beading is made by Over twice, i.e. K.2, * yarn twice round needle, K.2 tog. *. Repeat to end of row.

Row 2: Purl, purling the double Over as one stitch only and dropping the second over.

Row 3: Knit the loose Over together with the stitch immediately over it to make a clean hole.

BELTS, SEPARATE

These can be worked in DOUBLE KNITTING.

Double Knitting. A Tubular Fabric constructed on two knitting pins is worked as follows:

Cast-on an even number of stitches and knit the first row plain.

Row 2: Knit the first two stitches. * Insert the needle into the third stitch and cast the yarn twice round the point of the needle and draw through a double loop. Pass the yarn between the needles to the front of work, and slip the fourth stitch purlwise, take the yarn to the back again. * Repeat these two movements from * to *. Knit the last two stitches.

Row 3: Knit 2.* Insert the needle into the third stitch, cast the yarn twice round the point of the needle as before. Yarn to front and slip next stitch, slipping the double loop as one stitch. Take the yarn to back again. * Repeat from * to *. Knit the last two stitches.

Row 3 is repeated throughout. Knit the last row and cast-off.

A Tubular Fabric made in this way will have no opening at all, and thus is only used for ties and belts. The final end can be opened if desired, before casting-off, by dividing upon two needles, taking one stitch alternately on to each needle, and then casting-off separately in the ordinary way.

Fig. 166. Border. Separate
KNITTING-UP

BORDER, SEPARATE. *Fig.* 166

Straight. A straight border of contrasting or matching colour is added to the sides of a fabric already knitted, as in *Fig.* 166. Hold the fabric in the left hand and insert the needle into the side of a loop from back to front as shown. The movement of the yarn, over and under the needle, is similar to a crochet action, and is more easily made when the yarn is held in the left hand. △ KNITTING UP in this way avoids any unsightly gap, and forms a neat connection. (*See also page* 238.)

Curved. A curved border added to a neck-line or finish to sleeveless cardigans is added in the same way, only △ the loops to be picked up will have been slipped, so that one loop is picked up for every two rows of knitting. This is necessary to obtain the curve, otherwise there would be too many stitches.

Frilled. On a straight edge, knit twice into every loop; on a curved edge, do not slip the stitches of the edge to be bordered, and knit-up every loop, as for a straight border. A frill at a neck edge would fold over, and need to be increased in size every third or fifth row, according to gauge, increasing every third or fifth stitch, according to width and depth.

BUTTONHOLES. *Figs.* 167—169

All buttonholes on garments must be evenly

A   B
Fig. 167.   Buttonhole.   Bébé

spaced, with the same number of knitted rows between each.

Buttonhole, Bébé. The smallest and simplest buttonhole is shown in *Fig.* 167 A, and is worked as follows: Over, K.2 tog. On the next row, the Over is purled as an ordinary stitch. This will form a small round hole which should be overcast to make it firm and strong, as in *Fig.* 167 B. The black spots indicate where the succeeding overcast stitches will be made to complete the hole. This buttonhole is principally used on children's garments.

Buttonhole, Horizontal. This is the most popular buttonhole, and is generally used down the front of coats and cardigans. Knit to the position for buttonhole (usually three or four stitches from the edge of the garment), and then cast-off three

A

B

Fig. 168. Buttonhole. Horizontal

or more stitches, according to the size of the button (*see Fig.* 168 A) and knit to the end of row.

Second row: Purl (or work in pattern) to the cast-off stitches, and here cast-on as many stitches as were cast-off in the previous row. This was three in *Fig.* 168 A (cast-on method to be used is *Fig.* 51 A, *page* 60), and complete row. The finished buttonhole is shown in *Fig.* 168 B.

Buttonhole, Vertical. This buttonhole, shown in *Fig.* 169, is generally used on pocket flaps. Knit to the position for buttonhole, and here the fabric is divided to form an opening, so that each side must be knitted separately. Knit in Garter Stitch. Turn. Knit back. Turn. Knit. Do this for seven rows to form

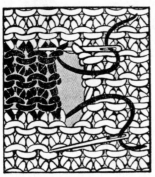

Fig. 169. Buttonhole. Vertical

the right side of the opening, as shown white in *Fig.* 169. An odd number of rows must always be knitted on this side in order to finish with the needle point and yarn just over the buttonhole and in the correct position to continue the knitting after the left side of the buttonhole has been worked up to this level.

Three or five rows are generally sufficient to form the depth of the bottonhole, but in fine yarn seven rows are necessary.

The left side of the buttonhole (shown black for instruction purposes) in *Fig.* 169 is now begun. With right needle facing in correct position, and the stitches of the right side still upon it, return to the bottom of the buttonhole and △ join on a new ball of yarn. Knit six rows, turning the knitting at the hole as before. This will bring the left needle to the top of the buttonhole. The second ball of yarn is then discarded, leaving an end of about 10″, and the knitting continues from the original ball, knitting straight across with the right-hand needle. If properly worked, there will be two loose ends of yarn, one top and one bottom of the buttonhole, as in *Fig.* 169. These are threaded separately into a darning needle and over-cast stitches made top and bottom of the opening, to form a strengthening bar or the entire buttonhole can be overcast, and this on a loose fabric is often a good idea.

This buttonhole should be worked in Garter Stitch, as in Stocking Stitch the sides roll under and fail to grip the button. Two Purl Stitches introduced on every other line, either side of the opening, would correct this, if a Stocking Stitch fabric is particularly desired.

BUTTON-STAND. *Fig.* 170

Where the knitting divides for the opening on a garment to be fastened with buttons and buttonholes, a separate stand for the buttons should be added, as in *Fig.* 170, by casting-on extra stitches at the end of the row. On a dress fastening at the back, these stitches will be added on the left side of the fabric at the end of a

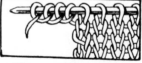

Fig. 170.   Button-stand

Purl row, fastening in the front, on the left side at the end of a Knit row. Sew neatly in position with matching yarn when garment is complete. Button-stands for fly openings are made in the same way.

CUFFS

Turn-back cuffs should be knitted first on small needles and then change to original for knitting the turned back portion. If necessary, an intermediate size of needle can be used. Cuffs treated in this way will have a snug fit.

COLLAR, SEPARATE

This is made to shape required, *see page* 174, and sewn on from the inside, loop for loop. Find the centre of the back.

GRAFTING OR WEAVING. *Figs.* 171—174

Grafting is a method of uniting two knitted fabrics horizontally in such a way that the join is absolutely invisible.

The work is done with a blunt wool needle and matching yarn, the grafting stitches being made to imitate those of the knitted fabric. The yarn must be of sufficient length to complete the work, as no join can be made. The fabrics so joined can be straight or formed at an angle by TURNING, as in shoulder seams. This matters not, providing the same number of stitches are contained on both sides to be united. The loops must be arranged to sit evenly and

GRAFTING   opposite each other, and the grafting

stitches must be of the same tension as the knitting, otherwise the join will appear as uneven knitting. The needle enters each loop twice, with the exception of the first or last stitch in the row, in its journey across the fabric.

Knit Fabric. Fig. 171 A shows the method of joining the top of one piece of knitting to the top of a second piece, as in joining shoulder seams. Commence as shown. The yarn is broken in a long length from the ball and threaded into a wool needle. This is shown black in the diagram, so that the journey can be better seen. The knitting should be laid flat on the table and the needles withdrawn loop by loop with the

A

Fig. 171
Grafting
Knit

B

progress of the work, as shown in *Fig.* 171B. *(See also page* 228.)

Purl Fabric. The method of work on a Purl fabric is shown in *Fig.* 172.

Fig. 172. Grafting. Purl

Garter Stitch. (*Fig.* 173.) In uniting a fabric of Garter Stitch, △ the two methods of work, Knit and Purl, must be combined horizontally in order to form the correct fabric, the top stitches being as for a

Fig. 173. Grafting. Garter

Purl fabric, and the bottom as for a Knit. This necessitates three separate movements for each stitch, as shown by the needle and the two arrows. The needle is inserted downwards through the top loop, then through the two bottom loops as indicated by arrow, and up under the same top loop again.

Ribbing. This also combines the Knit and Purl grafting movements, but △ vertically. The method of commencing is shown in *Fig.* 174 A, and the grafting further in advance in *Fig.* 174 B. Note the continuation of the journey as shown by the arrows, the second arrow indicating the change from a Purl to a Knit Stitch. In grafting two separate ribbed fabrics together at the top, such as in a shoulder seam, there is a difference of one

A   B

Fig. 174. Grafting. Ribbing

half-stitch to rectify at the beginning (*see also page* **239** for correcting half-stitch). In uniting a ribbed fabric to another ribbed fabric, both of which have been worked in the same direction, there is no discrepancy. In changing from Knit to Purl, watch the tension of the grafting yarn.

HEM, SEWN. *Fig.* 175

A hem is sometimes used at the top of skirt or knicker where an insertion of elastic is necessary, or when knitting is divided to shorten, and secured with a turned hem.

For the former, the stitches are not cast-off in the usual way, as this would form a bulky line, but are sewn straight off the needle, as in *Fig.* 175. The knitting must finish on the △ Knit row, so that the point of the needle faces as in the diagram, and the yarn broken off leaving sufficient length to thread straight into a large needle, and sew the loops in position.

In commencing this hem, △ see that the first two loops (AA) group closely into the edge of the knitting, and that the head of the stitch picked up below is immediately under that on the needle; stitch A fitting over stitch A at the extreme edge, and B over B, and so on, △ otherwise the hem will fall on the bias at the opposite end of the knitting.

Fig. 175. Hem. Sewn

Make certain to pick up the head of the stitch △ in the same row of knitting each time, and so keep the hem straight. This is rather difficult on a hem of any length, and a useful tip is to knit or weave in a coloured cotton on the row to which the hem will be turned, as the white line in the diagram. This ensures the correct stitch in the correct line being picked up, and is worth the trouble, as this is a tricky hem to unpick and straighten.

HEM, PICOT—OR HEM WITH TREASURE TEETH

This hem makes a dainty finish to any garment, jumpers, undies, socks or cuffs, and is very simple to work.

Cast-on an even number of stitches, using the two-needle

method (*see Fig.* 53, *page* 64), and knit the second row into the front of the stitches. Knit to the required depth of the hem, and then knit a row of holes: K.1, * Over, K.2 tog. *. Repeat. *See Fig.* 176 A. Always knit the first and last stitches of the row. In the next and

"TREASURE TEETH" HEM

Purl row, the Overs must be purled as ordinary stitches.

When this is completed, continue knitting as before, working the same number of rows △ plus one extra, so that the knitting will end on the Purl row. With the second needle, pick up the loose stitches of the cast-on edge, the number of which should equal those already contained on the other needle. Place both needles together and with a third needle knit the two together, as in *Fig.* 176 B, taking one stitch from the front and one from the back needle, and knitting them both

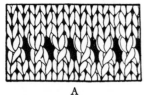

A

off as one stitch, as in *Fig.* 176 C. This will join the fabric together, and form a hem with a picot edge, or hem of "treasure teeth," as the Austrians call it.

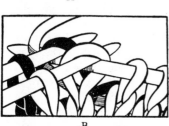

B

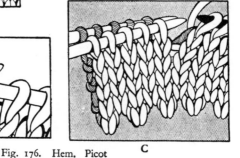

C

Fig. 176. Hem. Picot

NECK-LINES. *Figs.* 177—179

NECK, POLO

Knit to the throat, and here make the distance AA (*see Fig.* 177 A) about 2″. △ If this distance is too wide, either front or back, the collar will pull a hole. Put these stitches on a holder and proceed to turn, completing one side before beginning the other. Turn one stitch before the last at the end of the Purl row for right side of neck, and one before the last every Knit row for left side of neck, for about 1″. Then knit straight to the shoulder. The correct number of turns should be measured against own pattern. The size of opening for a polo neck should be the size of the head, minus 1″. For the back, only two or three turns are necessary, according to thickness of yarn.

When completed, divide the stitches on four needles. Knit with a fifth, ribbing to a depth of 6″ or 8″, as required. The neck will fit better if ribbing is commenced on needles two sizes smaller and changed after 2″ or 3″ of ribbing.

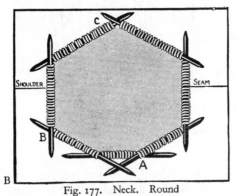

NECK, ROUND

A round neck can be of any depth and is usually finished with a ribbing. The depth of ribbing required should be marked off on own pattern (*see also Fig.* 158, *page* 157), making equal measurements all round. The greater the depth, the greater in number will be the stitches taken with each turn. *Fig.* 177 A is a diagram showing the method of work. The garment is knitted to AA′. The curve between A and B is derived by turning (as in *Fig.* 186 A to D). Turn

Fig. 177.   Neck.   Round

at end of Purl row for right side of neck. The number of turns will vary with the depth of the neck. The diagram shows three turns of three stitches, two of two stitches, and the remainder of one stitch. When the turning is completed, put the stitches from A' to B on a stitch-holder and knit straight, completing the right shoulder. Knit the left to correspond. The number of turns for the back will vary with depth, but as *Fig.* 177 A shows a deep curve, this is the same as the front—turning from C to D—which represents the shoulder line. When both sides are completed, either cast-off, or graft the shoulder seams together. Take the stitches from the holder and arrange on six or seven needles as in *Fig.* 177 B. Rib for the necessary depth, refining the fabric every 4th or 5th round, by changing to smaller needles. (*See* Regauging, *page* 41.) The stitches from A to B can be cast-off instead of turning, and afterwards knitted-up, and the ribbing decreased instead of regauged, though it is not so professional.

NECK, SQUARE

The simplest square neck is shown in *Fig.* 178 A. Knit in pattern to A. Here change to Garter Stitch. Width of about 6″ for a child, and 8″ or so for adult. Knit across to required depth (1″ for a child) and cast off middle section. Knit each shoulder separately, changing to Garter Stitch at CC′. Slip first stitch every row at neck edge. Knit the back to correspond.

NECK, SQUARE RIBBED

Change to ribbing at A in *Fig.* 178 B. Knit across, keeping middle section in ribbing. Cast-off at B, middle section. The ribbing at D is added separately. Knit the shoulder C in pattern, straight, slip stitches at neck edge. Knit other shoulder to correspond. Knit the back. The stitches along the neck edge of C are then knitted-up as in *Fig.* 166. Use smaller needle and change on the next row. Knit ribbing D as directed for this by lines in diagram. Cast-off. The corners should be knitted-up at the end of each row, or seamed together afterwards.

KNITTING UP
THE NECK

NECK, V-SHAPED.

The simplest V neck for a child is knitted in Garter Stitch, similar in manner to the square neck in *Fig.* 178A. Find the centre of garment about 1″ before dividing for neck. On a Stocking Stitch fabric do this on the Purl row, and, on coming to this centre stitch, knit it. On the next Purl row knit

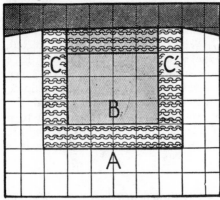

Fig 178 A

3 centre stitches, on the next 5, and so on, until there are about 14 stitches building up a V shape in Garter. Divide for neck. Take 7 of 14 for one side and still keep these in Garter Stitch as follows:

Row 1: Knit 7 and decrease (K.2 tog.). Do this on every Knit row until the V is of sufficient width, and then knit straight to shoulder. Knit the other side to correspond.

NECKS, "V" RIBBED

A "V" neck with ribbing, as in *Fig.* 179A, can be finished in three different ways, though in all three the preparation is the same. The garment divides in the centre at AA',

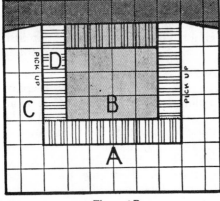

Fig. 178 B
Necks. Square

and shoulder B is knitted in pattern, decreasing on the Kni rows after the first stitch at the neck edge (K.2 tog.). Then knit straight to shoulder. The edge stitches must be slipped knitwise on the right side (Knit row) and purlwise on the left (Purl row) for B' to match. Knit the back, turning to shape as required, and cast-off. Add ribbing.

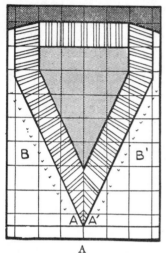 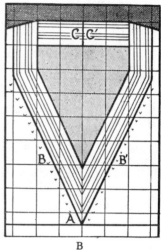

A   B

Fig. 179. Neck. "V" Shape

Ribbing. Method 1. Knit-up the stitches round the neck edge on a circular needle, commencing at A and finishing at A'. Knit backwards and forwards on this needle in Flat Knitting.

Commence from A. K.2 tog. Rib right round to A' and here S.1, K.1, p.s.s.o. Rib the next row without decreasing. Repeat these two rows, decreasing each alternate row, until the ribbing is of sufficient width. In a 1 and 1 rib, the two decreased stitches on the right will be one Purl and one Knit, and, on the left, one Knit and one Purl. Keep in pattern. Sew the mitred points together in the middle after casting-off.

Method 2. Knit-up the stitches all round the neck edge as before, but using four or five needles, and rib in round knitting. make a Decrease (chain, *Fig.* 78) at centre. If the ribbing is wide, it will set better by finishing the last few rounds with smaller needles. If very wide regauge, 3 times.

Method 3. Take the measurement of the neck edge and cast on the required number of stitches on one needle. This may be some two to three hundred stitches. Cast-on an odd

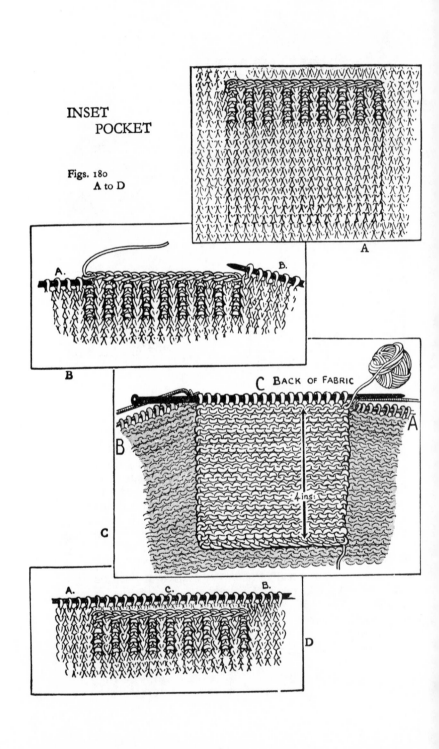

INSET
    POCKET

Figs. 180
    A to D

A

B

C BACK OF FABRIC

A

B

4 ins.

C

A.   C.   B.

D

number and find the centre stitch. The ribbing is then worked on two needles, to the depth of 1″ or 2″ as required, being careful to decrease either side of the centre stitch every other row to form a V point. Cast-off and sew strip to neck.

NECK SEPARATE "V". *Fig.* 179 B

Knit in Stocking or Moss Stitch, and commence at A, *Fig.* 179 B, building a V shape with a central increase as in *Fig.* 65, *page* 78. When this is deep enough, divide the stitches, putting one half on a stitch-holder, and knit up one side to C. Return and knit the other side to C′, and here graft the two ends together. If the strip is worked in Stocking Stitch, the two edge stitches must be knitted plain on each row at the neck edge, otherwise the fabric will curl. Join strip to fabric. This is a useful neck when the garment is in lace stitch, and ribbing for the neck is not desired.

POCKETS. *Figs.* 180—183

INSET POCKET. *Fig.* 180 A

An Inset Pocket, should finish with a border of ribbing, which is knitted in line as the garment is constructed. The ribbing in *Fig.* 180 A has 17 stitches and these are then cast-off, as in *Fig.* 180 B, and the yarn broken. Transfer the stitches on needles A and B to a stitch-holder. Knit a separate square for the inside of the pocket. Cast-on 17 stitches, $\triangle$ the same number that were cast-off, and knit about 4″. *Fig.* 180 C shows this completed and in position on the back of the work, ready to be inserted in the space left between A and B in *Fig.* 180 B.

Restore the stitches on holder A to the knitting pin and knit these off on the same pin (C) as contains the pocket, knitting to the end of the row. This will bring A, which was left a row short in *Fig.* 180 B, into alignment with C. Purl the next row, and, on reaching B, transfer the stitches from holder to knitting pin and purl to the end of the row. The knitting will now be in the position as shown in *Fig.* 180 D, ready to complete the garment. The three sides of the pocket are sewn into position after the garment is completed.

INSET POCKET

An Inset Pocket on a garment worked in jazz colours, such as Fair Isle designs, stripes, hoops, etc., is formed a little differently, as the ribbing at the top of the pocket is added later, when the garment is completed, and generally in a plain colour.

The pocket stitches are cast-off as in *Fig.* 180 B, but at △ border level and the pocket added as before. Later these cast-off stitches are knitted-up and a border is added in plain colours.

On a cardigan, the front edges are similarly treated, being knitted-up on a circular needle, and a narrow border added in one colour, to match the pocket border. (*See also* Zip Pocket, *Fig.* 184.)

POCKET, LOOSE, WITH BORDER

Method 1. This is a useful and practical pocket, as it does not drag the garment (*see Fig.* 181 A). The border to the pocket is added separately.

Knit to the position for top of pocket, minus the border, and then continue knitting in a strip as in *Fig.* 181 B, meanwhile transferring the stitches either side to a stitch-holder, A and B. Knit about 8″, and then fold to form the pocket as in

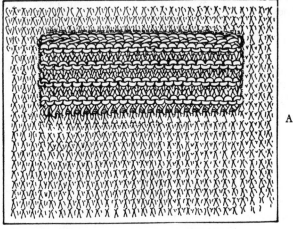

Fig. 181 A.   Pocket.   Loose, with border

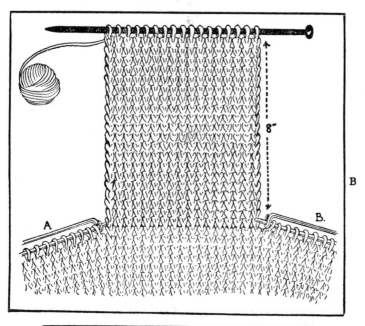

B

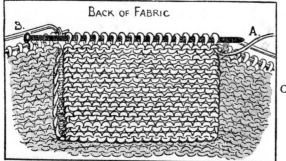

BACK OF FABRIC

C

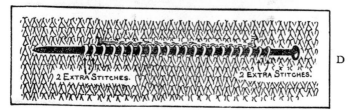

2 EXTRA STITCHES.   2 EXTRA STITCHES.

D

Fig. 181 B, C, D.   Pocket, Loose

Fig. 181 C, △ which is the back of the work. From here the method continues as in *Fig.* 180 C, the knitting being continued from the pocket along the stitches on holder A. In the next and Purl row those marked B will be purled, and the original number thus restored to the needle. The Garter Stitch pocket top is added when the garment is completed as follows:

Border. The stitches along the fold of the pocket are picked up as shown in *Fig.* 181 D, plus two extra, one either side, in order to avoid a hole. Knit backwards and forwards in Garter Stitch or ribbing on these stitches until the required depth is obtained, about 8 rows being generally sufficient. (*See Fig.* 181 A.) By knitting an even number of rows, the cast-off edge falls on the outside, to form a decorative finish.

When knitting the first and last stitch of each row, pick up and knit a stitch from the garment, knitting both stitches off together. This holds the border in position, and the sides can be sewn later. (*See also* Zip Pocket.)

POCKET, PATCH. *Fig.* 182.

A Patch Pocket is made complete with border, after the garment is finished, and sewn in position as required. To attach the pocket invisibly, work as shown. Bring the needle out in the middle of a stitch and slide it through the second loop above, as shown. Insert needle again in same loop as

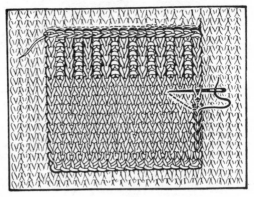

Fig. 182.   Pocket.   Patch

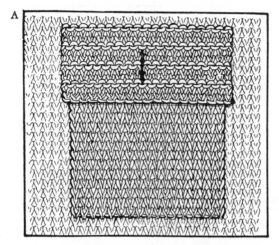

Fig. 183 A, B, C.   Pocket.   Patch with Flap

from which it emerged and take it through △ both pocket and fabric beneath and bring it out in middle of loop above. (*See also* Swiss Darning, *Fig.* 148, *page* 143.) The loose end of yarn on opposite side is the finish of pocket, and must be darned in. The pocket can be left as complete at this stage, or finished with a flap.

POCKET, PATCH WITH FLAP

A pocket flap must be added in when knitting the fronts of the garment. A Patch Pocket complete with flap is shown in *Fig.* 183 A.

Knit to the required position for the △ top of the pocket, a depth of about 7″ or 8″, and leave the work here on the △ Purl row. The flap is knitted separately (*see Fig.* 183 B), adding a button- hole vertically or horizontally as re- quired. The width of the flap must be governed by the number of stitches used for the pocket,

PATCH POCKETS

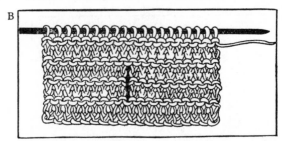

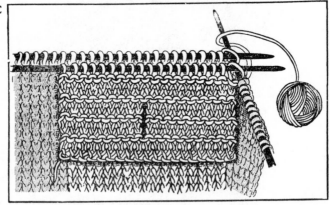

Fig. 183 A, B, C.   Pocket.   Patch with Flap

plus two extra. Knit the flap to a depth of an inch and a half, or as required, and then resume the knitting on the garment. Knit to the position for the pocket, and here the needle containing the pocket flap is placed against that containing the garment stitches (front of fabric) and the two are knitted off together, as in *Fig.* 183 C. The yarn used to knit the flap is then broken, leaving an end of about 6″, which is darned in from the back. The two extra stitches allowed in the width of the flap are distributed either side of the pocket, as shown in *Fig.* 183 A.

POCKET, ZIP

Upon arriving at the position for the pocket, take another yarn of a different colour, and with this yarn knit the required number of stitches forming the pocket △ stranding the original yarn across the back. On the next and Purl row, purl the coloured stitches in the ordinary way. When the garment is completed, remove the coloured yarn as in *Fig.* 184, and pick up the stitches top and bottom, on separate needles. Take a separate yarn to match garment, and cast-off the stitches on both needles. Prepare a Loose Pocket and attach this to a zip fastener, and insert the fastener into the space prepared.

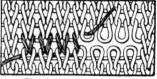

Fig. 184. Pocket. Zip

Both Inset and Loose Pockets can be added in similar way, and on a jazz-coloured garment the method is particularly useful, △ as it permits of the pocket being inserted later without disturbance to the design of the fabric. After removing the coloured yarn, pick up the released stitches on two needles. On the top needle knit a length according to pocket desired, as described in *Figs.* 180 or 181, and drop this inside. For a Loose Pocket, knit long enough and turn under to meet the stitches on the second needle, then knit the stitches off both needles together. Add border in ribbing or band of Garter Stitch as explained. For Inset Pocket, the border would be knitted on the bottom needle.

SEAMS, VERTICAL

Two knitted fabrics that are to be joined by seaming should be knitted with a firm edge. Knit the first and last stitches in the Knit row, and purl the first and last stitches in the Purl row (*see page* 71). This results in an edge as shown in *Fig.* 185 A. When

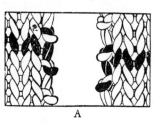

A

B

Fig. 185. Seaming. Vertical

two fabrics knitted thus are faced for joining, the knit stitches lock together as shown. Thread a needle with matching yarn and pick up the △ head of each stitch alternately from side to side, as in *Fig.* 185 B.

Be sure to take the head of the stitch, as shown. This ensures the correct △ pull to the knitting, and avoids the dragged effect which a mere overcast seam (made without any regard to the construction of the fabric) will produce.

SEAMS, HORIZONTAL

See Grafting.

SHOULDERS

A shoulder must finish with a diagonal selvedge, which on a knitted fabric is acquired in two different ways.

Method 1. By casting-off a few stitches at the time, at the beginning of each alternate row, until the desired angle is acquired. For the right shoulder cast-off at the beginning of the Purl row, at the shoulder edge. For the left shoulder, cast-off at the beginning of the Knit row at shoulder edge.

The number of stitches to cast-off will vary with yarn and the number of rows necessary to form the shape of shoulder. For a 3- or 4-ply yarn, three stitches are cast-off; in a fine yarn more, 5 or 6. Casting-off in this way leaves the selvedge in steps. Make the back shoulder according, casting-off to shape of pattern, and then overcast the back and front shoulders together.

Method 2. By turning, instead of casting-off, "steps" are avoided and a clean diagonal line is formed, which can then be cast-off in one line. The left shoulder is turned on the Knit row, the right on the Purl row. The back should be turned in the same way, and cast-off, and the two when united will make a better join. In sewing shoulder seams together, sew stitch by stitch, and then there is no contraction or gaps.

The better method of shaping and joining shoulders is to "turn" and to avoid casting-off by grafting (*see Fig.* 171) the front and back shoulders together. By this means there is no apparent join in the fabric at all, and, as stitch is linked to stitch, there is no likelihood of dragging, providing, of course, the right angle has been formed when turning. Always check

shoulders carefully against Block Pattern, △ as they affect
and control the fit of the neck. A shoulder seam that is grafted
must be first turned.

TURNING

Turning is a means of forming a diagonal line across the
fabric, and can be employed to form any required angle. A

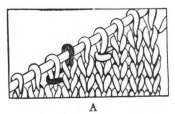

Fig. 186 A. Turning. Knit

"turn" made every one stitch will
form a very steep angle. In
shoulder seams the turn is usually
made after every three stitches,
but a turn can be made after any
number of stitches, and can be regular or irregular, according
to requirements.

Fig. 186 B, C. Turning. Knit

A Diagonal Line sloping to the right is formed as in
Fig. 186 A, which shows a turn after every third stitch.

Knit to the last three stitches.* Bring the yarn forward
as though to purl. Slip the next stitch (which is the third
from the end of left needle) and pass the yarn round and to
the back again (*see Fig.* 186 B). Return the slipped stitch to
the left needle again, △ without knitting it (*Fig.* 186 C).
Turn and purl back. * Repeat from * to * until shaping is
completed as in *Fig.* 186 A. This method is employed to
shape the left shoulder.

A Diagonal Line sloping upwards
to the left must be turned on the
purl side of the fabric (*see Fig.*
186 D). The yarn is already forward, so, on reaching the third
stitch from the end, △ just slip

Fig. 186 D. Turning. Purl

this on to the right needle without purling it, and pass the yarn round to the back, and return the slipped stitch again to the left needle. Turn the work and knit back. Repeat as before.

Turning a Corner. The turn is made on the Purl row (*see Fig.* 186 E) and the whole turn pivots on stitch A in the Knit row 1.

Example. — Cast-on 11 stitches and knit in Stocking Stitch. Knit two rows, and then begin the turns.

Row   1. Knit 11.
Row   2. Purl 10. Turn. Knit back.
Row   4. Purl 8. Turn. Knit back.
Row   6. Purl 6. Turn. Knit back.
Row   8. Purl 4. Turn. Knit back.
Row 10. Purl 2. Turn. Knit back.
This is the centre of the corner, and the next row is important.

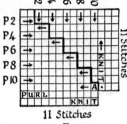

Fig. 186 E. Turning a corner

Row 12. Purl 2. Knit back 2.
Row 14. Purl 4. Knit back 4.
Row 16. Purl 6. Knit back 6
Row 18. Purl 8. Knit back 8.
Row 20. Purl 10. Slip the last stitch, A, which will be the original A in Row 1, without knitting it.

The corner is now complete as in *Fig.* 186 E. The next Knit row will be full width and commence in pattern. In turning, Rows 1 to 10 △ turn as in *Fig.* 186 D, taking the yarn round the stitch beyond, otherwise there will be spaces left when the corner is completed. In Rows 12 to 20 this is not necessary, as the stitches are encroaching.

TURNING

SHETLAND SHAWLS

HETLAND KNITTING—or "Macking," to use the native term—is amongst the most beautiful in the world, having survived the machine age intact with all the ancient traditions and knowledge of the work. Ancient knitting terms still prevail. Knitting needles are still known as "wires," and those of wood home-made, while the use of a knitting belt or pouch is still customary. (*See also page* 20.)

The old knitting terms are interesting, as, in common with those of several European nations, these refer to Knit and Purl as Right and Wrong stitches.

Macking	means Knitting	
Single Macking	,,	Flat Knitting
Plain Macking	,,	Stocking Stitch
Reggies	,,	Garter Stitch
Ridge	,,	Two rows of Garter Stitch
Loop About	,,	Plain and Purl
Lay-up	,,	Cast-on
Loops	,,	Stitches
Right Loop	,,	Knit Stitch
Wrong Loop	,,	Purl Stitch
Cast-up	,,	Over
Take in	,,	Decrease
Wires	,,	Needles

Until about 1920, Shetland garments were circular, without shape for the armhole, being similar to the peasant styles of other nations. The sleeves, also circular, were picked up at the armhole and knitted to the wrist and cast-off. The work was done on two needles, a third being used for knitting. These peasant garments, highly decorated with borders of colour knitting (*see page* 93) then captured the attention of the world, and Fair Isle cardigans, pullovers and jumpers became a craze of the fashionable set. The knitting was a home industry from beginning to end, the wool being home-spun, and hand-dyed from the lichens and seaweed which abound round the islands.

The knitted shawls of Shetland are world-famous, and are so

fine and lace-like in texture that they can, as the fairy tales have told us, be drawn through a wedding-ring. They are in truth knitted "webs," with neither beginning nor end. (*See page* 8.)

HOW A SHETLAND SHAWL IS MADE

Materials. The yarn used for knitting a Shetland shawl is hand spun and as fine as a hair of the human head.

SHETLAND SHAWL MATERIAL

The knitting is done upon steel wires about 14" long, size 12 being the most popular. For thicker shawls a little thicker wire is necessary and for fine shawls a little finer, but the No. 12 is the average size. Once a shawl is commenced, it is knitted throughout on the same wires.

SHETLAND PATTERNS

A beautiful example of a Shetland shawl from Unst is shown in *Fig.* 188. It is worked in the finest 2-ply wool and according to all the traditions of Shetland shawl-knitting. The centre square is in Garter Stitch, and the wide surrounding border is in Old Shale Pattern, known erroneously to the world as Old Shell. The pattern imitates the undulations of sea upon a shale beach, and all the traditional patterns of Shetland, simple and pure in character, aim to reproduce some such simple design of nature. They are few in number, only ten being truly native, as shown in *Fig.* 187, together with their delightful names, all inspired by nature herself.

These patterns may be worked on a Garter Stitch or Stocking Stitch ground—it matters little to the knitter, who can as easily form the pattern on either ground. This variation of background does not change the name of the pattern, which is often perplexing to a stranger. Old Shale, for example, as produced by Mrs. A, may show a line of Purl every seventh row, while Old Shale as worked by Mrs. B might have no Purl rows at all, while Mrs. C might have a Purl every third row, and so on, different families and knitters having their own traditions, which they neither vary nor copy. Garter Stitch, however, is characteristic of all families, and so characteristic of Shetland knitting.

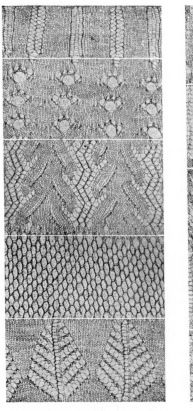

Knitted by Miss Ruby Eunson of Shetland

1. Ears o' Grain
2. Cat's Paw
3. Print o' the Wave
4. Bird's Eye
5. Fern

6. Fir Cone
7. Spout or Razor Shell
8. Old Shale
9. Acre (ploughed)
10. Horseshoe

Fig. 187.   Shetland Knitting Patterns

WORKING METHOD

A Shetland shawl has neither cast-on nor cast-off edges, but is built up from one corner of the lace border. The method is ingenious, and accounts for the remarkable elasticity

By kind permission of the Shetland Industries
Fig. 188.   Shetland Shawl from Unst

of all the edges and the soft, caressing feel of the shawl as it enfolds the shoulders.

The shawl commences at A in *Fig.* 189 with two stitches, increasing in pattern to a narrow lace with a scalloped edge. This is knitted the length of one side of the shawl, as directed by the arrow. This edging can be clearly seen in *Fig.* 188. When this is completed, △ all the loops along the straight edge of the lace are picked up, commencing at B, and finishing at end A (*Fig.* 189). These loops will total some two or three hundred, and form the basis upon which the deep inner border, C on *Fig.* 189, is constructed.

This border proceeds in the direction of the arrow, decreasing either side as follows: knit about 3 inches, and then decrease one stitch at the beginning and end of each alternate row to form mitre as shown. Actually about thirty stitches are decreased in this manner. Some workers do this by taking in ten stitches on each side and ten in the middle. It is just a matter of convenience and pattern.

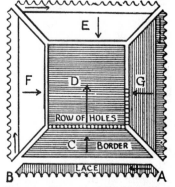

Fig. 189. Diagram of Shetland Shawl

When this wide inner border is completed, △ a line of holes (K.2 tog., Over) is worked, and then the centre square, marked D in *Fig.* 189, is knitted in Garter Stitch. This must be constructed to form an exact square, which is accomplished by knitting as many Reggies (double rows) as there are stitches on the needle. When this square is completed, △ the stitches are left on the needles, and a second lace border and wide inner border (E, *Fig.* 189) is knitted as before, but, instead of working a row of holes, △ this border is grafted to the centre square. The stitches of border E and those

FAIR ISLE DYEING

of the square D, each, of course, containing the same number of stitches, are held together. A darning needle is then threaded with matching wool, and the two are joined by drawing two stitches from the centre needle through two stitches from the border needle. This will form an openwork border similar in appearance to the line of holes on the opposite side of the square. △ In joining, the centre of the shawl is always kept towards the body and the borders on the outside, by which means all sides are joined alike.

Two similar lace and inner borders, G and F, are then knitted as before, and the side stitches along the edges of the centre square are picked up and the borders grafted, as described. The shawl is now completed with the exception of joining up the four corners.

To do this, the stitches of the border are picked up on two separate knitting needles and grafted together, taking one stitch from one needle and one stitch from the other in a herring-bone movement, and drawing the two well together (*see Fig.* 188).

The shawl is then washed and dressed, and for this purpose special large wooden frames, as large as a bed, are needed. The shawls are laced to the frames by lacing through every point along the edge of the scalloped lace border. This stretches the scallops to little points, the effect of which is still apparent on the shawl shown in *Fig.* 188.

Quite a number of Shetland knitters do not possess a frame, but merely peg their shawls out on the grass, and so keen and accurate is their eye that they will do this without measuring, and rarely be a fraction out in their calculations.

NOTE

To dress a shawl at home, do so on the floor, over a sheet spread out on a carpet. First pin the opposite diagonal corners and then along the sides, placing a pin through each point of the lace border. The shawl must be kept taut and square in this manner until dry.

IMITATION SHETLAND SHAWLS   HORSESHOE PATTERN

So-called Shetland shawls are often made as in *Fig.* 190, but are only Shetland inasmuch as they were at one time made of Shetland wool. △ The square is made first. Cast-on the required number of stitches at A, and work the centre square. Change to border pattern, and work the first border and cast-off at edge. This portion of the shawl is shown in shadow on *Fig.* 190. Work borders B, C and D by picking up the stitches of the centre square and working outwards in the direction of the arrows as shown. Cast-off and sew up the corners.

This makes quite a good shawl, but there is all the difference 'n the world between this and the genuine Shetland shawl. One is like a spun web, the other has joins and cast-off edges.

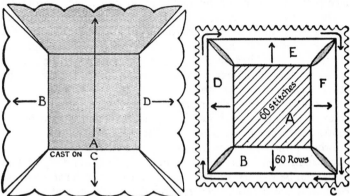

Fig. 190. Diagram of Square Shawl   Fig. 191. Diagram of Diagonal Shaw

SHAWL WITH DIAGONAL CENTRE

Another shawl, the working method of which is shown in *Fig.* 191, has a diagonal centre. This is English and not Shetland in origin. It was a great favourite with Victorians, and always referred to as a Shetland shawl, because it was knitted in Shetland wool. To work diagonal centre (A), cast-on three stitches. Knit in Garter Stitch. Every row commences with an Over, as a means of increasing. The order is: "Over, Knit to end of row." Repeat this until there are 60 stitches on the needles and then start decreasing as follows. Over, K.3 tog. on each row, until three stitches are left, K.2 tog., K.1. Cast-off the remaining two stitches. Diagonal stripes of different colours may be introduced by knitting four rows in one colour and four in another.

To make the border, △ keep the front side of the shawl towards you and pick up and knit the stitches along one side. Then work border B in pattern on these stitches, increasing after the first and before the last stitch, or by an Over at the beginning of each row as usual. Do this for 60 rows, or for as many rows as there were stitches forming the central row of the square.

At the end of the 60th row, △ do not cast-off, but cast-on 12 extra stitches, or the number of stitches necessary to knit a lace edge (C, *Fig.* 191). This can be 12, 16, 18, according to lace pattern. Take shorter needles and knit a lace border on these 12 cast-on stitches, knitting up a stitch from the border needle each time on the Purl row until all the stitches on the long border needle have been knitted off. When completed, slip these 12 stitches on to a holder, △ as they will be carried forward along the next border edge, D, after picking up the stitches from the centre square and knitting as before.

The lace edging as described is continued all round the four sides of the shawl as shown by the arrows, and is then finally grafted together where it meets. The side borders of the shawl are then joined together in herringbone stitch.

Another Method. The wide borders, B, D, E and F, of this shawl can be worked on four needles, using a fifth for knitting. First knit the diagonal centre, and then pick up and knit the stitches along all four sides of the square. At each corner knit twice into the last stitch and twice into the first on the needle, but between the two make an Over, which drop in the next round. Do this at all four corners and on each subsequent row.

TRIANGULAR SHAWL

To make a triangular shawl, *Fig.* 192, work in Garter Stitch and increase in Garter Stitch (i.e. with an Over as shown in *Fig.* 67 C, *page* 80) after the first and before the last stitch. Continue increasing thus for 12 ridges and then increase also in the middle, i.e. before and after the 5 middle stitches, and continue parallel to edge as AB, AB'.

When the triangle is completed, surround with a lace border as previously directed, forming a mitre at centre corner.

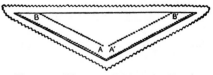

Fig. 192.   Diagram of Triangular Shawl

GLOVES

GLOVES are constructed in Round Knitting on either four or five needles. The manner of adding the fingers to a glove varies but little, but that of the thumb can vary considerably, as here the glove is given character, distinction and fit.

This was realised by the old knitters, as is shown by the

Fig. 193.   Spanish Gloves (ecclesiastical) of the 16th century, knitted in red silk and gold thread

16th-century gloves in *Fig.* 193. The gauntlet glove is a specimen of the brocade period, knitted in gold (still untarnished) and red silk. The threads are not stranded, but woven, and the inside of the glove is as neat as a modern machine-woven brocade. It is a magnificent specimen, and one of a pair in the Victoria and Albert Museum.

The thumb is knitted separately and lined with a knitted fabric of red silk, which is sewn in from the wrist to the thumb division, where it joins with a long graceful triangular gusset, and finishes in Round Knitting, like the fingers. The thumb is outlined with gold gimp, while an impression of forchettes is given to the fingers by a twisted thread of gold, arranged to imitate the seam stitching on a leather glove. Both the hand and the gauntlet are also lined.

The second glove is more modest though most interesting, as the shaping for the base of the thumb is on the back of the hand and coincides with the hand muscles, suggesting that the gloves were made from a drawing, by one familiar with knitting, though unfamiliar with glove technique.

The top of the thumb is added to the palm as in *Fig.* 208. The fingers are quite flat and without forchettes, and so naturally show signs of splitting at the divisions. The gauntlet and medallion of gold on the back are both lined with yellow silk.

The ecclesiastical gloves of this period were of great beauty, and with reason, as the glove is said to have been invented by St. Augustine, and to this day remains part of a bishop's regalia.

During the 17th and 18th centuries long cotton gloves, knitted in Lace Fabrics, became very fashionable, while knitted mittens, of silk or cotton, remained fashionable until the late 19th century.

YARNS

Gloves can be knitted in any yarn, wool, silk, metal, cotton or string. Winter sports and country gloves are generally in wool, used single or double; golf and riding gloves in double cotton or string; evening gloves in silk. Metal threads are rarely used now, though there is no reason for this other than fashion, or, perhaps, because the untarnishable variety is rare and expensive.

NEEDLES

Sets of 4 or 5 needles are necessary, and the shape of a glove can be considerably improved by varying the gauge in shaping the tips of the fingers, thumb and wrist, changing to needles two or more sizes smaller for this purpose. It is often expedient to work the gauntlet of a glove on larger needles and use the yarn double. The fingers and thumb are more easily worked on short glove needles specially made for the purpose. The needles, together with the yarn, will determine the gauge. (*See page* 42.)

MEASUREMENTS (HAND)

The measurements for a glove are made in △ width and length. The width measurement gives the number of stitches to cast-on, the length the number of rounds to knit.

The Width of a glove is measured round the broadest part of the hand—the knuckles (*see* Measurement 1, *Fig.* 194). This measurement will give the number of stitches to cast-on. The second width measurement is made at 2, and the difference between this and the previous measurement will give the number of stitches contained in the thumb. Supposing the difference to be 2½″. With 8 stitches to the inch, increase 20 stitches. This will necessitate

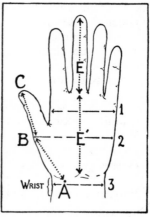

Fig. 194. Hand Measurements

eleven increasing rounds, with two increases in each round. This increase is for the thumb. △ In many directions this is termed the "gusset," which is not strictly correct, as the thumb gusset is the triangular inset between the thumb and first finger.

The Length measurements of a glove are also shown in *Fig.* 194. Notice in particular that the △ thumb commences at A, the wrist, and the measurement from here to B (the thumb joint) should be the same as from B to C (the joint to the tip of the thumb). AB then equals BC. △ Never underestimate or skimp the thumb measurement, as this is the most important member of

HAND
MEASUREMENT

the hand, and must accordingly be treated with dignity.

E = E', the length of the middle finger, which is about the same as the length of the palm.

These measurements represent the average hand. Individual measurements will vary considerably, as the palm may be of greater length than the fingers, or vice versa, and the glove, to fit, must be knitted accordingly.

The length of the wrist is about 1". This space should be allowed between the ribbing and the commencement of the thumb shaping, $\triangle$ otherwise there is no clean fit at the wrist. This measurement is the most important in glove-knitting, yet one so often omitted.

Gauntlet measurements should be made over the sleeve of the coat. A knitted glove should not fit too tightly, otherwise it retards the circulation, and defeats its object, which is warmth. Sports gloves should be large and roomy, and a larger gusset made at the division for the thumb.

THE PARTS OF A GLOVE

Gauntlet or Ribbing = the part above the wrist.

Wrist = part between gauntlet and commencement of the thumb.

Gusset $\triangle$ = the small triangular portion between the thumb and first finger.

Forchettes = the finger gussets.

THUMBS

Straight Thumb = *Fig.* 195 set to straight of hand.

Palm Thumb = *Fig.* 203 starts on palm from root of thumb.

Stocking Thumb = *Fig.* 208 commences at the thumb joint.

CASTING-ON

The cast-on edge of a glove is important, as it is meant to show, and should therefore be decorative, and well constructed. Gloves knitted in silk and cotton should commence with a picot cast-on (*Fig.* 56, *page* 67). Cable cast-on, *Fig.* 54, *page* 65, is effective on a woollen glove with gauntlet. Invisible cast-on (*Fig.* 55, *page* 66) should be used if a separate gauntlet, open at one side and knitted in a different yarn, is to be added after the glove is finished, as it can then be united without any apparent join.

INCREASING

The method of increasing used throughout in Glove Knitting is M.1 by △ raising and knitting the running thread. (*See Fig. 65, page* 76.) This increase must be understood throughout this chapter wherever M.1 occurs.

GLOVE. STRAIGHT THUMB AND GUSSET

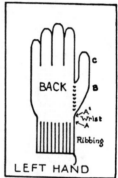

Steel needles sizes, 12 and 14. Set of five. Glove needles size 12.

Yarn, 3-ply Fingering.

Gauges: 8 stitches to 1". 11 rounds to 1".

Glove (measurement, knuckle) $7\frac{7}{8}"$.

Fig. 195. Cast-on 63 stitches on 4 needles (leave yarn end for guidance and darn in when glove is finished).

Ribbing. K.1, P.1 for 4".

Wrist. AA'. *Fig.* 195. Change to smaller needles.

Fig. 195
Glove with Straight
Thumb and Gusset

Rounds 1–13. Knit. Revert to original needles.

Palm and Thumb (*Fig.* 196). Round 13. M.1 before the first needle. Knit round.

Rounds 14–15. Knit.

Round 16. M.1 as before. K.1, M.1. Complete round. (Sometimes the stitch before the first increase and after the second is purled throughout, to form dividing line for thumb. In which case Bar increase is used.)

Rounds 17–18. Knit plain.

Round 19. M.1 as before. K.3, M.1. Complete round.

Rounds 20–21. Knit plain.

Round 22. M.1, K.5, M.1. Complete round.

Rounds 23–24. Knit plain.

Continue thus until there are 21 stitches for the thumb, as in *Fig.* 196. Then knit one plain round.

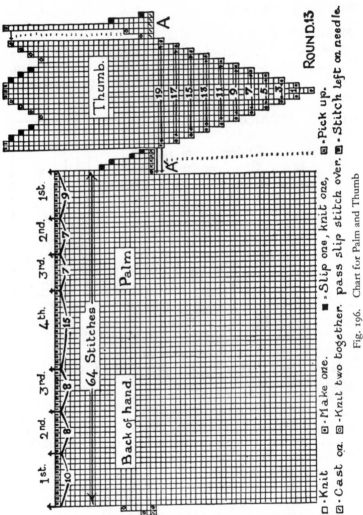

Fig. 196. Chart for Palm and Thumb

This thumb is for a normally proportioned hand. If the thumb is short and thick, knit 3 (more if necessary) instead of one stitch between the increases made in Round 13 and then continue increasing to left and right as before. The number of rounds knitted between the increasing rounds will be decided by the length of the thumb. Two rounds are usually sufficient; occasionally a third for an extra long thumb, or only one for a short thumb.

Thumb. Divide the 21 stitches upon three short glove needles, putting 7 upon each. On a fourth needle cast-on 5 stitches, making 26 stitches in all (*see* A, *Fig.* 197). Knit 2 rounds, then decrease for the gusset. This is done by decreasing the 5 cast-on stitches until only the middle one is left, as shown in *Figs.* 196 and 197 (B). Knit 2 rounds between each decrease, decreasing 2 stitches for the first decrease. Knit 2 rounds. Then decrease 1 stitch. Knit 2 rounds, decrease another. (*See Fig.* 196.) There are now 22 stitches. These are rearranged so that the last of the five stitches becomes the centre of six. Arrange 6 on two needles and five on the other two as at C in *Fig.* 197.

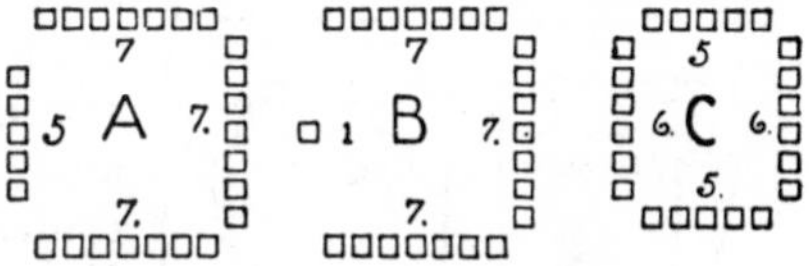

Knit the thumb as many rounds as were between the wrist and gusset and then Decrease

Fig. 197

Arrangement of Stitches for Thumb

on all four needles, doing so at the beginning of one and the end of the other, as follows: S.1, K.1, p.s.s.o. at the beginning of needle 1, K.2 tog. at the end of needle 2, and so on. This makes the decreases run up either side of the thumb. It is easier to do this on two needles like the toe of a sock (*see Fig.* 229, *page* 225). Decrease until there are six stitches left.

Finishing the Top. There are three methods of finishing. (1) These six stitches can be grafted together. (2) The glove turned inside out and the stitches overcast together. (3) Run a thread through the six stitches, turn inside out, and tie. Thread yarn end into darning needle and secure. On gloves of silk or cotton this finish is most attractive. On sports gloves and men's gloves it is better to graft.

Palm. Return to the base of the thumb, and pick up the

5 cast-on stitches and M.1 either side to number 7 in all. *See Fig.* 198 how rearrange stitches. Take 5 of these and place them on the palm needle, and put the other 2 on the outside

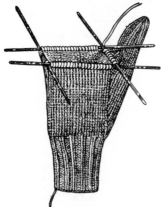

needle. This brings the thumb to the inside and $\triangle$ decides if the glove is for the right or left hand. The glove charted in *Fig.* 196 is for a right hand, so the palm needle must be needle 1, and the beginning of a round. On a left hand it would be needle 4, and the end of a round (*see Fig.* 199).

Fig. 198. Thumb Gusset

The gusset is continued up the inside of the hand, so these seven stitches are all decreased as before, until only one is left, making more decreases on the palm needle than on the other. Between the thumb and the fingers there are 20 rounds, and the decreasing is made with an interval of one round between each decrease (*see Fig.* 196). This will leave 64 stitches on the needle. Divide for the fingers, arranging the stitches as shown in *Fig.* 200. Note that the number of stitches for the first three fingers is the

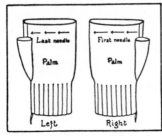

Fig. 199. Position of Rounds

same (21, 21, 21), but two less (19) for the little finger. These are derived as follows.

First Finger. Fig. 200. Take 9 stitches from the palm needle and 10 from the outside needle and arrange these on 3 needles

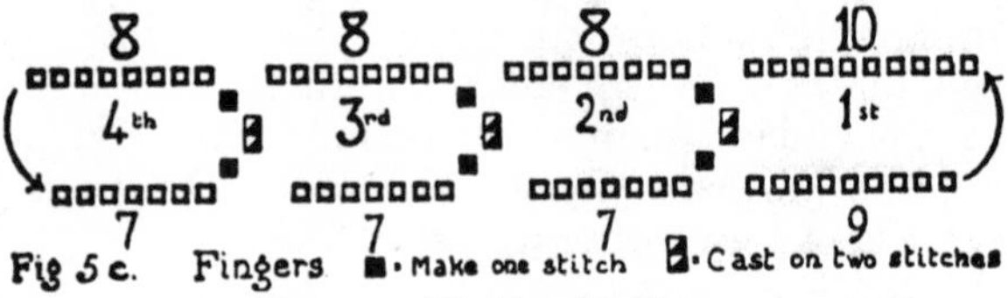

Fig 5 c.   Fingers ■ = Make one stitch ◼ = Cast on two stitches

Fig. 200. Division for Fingers

(slip the unwanted stitches on a string), as shown, until required (*see Fig.* 201). Cast-on 2 stitches between the fingers for the forchette, making a total of 21 stitches. Knit 2 rounds, and then decrease one on the inside forchette. Knit another 2 or 3 rounds, and decrease again if necessary. Knit the finger the required length and finish like the thumb.

Fig. 201

Arrangement of stitches

Second Finger. See Fig. 200. Pick up the 2 cast-on stitches and M.1 either side of these 2 stitches to make 2 extra stitches. This makes 4. Take 7 stitches from the palm and 8 from the outside. Cast-on 2 stitches between these for the other forchette, making 21 stitches in all. Decrease as required. Knit the finger the required length and finish off.

Third Finger. Same as the second.

Fourth Finger. Pick up the 2 cast-on stitches, and M.1 either side as before. With the 15 stitches left over, this makes 19. Divide these upon 4 needles, and knit the little finger, shaping at the forchette as required.

The number of stitches to cast-on for the forchette will vary with the thickness of the fingers. Two is the average number. Always measure the fingers to be sure of a good fit. Make the second glove to pair, △ and be careful not to make two gloves for the same hand.

ALTERNATIVE METHOD

Knit to the position for the thumb gusset, AA′ in *Fig.* 196, increasing from wrist as before, and here take the stitches which will form the thumb and put them on to a separate thread. Cast on 4 or 5 stitches (according to yarn) at the end of the gusset; and round for the fore. Knit decrease as be- fingers. By to position for this method the arrangement of stitches for the $\triangle$ first finger will denote the right or left hand glove.

Right Hand. Decide the stitches for the first finger and arrange these upon 3 needles, taking one-third of the number from the first needle (commencement of round; *see Fig.* 199), and the other two-thirds from the end of the previous needle, i.e. from the end of the previous round. Knit the stitches on the first needle, then take a fourth needle and cast-on 2 stitches for the

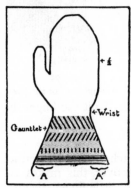

forchette. Continue knitting on the finger stitches; shape and finish the finger. Knit the other fingers as previously described.

Left Hand. For the first finger of the left hand the order is reversed (*see Fig.* 199), as one-third of the finger stitches are taken from the $\triangle$ end of the round, and two-thirds from the beginning of the round. Cast on two stitches for the forchette and knit finger as before.

Fig. 202
Mit with Straight Thumb

SPORTS MITS

A glove without finger divisions, as in *Fig.* 202, is made with a gauntlet and often worn over other gloves.

Take the measurement of the coat sleeve in order to know the number of stitches to cast-on for the gauntlet. The difference between these and the number needed for the mit (Measurement 1, *Fig.* 194) will give the number to be decreased, to wrist. Usually this is one decrease either side every three rounds. The number of stitches to be decreased for this mit are shown between A and A′, *Fig.* 202.

Take the hand measurement and stitch gauge to make certain. Knit the wrist on smaller needles and revert to original needles and knit the rest of the mit, adding a straight thumb and shaping as before. Omit

GAUNTLET

Fig. 204. Gloves in Pattern from Lithuania

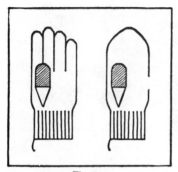

Fig. 203
Palm Thumb (Glove and Mit)

the fingers and shape the top as for the toe of a sock (*see Fig. 229, page 225*), commencing to shape for the little finger 1″ before commencing to shape the opposite side.

PALM THUMB

Fig. 203 shows a glove and mit with palm thumb. This is a simple method of work, and is used when gloves are knitted in pattern, as in *Fig.* 204, since it permits of the design on the back of the hand being worked in stranded knitting without interruption as follows:

LITHUANIAN GLOVES

These gloves from Lithuania are knitted in traditional style and pattern. The yarn, showing commencement of glove and

Palm.   Back of hand. (LEFT)

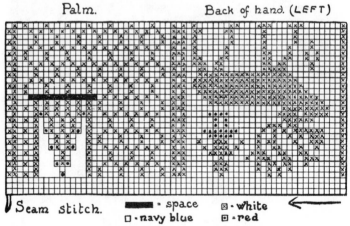

Seam stitch.   ▬ = space   ⊠ = white
                □ = navy blue   ▣ = red

Fig. 205.   Chart for Pattern Gloves

seam stitch, is shown in photo, as a guide. The hand of the glove in *Fig.* 204 is charted in *Fig.* 205 to show the construction of the base of the thumb. The colours are red, white and navy. Rib as in *Fig.* 204, finishing with three rounds of navy.

Round 1, which now commences the pattern of the glove (left hand), knit the round until six stitches before the seam stitch, and, before knitting this sixth stitch, pick up the running thread and M.1 as described. Knit to end of round.

Round 2. Knit in pattern.

Round 3. Knit in pattern, but 7 stitches before end of round M.1, K.1, M.1.

Rounds 4 and 5. Knit.

Round 6. Knit and M.1 before the 8th stitch. K.3, M.1.

Rounds 7 and 8. Knit.

Round 9. Knit. M.1 before 11th stitch. K.5, M.1.

Rounds 10 and 11. Knit.

Round 12. Knit and M.1 before 13th stitch. K.7, M.1.

This increases nine stitches as shown in the chart.

Rounds 13 and 14. Knit in pattern.

Round 15. Knit, but, upon arriving at 17th stitch before the seam stitch, take a different colour yarn and knit 13 stitches in this colour, stranding the original yarn at the back. Continue in pattern, and complete the glove. When this is finished, return to the 13 stitches, and unfasten the yarn, as shown in *Fig.* 206. Pick up the released stitches on 4 needles and complete the thumb, as charted in *Fig.* 207.

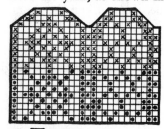

Thumb.

Fig. 207
Chart for top Thumb

Fig. 206. Removing the
Coloured Thread

STOCKING GLOVE

A sports glove for skating, ski-ing, driving, etc., with the fingers arranged for grip and the thumb free and unrestrained, is shown in *Fig.* 208. The △ wrist must be kept snug and well fitting, and the glove can be made with or without a gauntlet. After completing wrist, M.1 between first and last needles for seam stitch which purl. Knit straight to thumb without shaping. Here knit 12 stitches in a different coloured yarn as

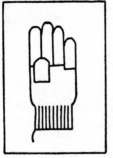

Fig. 208

Stocking Glove

before (*Fig.* 206), stranding the original yarn at the back. (There should be a distance of $\frac{1}{2}''$ between these and the seam stitch.) The position for the thumb should coincide with the line B.2, *Fig.* 194. On the next round knit these coloured stitches as ordinary stitches. Continue knitting to position for fourth or little finger. This is knitted first (*see Fig.* 208), about three rounds before the other fingers (this number will vary with yarn and needles). Divide the stitches for the fingers and put those for the little finger on to short glove needles (*see Fig.* 200). Cast-on 2 stitches for the forchette and knit the little finger. When this is completed, pick up the 2 cast-on stitches and M.1 either side. Knit another four rounds. Divide the stitches for the other three fingers and knit as before. Return to the thumb and remove the coloured yarn as shown in *Fig.* 206. Pick up the released stitches on 4 needles and knit the thumb straight, without any gusset as in *Fig.* 207, shaping the top.

MITTENS

These are knitted as for gloves, only the fingers stop at the first joint.

MARKINGS

To add stripes, or patterns of contrasting colours, to the back of the glove, work as described in Festive Knitting, *page* 111. By this means the stripes or pattern is worked backwards and forwards in colour on the back of the hand, as in Flat Knitting, while the glove itself is constructed in Round Knitting.

Stripes worked in this way can be made to take the same radiated markings as those on gloves of other fabrics.

SOCKS AND STOCKINGS

HO KNITTED the first pair of socks? Who turned the first heel? These questions will never be answered, though the Sandal Socks in *Fig.* 209 show the methods were already known in the 4th and 5th centuries. These socks are a rare find, a pair! This is very unusual, as one is all too often

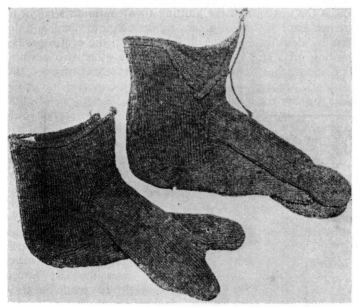

Fig. 209.   Sandal Sock with Toe Division, 4th to 5th century

found without its mate. They are a woman's size, knitted in red wool and with a big toe division for wearing with sandals. They were excavated in Egypt.

The method of knitting is interesting, as it reveals the heel flap to be "turned" and therefore worked backwards and forwards on two needles, necessitating a knowledge of both Knit and Purl stitches. The knitting is in Crossed Stocking Stitch, and a half-finished sock of the 12th century found in a Turkish tomb is also in this fabric. A difference of seven or eight centuries divides the two, and intermediary finds are also in this fabric, suggesting that Crossed Stocking Stitch had a long run before it was succeeded by the uncrossed variety as now preferred for socks and stockings.

The Sandal Sock in *Fig.* 209 is commenced from the top on two needles, and knitted to the side opening. Here the knitting forms into a round, with an overlap of 5 stitches, to provide a stand for the lacing. A certain number of stitches are cast-off across the instep, and the knitting then continues straight to the heel flap. Here the stitches are divided into three, and the knitting done backwards and forwards on the centre needle, knitting off a stitch either side from the other two needles. The side stitches are then knitted-up, also the cast-off edge, and the work proceeds straight to the little toe, decreasing at the sides to shape the division of the four toes. A separate division for the big toe was then made after this was finished.

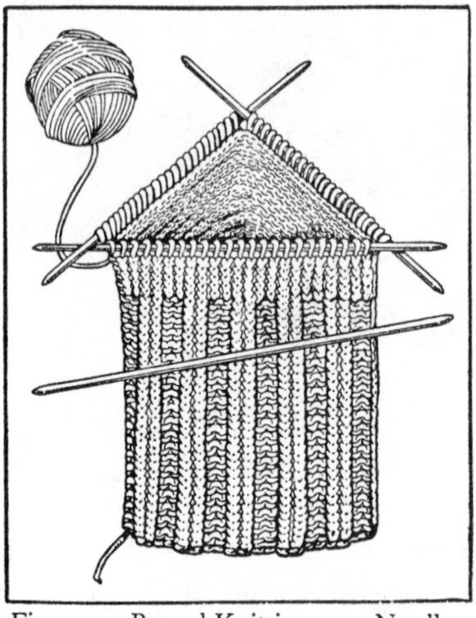

Fig. 210.   Round Knitting on 3 Needles

The sock has no gusset, as the broad heel flap shapes the ankle according to the fashion of the day, and the tops were tied or probably laced together.

How many hundred years had it taken to evolve such perfection? Sock construction over the last fifteen centuries has made but little change.

MODERN HOSE

Socks and stockings are knitted with either 4 or 5 needles, according to preference, all of which must be the same size (*see Figs.* 210 and 211).

Stocking knitting is called Round Knitting, as it is always

worked in one direction, round and round in a continuous spiral, the natural action of which automatically produces the well-known fabric Stocking Stitch. *Fig.* 210 shows Round Knitting on 3 needles, worked with a fourth, and *Fig.* 211 on 4 needles, worked with a fifth.

A Round is completed when all the stitches on all three or four needles have been knitted, and the end of a round should coincide with the tag end of yarn which is always left at the commencement when casting-on. This is darned in when the sock is completed, and should be left long enough for this purpose. This tag end is an invaluable guide to position of seam stitch, decreasing and forming the heel, and should never be cut off after casting-on.

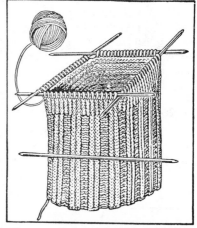

Fig. 211. Round Knitting on 4 Needles

Yarn. Use the best (*see page* 33), and, if wool, choose a worsted variety.

Casting-on should be loose, and the thumb method, *Fig.* 52, *page* 61, is the best, as it is more elastic, and permits of the first round being knitted through the front of the stitches △ and not through the back, which twists and breaks the edge.

Fig. 212. Round Knitting. Casting-on

All the knitting diagrams shown here depict Round Knitting on 4 needles, and *Fig.* 212 shows the arrangement, the stitches being equally divided on 3 needles, the fourth being inserted through the first stitch ready to commence the first round.   Notice the tag end beneath this stitch.

Tension should be easy, and knitting even—neither tight nor loose, but sufficiently firm to prevent the needles slipping out when knitting or when laid aside. A child commencing Round Knitting should begin two socks simultaneously, and knit a distance on one and then on the other to learn correct tension. This also impresses better the lesson of turning the heel. To ascertain the number of stitches to cast-on, measure the leg, and knit a tension square and count the number of stitches to the inch (*see page* 42). The number varies.   On half hose (men's) the average is from 80 to 90. A child's sock varies from 60 to 70.

LENGTH MEASUREMENTS

To measure the length of a sock let it hang naturally from the top of a yard-stick or tape. Granny's idea of ascertaining length is shown in *Figs.* 213 and 214. Measure the length of the foot.

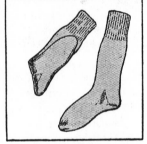

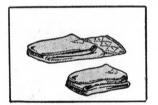

Fig. 213.   Granny's
Measurements for Stockings and ¾ hose

Fig. 214.   Granny's
Measurements for Socks

Full-length Hose. Three times the length of the foot gives the length for a stocking, folded as in *Fig.* 213. The second fold also gives the position for shaping the leg.

Three-quarter Hose. Twice the length of the foot gives the correct length for leg of boy's school sock or golf hose, measured, as in *Fig.* 213, below the fancy top, which is turned back, as shown, when measuring.

Half Hose (Socks), *Fig.* 214. The length of the foot is equal to the leg measured beneath the ribbing.

TOPS

Ribbed Tops. All socks and stockings are commenced with a ribbing, which contracts the fabric and helps to maintain the position, and prevents rolling over at the top. *See Fig.* 209, which is not commenced with ribbing. The most popular ribbings are 1 and 1 or 2 and 2, as shown in *Figs.* 210 and 211. The depth of ribbing is:

Stocking, 1″ or 1″ hem with picot hem.
Three-quarter Hose, turn over 3″ or 4″.
Half Hose (Socks), 4″ or 5″. Children's, 1½″.
Ankle Socks (Sports), turnover 8″.

Suspender Tops. Fig. 215. The ribbing should be knitted in Crossed Stocking Stitch, as it has better elastic qualities, and a little more than half the width of the ribbing is cast-off, as shown, and the same number of stitches are then cast-on again.

Fig. 215
Suspender Top

Fancy Tops. These are turnovers, and consist of patterns in different colours, either Stranded or Woven, as in Colour Knitting, *page* 91, where some designs suitable for this purpose are given. Fancy tops can also be worked in one colour only, changing the pattern of the fabric, but not the colour. When the top is completed, the knitting is turned inside out so that the turnover will appear on the right side.

SEAM STITCH

The seam stitch commences after the ribbing or turnover top is completed, △ thus avoiding an odd stitch. It is a Purl Stitch made M.1, "lifted" after the last stitch of the third needle. Its position thus is next to the first or tag stitch and can always be checked. This Purl Stitch gives a dividing line to the fabric down the middle of the calf. It denotes the end of a round and is a guide when shaping and turning the heel.

SHAPING

Full-length hose (stocking), also a gaiter, is shaped by increasing above the calf and decreasing below, making about 2 increases and 5 decreases. This is the only occasion on which increasing is employed in hose knitting. To shape a three quarter hose, make about 5 decreases. For half hose (socks) make 2 decreases, or, if leg is slim, no decreases at all. Ankle hose, no decrease, but change to smaller needles for last 4″ of ribbing to improve the shape of the turnover.

The methods of increasing and decreasing are important, as they form a decoration to the back of the hose. They must be strictly paired and kept at equal distance either side of the seam stitch, being made on the second or third stitch either side and strictly above each other.

To decrease on the first needles always K.2 tog., and on the third, S.1, K.1, p.s.s.o. On a sturdy leg the number of rounds between the decreases are fewer than on a long, thin leg. For the former, three rounds are enough; for the latter, five or seven are necessary. The last decrease must be made just below the calf. From here knit straight to the ankle (see Fig. 216), knitting as many rounds as half the number of stitches on the needle. Then divide for the heel.

A stocking knitted throughout in a ribbed fabric is decreased as follows:

First decrease, on fourth rib either side of seam stitch.
Second decrease, on third rib either side of seam stitch.
Third decrease, on second and last but one rib of round.
Fourth decrease, on first and last rib of round.

FABRIC

Hose can be knitted in any variety of fabric, as desired, but the heel flap and sole and toe are always knitted in Stocking Stitch.

HEEL FLAP

There are many different methods of forming the heel, but, once the principle is known, it is a simple matter to create any type of heel. The secret is the readjustment of the stitches on the different needles, and the positions for the decreases,

which must be strictly paired in order to keep the pull of the
stitches correct, and avoid gaping at the instep.

The different redivisions necessary in forming the heel and
toe are shown here in progress order, and should be studied
progressively, as in this manner they become self explana-
tory, and, learnt thus, will never be forgotten. *Fig.* 216 shows
the sock shaped and knitted to the ankle, and *Fig.* 217 shows
how the stitches appear on the needle (64 in all—19, 25 and
20). The arrows indicate the first redivision.

The total number of stitches (no matter what number) are
divided in half, arranging one half either side of the seam

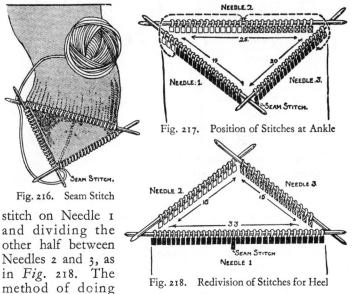

Fig. 217.   Position of Stitches at Ankle

Fig. 216.   Seam Stitch

Fig. 218.   Redivision of Stitches for Heel

stitch on Needle 1
and dividing the
other half between
Needles 2 and 3, as
in *Fig.* 218. The
method of doing
this is shown in *Fig.* 217. Knit 16 stitches from Needle 1,
and slip the remaining 3 on to Needle 2. Turn. Slip the first
stitch and Purl 15, and on the same needle Knit the seam
stitch and Purl 16 beyond from Needle 3. Leave the remaining 3 on the needle and take 12 from Needle 2. The instep
is now divided on Needles 2 and 3 and left thus until the heel
is turned.

In making this redivision, allocate an odd number of

stitches on Needle 1, to keep the seam stitch the centre stitch. This in *Fig.* 218 necessitates 16 stitches on Needle 2 and only 15 on Needle 3, which does not matter. The thing that does matter is the central position of the seam stitch.

The heel flap is knitted on Needle 1, as shown in *Fig.* 219, and in Stocking Stitch. For extra strength this flap is some-times knitted in Heel Stitch as follows: Row 1: K.1, S.1. Row 2: K. Row 3: S.1, K.1. Row 4: K. Repeat these four rows. The heel can also be woven (*see Fig.* 107, *page* 106), weaving in a length of yarn from a second ball. The heel flap

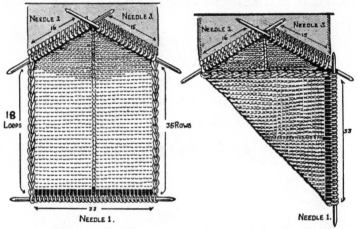

Fig. 219. Heel Flap   Fig. 220.   Measuring Heel Flap

is a square and should finish on a Purl row. The first stitch in every row is slipped, to provide a smooth edge and the necessary loops for knitting-up. Knit 34 rows and then fold the flap over and measure in granny's way, as in *Fig.* 220. This completes the flap. The next process is to turn the heel, which can be done in many different ways to form many different heels. Two methods only are given here, one for a Round Heel and the other for a Square Heel (Dutch Heel).

ROUND HEEL

This is a comfortable heel, with plenty of spring to the instep. The working method is shown in *Fig.* 221, and is

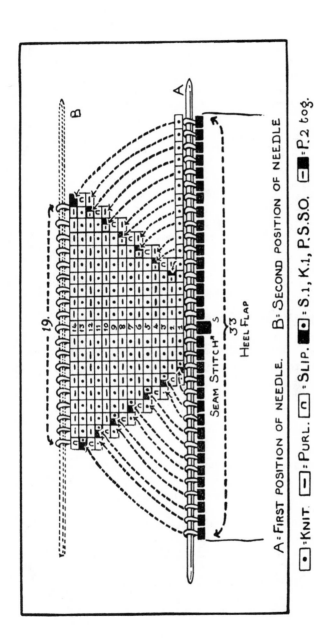

A = First position of needle.   B = Second position of needle.

⊡ = Knit.   ⊟ = Purl.   ⊓ = Slip.   ■ = S.1, K.1, P.S.S.O.   ⊟ = P.2 tog.

Fig. 221.   Chart for Round Heel

called "turning" the heel, as the knitting is turned after every decrease. For a Round Heel turn △ one stitch further in each row until all the stitches are knitted off and the heel appears as in *Fig.* 222. Knit as shown on the chart, *Fig.* 221. Knit to the seam stitch, purl this, and knit 2 beyond and here decrease. S.1, K.1, p.s.s.o., K.1. Turn. (The seam stitch can be discontinued here if desired, but is shown throughout as it simplifies the explanation of dia-

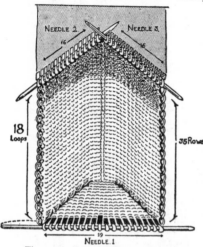

Fig. 222. Round Heel Completed

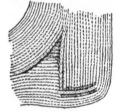

Fig. 223 A
Dutch Heel and Gusset

grams.) Slip the first stitch (on both Knit and Purl rows). Purl 7, P.2 tog., P.1. Turn. S.1, K.8, S.1, K.1, p.s.s.o., K.1. Turn. And so on as shown in the diagram for 15 rows, decreasing until all the stitches are exhausted from A and 19 stitches are left on needle B.

DUTCH HEEL

Having turned one heel, it will be easy to follow Dutch Heel and gusset shown in *Fig.* 223 A and charted in *Fig.* 223 B. The charts for both heels should be compared as for Dutch Heel. All the decreases are made the same width apart instead of graduating to take the heel shape, as in *Fig.* 222. This is a good heel, and has a broad fitting, and is very similar to the ancient heel in *Fig.* 209. Knit to the seam stitch and purl this and knit 5 stitches beyond. Then S.1, K.1, p.s.s.o. Turn.

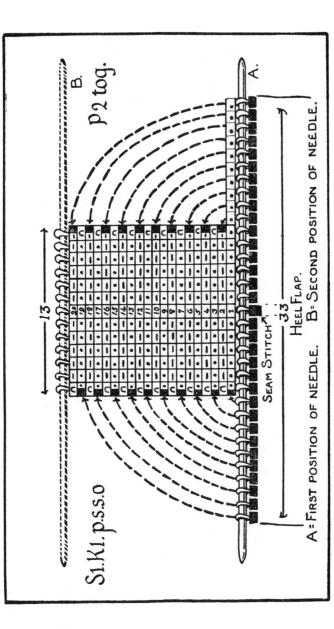

S1. K1. p.s.s.o

P2 tog.

B.

13

A.

SEAM STITCH.

33

HEEL FLAP.

A = FIRST POSITION OF NEEDLE.   B = SECOND POSITION OF NEEDLE.

● = KNIT.   ⬜ = PURL.   C = SLIP.   ■ = S.1, K.1, P.S.S.O.   ■■ = P.2 tog.

Fig. 223 B.   Dutch Heel.   Chart

(Slip the first stitch as before at every turn.) P.11 and then P.2 tog. Turn, and continue as in chart for 20 rows, or until 13 stitches are left on needle. This heel can be any width, as the turn starts and finishes with the same number of stitches. For this reason is a popular heel to use when re-heeling.

GUSSET

Fig. 224 A shows the appearance of the knitting after turning for Round Heel (*Fig.* 221). There are 3 needles containing the stitches and 2 lengths of fabric between. (The method of work from here is the same for Dutch Heel.) In Round Heel, there were 19 stitches left on the needle after "turning." *Round* 1 (Needle 1). Knit the 19 stitches forming the heel flap, as shown, and with the same needle knit-up 18

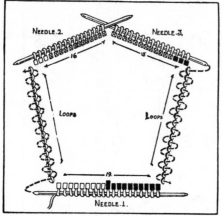

Fig. 224 A
Work at Completion of Heel

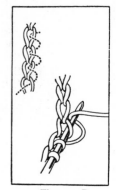

Fig. 224 B
Knitting-up

loops, taking the inner loop of the chain each time, as in *Fig.* 224 B, and knitting rather tightly. Continue, and knit 3 stitches from instep, Needle 2. Take another needle and knit 25 instep stitches, knitting 13 from Needle 2, and 12 from Needle 3. Commence a new needle and knit the 3 black stitches from Needle 3, and then knit-up the 18 loops down the side and continue knitting on this needle to the seam stitch. The

Round now begins in the middle of the sole, the new redivision being shown in *Fig.* 225 ready for making the
gusset. The stitches
to be decreased
(13) are indicated
either side by a
bracket.

Round 2. Knit
plain.

Round 3. Knit to
last six stitches and
here K.2 tog.
Needle 2, Knit
without decreas-
ing. Needle 3,
K.4, S.1, K.1,
p.s.s.o., complete
the round. Repeat
rounds 2 and 3, de-
creasing thus on
each side until the
13 stitches are ab-
sorbed and the
gusset completed.
This leaves the
stitches as shown
in *Fig.* 226, the
arrows indicating
another redivi-
sion, as the three
stitches either
side are restored
to Needle 2.

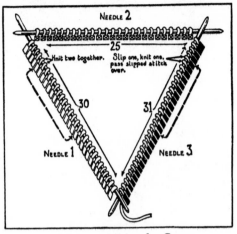

Fig. 225.   Redivision for Gusset

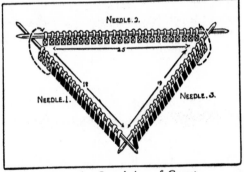

Fig. 226.   Completion of Gusset

(They were placed here in order to avoid a gap when decreasing.)   This new redivision is shown in *Fig.* 227, the two
sole needles being now equal in number to the instep needle.
From here knit the foot until position for toe, knitting the
instep needle in pattern, if other than Stocking Stitch fabric
has been used for the leg.

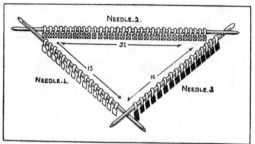

Fig. 227.   Redivision for Foot

SEPARATE SOLE

A separate sole as in *Fig.* 228 can be added as follows: The work is the same up to *Fig.* 225. The 3 stitches on Needles 1 and 3 must be returned to Needle 2, as shown in *Fig.* 226, and the gusset then knitted as directed but on the two sole needles only, knitting backwards and forwards in Stocking Stitch, decreasing on the Knit rows, but not on the Purl. The knitting can be on two needles if more convenient. Knit the sole and form the toe. Knit the instep and toe, and seam the two together when complete. Knitted thus, a sock is easily re-footed.

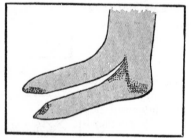

Fig. 228.   Separate Sole

TOES

Two toes are given here—Long toe for a long foot, Short toe for a broad foot. The difference in the number of rounds should be allowed in calculation.

LONG TOE

Toes are always knitted in Stocking Stitch. For Long Toe the number of stitches on the instep needle must equal those on the two sole needles, so the division shown in *Fig.* 227 is still correct. Arrange these on two needles, putting the stitches on Needles 1 and 3 together on one needle as in *Fig.* 229. To do this, continue knitting from Needle 3 along 1 to last three stitches. Here K.2 tog., K.1. Always knit one stitch before making a decrease and one after. The decrease at the beginning of a needle is S.1, K.1, p.s.s.o., and that made at the

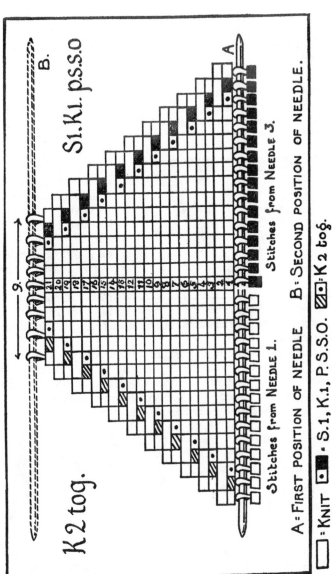

B.

S1. K1. p.s.s.o.

K2 tog.

9.

21
20
19
18
17
16
15
14
13
12
11
10
9
8
7
6
5
4
3
2
1

Stitches from Needle 1.

Stitches from Needle 3.

A = First position of needle   B = Second position of needle.

☐ = Knit   ■ = S.1, K.1, P.S.S.O.   ▨ = K 2 tog.

Fig. 229.   Long Toe.   Chart

end of a needle is K.2 tog. Knit one plain round as shown between each decreasing round, and continue decreasing so until only nine stitches remain on the needle. Graft toe together.

SHORT OR ROUND TOE

In order to shorten the length of a toe, make a greater number of decreases in each round. For Long Toe, only four

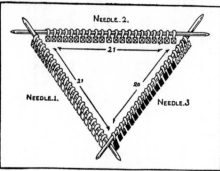

Fig. 230.   Redivision for Short Toe

decreases were made in each round, but for Short Toe there are six in each round. This necessitates a redivision of stitches so that an equal number is contained on all three needles (*see Fig.* 230). The decreases are still made at the begin-ning and end of each needle and in the same order as before, but on three needles instead of two.

The new redivision in *Fig.* 230 reveals Needle 3 as one stitch short. This must be rectified by omitting the sole decrease on Needle 3 on the first round, after which the number will be equal. Knit one round plain between every decreasing round, and keep the decrease paired as shown in the chart, *Fig.* 231. Decrease thus until four stitches remain on each needle. Then divide on two needles and graft together.

REDIVISION

JOINING THE TOE

Toes can be joined to-gether in three different ways.

1. The stitches can be cast-off in the usual way and the sock turned inside out and the stitches sewn together. Leave a long end of yarn when breaking for this purpose.

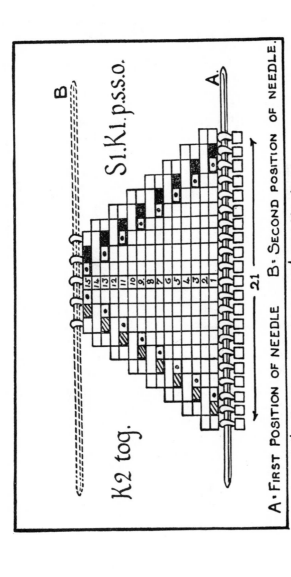

S1.K1.p.s.s.o.

K2 tog.

B

A

15 14 13 12 11 10 9 8 7 G 5 4 3 2 1

21

A. FIRST POSITION OF NEEDLE   B. SECOND POSITION OF NEEDLE.

Fig. 231. Short Toe.   Chart

□ = KNIT | ☐• = S.1, K.1, P.S.S.O. | ☒• = K 2 tog.

2. The stitches can be equally divided upon two needles and knitted together as in *Fig.* 232. Knit and cast-off at the same time.

3. The toe can be grafted together as in *Fig.* 233 and the join quite invisible.

GRAFTING THE TOE

Divide the stitches evenly upon two needles. Keep the yarn on back needle. Thread a wool needle and begin. The first two movements are preparatory.

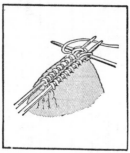

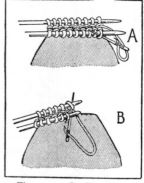

Fig. 232.   Joining Toe   Fig. 233.   Grafting Toe

Front Needle: Insert needle as if to purl as at A. Draw through the yarn, leave stitch on needle.

Back Needle: Insert needle as if to knit. Draw through the yarn, leave stitch on needle.

The following movements are repeated from * to *.

* *Front Needle*: Insert needle as if to knit (same stitch as before), and slip it off the needle. Insert needle in next stitch as if to purl, draw through, but leave it on needle.

Back Needle: Insert needle as if to purl, take it off. Insert in next stitch as if to knit (*see* B). Draw yarn through but leave stitch on needle. *

Song of the Knitting Graft
Front Needle:

> Take off as if you were going to knit.
> Prepare as if you were going to purl.

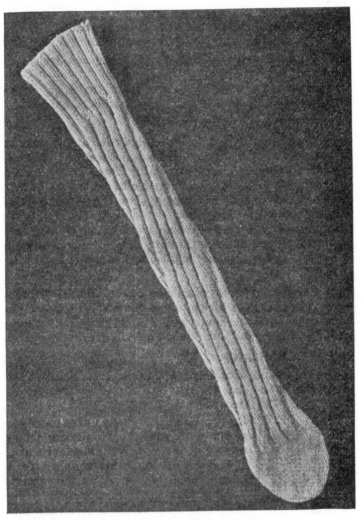

Fig. 234 A.   Stockings in Spiral Ribbing and without Heels

Back Needle:

> Take off as if you were going to purl.
> Prepare as if you were going to knit.

The song omits the two preparatory movements, which are necessary.

In passing the wool needle from back to front, do so beneath the points of the needles, as shown in A and B.

HOSE WITHOUT HEELS

Socks and stockings are often knitted straight and without heels, the foot finding its own heel by adjustment. This stocking can be very uncomfortable at the instep unless knitted correctly, and then it is as comfortable as any other, the best fit being derived in Spiral Ribbing, shown in *Fig.* 234 A. A stocking knitted in this manner is adjusted on the foot by twisting it round until the ribbing appears straight. The heel then takes its position with comfort, and the instep is smooth and smart. Bed-socks made in this manner remain in position all night.

Note. Spiral Ribbing was often used by the old-fashioned folk when knitting jerseys for corpulent figures, as the fabric can be adjusted over the figure with a slick line. The knitting would be round, and often done on eight needles.

SPIRAL KNITTING

Cast on a multiple of 6, according to size and needles. Rib for 12 rounds in 2 and 2 (K.2, P.2). This is ordinary ribbing (see top of sock, *Fig.* 234 A).

Fig. 234 B
Spiral Ribbing

Row 13: Change and rib for 6 rounds in 3 and 3 (K.3, P.3). From here follow chart, *Fig.* 234 B, as the ribbing (3 and 3) now moves one stitch to the right every 6 rounds, moving thus until reaching the toe shaping. The length must be enough for the leg and foot (22″ for a sock), and then decrease for the toe in the usual way.

PEASANT HEELS

A straight sock with a peasant heel is shown in *Fig.* 235 A. The sock is knitted straight, and the heel is added afterward

Fig. 235 **A.** Peasant Heels

when the sock is completed, and is knitted in exactly the same way as the toe!

Knit to position for heel, and then take another coloured yarn and knit half the number of stitches in the round in this colour, stranding the original yarn at the back as shown in Fig. 235 B. Complete the sock and toe. The heel is then added by removing the coloured yarn as shown and picking up the stitches thus released on two needles and knitting another toe. This now becomes the heel.

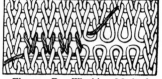

Fig. 235 B.   Working Method

The sock in *Fig.* 235 A is an interesting example of late 19th-century Stranded Knitting from Bulgaria. The fabric is in bands of colour, mauve, pink and scarlet, each of a different width. Two stitches in a contrasting colour are then grouped together with 3 plain between in every sixth round, the colour being stranded from stitch to stitch across the back. This makes a simple but effective pattern. The yarn is very coarse and scrubby, being peasant spun (*see page* 31), but the socks are generally worn over others of a softer texture.

RE-HEELING

Fig. 236 A shows the worn portion of a heel removed, and a reference to *Fig.* 219 reveals that this is merely the heel flap and turn, cut away. Knit another as described, and so add a new heel. Cut away the old heel, △ unravelling the last few rows to obtain a clear line of loops. Do not unravel beyond the instep level and gusset. Pick up the stitches as shown in *Fig.* 236 B, and knit the heel flap, backwards and forwards, on the middle needle as follows:

Fig. 236 A.   Re-heeling

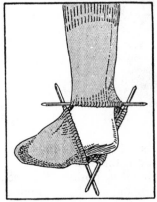
Fig. 236 B.   Re-heeling

* Knit to end of row, and here transfer one stitch off the side needle and knit it together with the last stitch. Turn and purl back. Transfer stitch as before, and purl this together with the last stitch on heel needle. * Repeat from * to * until heel flap is long enough. Count the stitches left for the sole and put on separate needle. Turn the heel in the same way as on the original heel, leaving the same number of stitches as on the sole needle. Graft the two together. Darn in odd ends, reinforcing the gusset to prevent any breaking away.

KNITTING HINTS

Alphabetical Order

BLOCKING

THIS PROCESS is useful in restoring baggy skirts and elbows to shape, and will also help to restore shape to an ill-fitting garment, though this is only temporary and until washed, when it must be done again.

Lay the garment on a flat surface and cover with a wet towel (not dripping). After two or three hours it will be damp enough to model to shape. Do this by laying it upon your own pattern (*see page* 151), and, where any discrepancies occur, smooth the fabric out with a firm hand until it takes the dimensions required. Straighten the lines of the fabric, and leave it thus until dry.

A damp yarn will take almost any shape. (*See also* Remodelling.)

COUNTING SIMPLIFIED

When casting-on a large number of stitches, a long coloured thread, knitted in with every tenth stitch, will save a lot of troublesome recounting. When working in fine yarns, the number of increases on a sleeve and decreases on a skirt grow proportionately more. To save recounting, knit in a strand (about 2″ long) of coloured wool on the increasing or decreasing row or round.

LEARNER

The decreases on a skirt are always made in a vertical line, and in working on a circular needle these are more easily located by weaving in a coloured yarn, arranged vertically and at the position of the different decreases. Break off a length about 30″ long, and weave this in between the stitches. Bring it forward between the stitch after the decrease and take it back after the next. Then forward, back, and so on, keeping a true vertical line. This will not only mark the position for decreasing with accuracy, but enable the number of rounds to be counted with ease. It can be done after every round, if preferred.

DRESSING

Silk knitting can be "dressed" by holding it before the steam of a boiling kettle; when damp, lay upon the table and pat into position and allow to dry.

Small articles and purses with steel beads can be dressed in the same way. Narrow Shetland scarves of wool are also treated in this way. For dressing a Shetland shawl, *see page* 194.

The old knitters never pressed any pure woollen garments, but dressed them over steam and patted them into position afterwards, and the modern tendency is to advocate the same treatment.

DROPPED STITCHES

A stitch dropped on a KNIT row is picked up as shown in *Figs.* 237 A to F. A. The dropped stitch. B. Insert right needle through stitch and strand from front to back. C. Insert left needle from back to front, through stitch only. D. With right needle draw through the strand and so re-form the stitch. E. The stitch is facing in the wrong direction, so must be corrected by inserting the left needle through the stitch from front to back, which transfers it to the left needle ready to be knitted.

DROPPED STITCHES

A stitch dropped on a PURL fabric is picked up as in *Figs.* 238 A to F. The movements are the reverse of those shown for the Knit Stitch. A. The dropped stitch. B. Insert right needle through stitch and strand from front to back. C. Insert left needle through stitch only, and, D, lift the stitch above the strand with the left needle to enable the right needle to draw through the strand as at E. This re-forms the stitch as at F, which in this case faces in the correct position and so remains.

GARMENTS, WASHING

Never soak knitted garments, especially those knitted in wool. Never use strong soaps, soda, washing chemicals, very

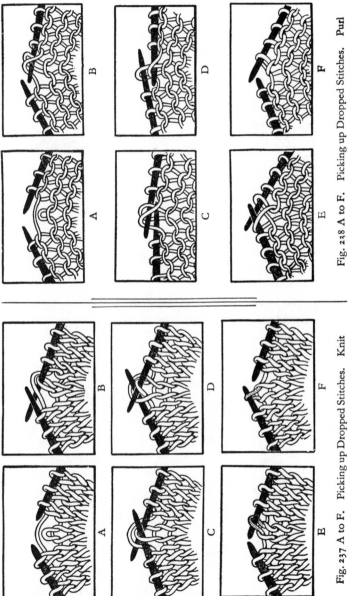

Fig. 237 A to F.   Picking up Dropped Stitches.   Knit

Fig. 238 A to F.   Picking up Dropped Stitches.   Purl

hot water, or dirty suds. Never allow woollens to lie in a wet state after washing. This is the worst crime of all!

Wool is a living substance, and to wash it in chemicals or hot water is to kill this living quality, reduce its warmth, impair its wear and spoil its soft caressing feel. Wool treated kindly in the wash-tub will respond to almost any modelling process demanded of it.

Wash quickly. Test the temperature of the water with the elbow. Use good soap flakes, and fluff up a lather before immersing the garment. Don't rub. Squeeze the dirt out of the garment. Don't be in a hurry. Do it properly. Rinse thoroughly in two lots of water. Do not wring, but squeeze the garment to remove the water. Part dry by rolling tightly in a towel, and bear upon this to squeeze it. Dry flat on a clean cloth arranged to admit an undercurrent of air.

Drying. Dry preferably in the open air, but in the shade. Hot sun, cold winds or frost will spoil most yarns, especially those of pure wool. If dried in the house, do so in a warm room, but never before a fire or on a radiator.

Shape. To ensure the garment drying a good shape, take your own pattern and outline this upon a cloth. Muslin will do. Make a permanent outline with a tacking thread, and keep this muslin especially for reshaping a garment after washing. This will ensure perfect fit. Lay the garment upon the cloth, arrange the neck-line and the base-line in position and pat the

intervening portions into shape, until the garment is flat and without wrinkles. Straighten out the pattern, arranging the lines of Stocking Stitch vertically. Pay attention to buttonholes and buttons, as these are apt to pull the fabric.

A garment prepared in this

way will dry to shape without pressing. Woollens are better without being pressed, as undue heat, administered over a damp cloth, will shrink them. This is indeed a shrinking process, and is used for this purpose. Properly prepared by patting, pressing can be avoided.

Silk and artificial silk garments must be treated with the same care, washed lightly, not wrung, and dried in a towel, remodelling to shape before drying.

Garments in artificial silks and mixtures may be pressed, but with a cool iron and through muslin, and left to dry flat before moving, otherwise they lose their shape again. (*See also* Dressing.)

Pressing. Yarns other than pure wool should be pressed, but through a muslin cloth, and not with a gliding iron movement, but with a light lifting movement. This is necessary because of the elastic nature of a knitted fabric. Yarns spun to a tighter tension need more pressing. Bouclé, Bouclette and Knobbly yarns should be pressed on the inside and then reversed, modelled to shape and allowed to dry. Each yarn needs its own treatment. Never press ribbing, as this destroys its character and objective, which is to contract the fabric. Fancy patterns in knobbly lace stitches are better dressed than pressed.

HANDS

Always wash the hands in warm water before commencing to knit a fabric in white or delicate colours, otherwise it will get so grubby in work as to need washing before worn. Keep the work wrapped in a white cloth and spread this in the lap when working.

LADDERS

A long ladder is more easily picked up with a crochet hook, and on a stocking surface this is a simple matter, as the loop is drawn through with the hook, as shown in *Fig.* 239, in one continuous journey up the ladder.

Picking up a stitch on a Purl fabric, as in *Fig.* 240, is not such a simple matter, as the hook must be removed after making each new stitch and inserted again, as shown, to pick up the next one.   These two movements must be alternated when picking up a "ladder" on a Garter Stitch fabric.

Fig. 239
Ladders on Knit Fabrics

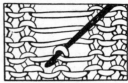

Fig. 240
Ladders on Purl Fabrics

KNITTING-UP

When knitting-up stitches for any purpose, such as a neck or stocking gusset, do so on a smaller needle, and revert to original needles on second row.   Diagram showing method of knitting-up is *Fig.* 166, *page* 166.

LENGTH.   TWO WAYS KNITTING

Too Short.   The simplest way to lengthen any knitted garment is to remove the cast-on edge and pick up the exposed loops upon a knitting needle, and knit in the opposite direction, and, provided the loops have been picked up correctly, there will be no suspicion of a join.   If the garment has been already seamed at the sides, the sewing stitches should be unpicked for about one inch, so that the fabric is released to its original width.

TWO WAYS KNITTING

The cast-on edge is then either cut or unravelled from A to B as in *Fig.* 241 A, and the loose threads pulled away, leaving a clear row of knitting loops exposed.

△ The last few stitches to the right of B must be unravelled in order to ensure a thread of sufficient length to join on a new

ball of yarn. The shaded loops in the third row of *Fig.* 241 A
will be left clear and ready to be picked up on the needle, and
form the foundation of the knitting, which will proceed in the
opposite direction.

△ The order in which the loops are picked up is important,
since if they are restored to the needle as exposed, and in their
original order, the knitting will be one half-stitch out in the
working. To correct this, △ the first half-loop, C, in the

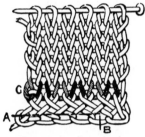 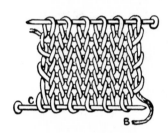

Fig. 241 A. Lengthening   Fig. 241 B. Lengthening

shaded row of *Fig.* 241 A, must become the first full loop or
stitch in the new row, *Fig.* 241 B. △ This necessitates the
second and each succeeding stitch also moving one half-loop to
the right. The new and correct loops to pick up have been
shaded alternately black and lined, in *Fig.* 241 A. These same
loops are shown picked up on the needle in *Fig.* 241 B in
the △ correct way in which they should lie to proceed knitting
on the next and Purl row in the opposite direction.

Too Long. To shorten a garment, remove a section of the depth
from the middle. △ Do not cut, but divide the fabric. Insert
a needle into the head of one stitch and pull as shown in
Fig. 242. Loosen the yarn across the
entire width of the fabric and then break
it, and the fabric will automatically fall into
two portions, leaving a clean row of loops.
These should be picked up on a knitting
needle, and the same process repeated
to remove the unwanted section below.

Fig. 242
Dividing a Fabric

Pick up the second lot of exposed loops and weave the two
portions together. (Weaving, *see page* 170.)

MEASURING

Knitting should be measured flat upon the table, as, held in the hand, it will stretch in all directions. Lay it flat and pat it into position, and then make the measurement. Do not stretch. When measuring knitting against a paper pattern, lay the pattern upon the table and place the knitting over it, and pat it flat and into shape and position. This is necessary because of the natural elasticity of the fabric. When knitting two pieces of fabric to the same size, count the rows or rounds of the first section, and knit those of the second to correspond.

MENDING

The yarn used for mending a sock or stocking should be a little finer than that used for the knitting.

REINFORCING

A Stocking Stitch web that has grown thin in wear can be reinforced by Swiss Darning (*see page* 141). Work over the existing web with care, and use a matching but finer yarn. Divide the plys of the same yarn, if matching is impossible.

Stocking heels are often strengthened in this manner before they are worn, though in knitting a stocking the heel can be reinforced as explained on *page* 218.

REPAIRING

(1) *Horizontal Damage*. A Stocking Stitch web can be rebuilt horizontally as shown in *Figs.* 243 to 245. Remove the weak and damaged threads, but unravel the last few loops so that the ends are long enough to turn back, as in *Fig.* 243 A. These must be fastened in some way—darning if length permits. If the hole is fairly broad, then at this stage pat it out flat on a paper until it is the correct shape, and tack it in position. If done in the hand, the fabric is likely to contract, and the repair will show. (For a stocking, place over a pad.) Take a length of yarn, the same as the fabric, and, if the garment has been washed, then wash and dry the yarn before using it.

Unite the loops top and bottom with long strands, as in *Fig.* 243 A. The short end is left to show the commencement of the journey, though this is, in reality, secured several stitches in advance either by darning it through the fabric, or tying it

to the head of a stitch, as in Swiss Darning. △ These strands
should not be drawn tightly, as, in building the new stitches
around them, they tighten up. Experience alone will give the
correct tension.

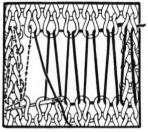
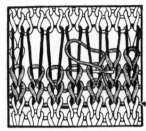

Fig. 243 A, B. Repairing Horizontal. Knit

When this is completed, attach the end securely and proceed
to build in the new loops as in *Fig.* 243 B. △ Notice how the
turn is made at the end of the row, by wrapping round the
stitch of the original fabric. It is easier to work the return
journey by reversing the work.

Fig. 244 shows how to repair a Purl web.

A ribbed web, 2 Knit, 2 Purl Stitches, is rebuilt as in *Fig.* 245,
the needle being about to complete the first Purl Stitch com-

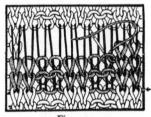

Fig. 244. Repairing Horizontal. Purl

Fig. 245
Repairing Horizontal. Ribbed

menced as in *Fig.* 244. △ The number of rows added will correspond to those removed. The new loops will straighten
themselves out to the correct dimensions with the addition of
the last row. Keep to the knitting tension throughout, as the
tendency is to tighten up in the first two or three rows.

(2) *Vertical Damage.* A stocking web can be rebuilt vertically
as in *Fig.* 246. This is a more convenient method when

the damage to be repaired is greater in height than breadth. Remove the damaged portion as before, and secure the loops top and bottom to prevent them running. Those at the bottom should be secured immediately, commencing two or three stitches in advance, and continuing two or three stitches beyond the part to be repaired, as shown. Secure the side portions and continue laying the foundation bars horizontally until com-

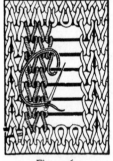

Fig. 246
Repairing Vertical

plete. This is more conveniently done on the back of the fabric. On the △ right side of the work, and in the left corner, build in the new stitches. △ Two vertical journeys are necessary to make one vertical web of Stocking Stitch. The needle shows the second and downward half of the journey. Build the first two or three lines over the existing stocking web to strengthen it. The first journey commences up under the first bar, and over and under the second, bringing the needle point to the right of the half-stitch as made. Descend as shown. The stitches and number of rows will, of course, coincide with those of the fabric.

REWINDING

Knitting yarn that has been already knitted and is crinkled can be straightened out in either of the following ways:

1. Rewind it into a skein by passing it round the back of two chairs. Then hold the skein taut before the spout of a steaming kettle, moving it backwards and forwards through the steam until the kinks have disappeared.

2. Wind the yarn round an aluminium hot-water bottle, and fill it with boiling water and leave until cool. When removed, the kinks will have disappeared.

SIZE

To enlarge or reduce the size of a garment when working from written directions, work as follows:

For each size larger than the one given in the directions, add the required number of stitches to make an inch to those stated in the directions. Should the needle gauge given be

8 stitches to the inch, and two inches extra are required, an addition of 16 extra stitches is necessary. (*See also page* 41.) Add one inch to the back section (8 stitches) and one inch to the front section (8 stitches).

If the garment is knitted in pattern, the repeat of this must be taken into consideration, and the addition made accordingly.

Having cast-on the extra stitches required, work according to the directions. Upon reaching the division of stitches for the neck, △ remember to count in these extra stitches, or the neck will be off centre. In shaping the armholes, allow a half-inch extra in depth, back and front; one inch extra if the garment has been increased two sizes. For a large armhole, shape as in *Fig.* 164, *page* 164. Add additional width to the neck at the back by casting-off two extra stitches. Increase the width of the sleeve by adding the necessary extra stitches when casting-on, and the length by knitting extra rows midway.

To reduce the size, deduct the required number of stitches. Average these according to the gauge.

The best plan is to construct your own pattern as on *page* 153 and work to this.

SLIPPED STITCHES

In forming a decrease, the stitch must be slipped △ knit-wise, otherwise when drawn over the succeeding stitch it will be crossed. In fabric construction (Fancy and Lace Patterns) it must be slipped △ purlwise, otherwise it will be crossed when purled in the next row.

TAKING-BACK AND UNRAVELLING

Taking-back. Mistakes are often made and need to be corrected. Sometimes this can be done by "taking-back" a few stitches, without unravelling. Insert the left needle into the stitch below that on the needle, and then withdraw the right needle from the loop above, and pull the yarn with the right hand to unravel this loop.

The left needle must be inserted into the loop correctly, otherwise the stitches will "sit" in the wrong direction upon the needle. The arrow in *Fig.* 247 shows how to insert the needle into a △ Knit Stitch on the front of the fabric, inserting it from △ front to back through every loop, and not from back to front as in the shaded diagram below, which is the incorrect method. In actually taking back, this stitch would be the one below that on the needle, but the diagram appears clearer drawn in this way.

Fig. 248 shows the method of work on the back of the fabric, or on a row to be △ Purled. It is the same. The needle is inserted from front to back, as shown, and *not* from back to front, which the shaded diagram below shows as incorrect.

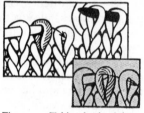 

Fig. 247. Taking-back, right and wrong methods. Knit

Fig. 248. Taking-back, right and wrong methods. Purl

Unravelling. After several rows of stitches have been un-ravelled, the row to be picked up, Knit or Purl, can always be ascertained by the position of the yarn. Lay the fabric front side uppermost on the table. If the yarn is on the RIGHT hand side of the knitting, the unravelling will have stopped at the completion of a Purl row. The next will be a Knit, so the stitches will be picked up on the △ front of the fabric as in *Fig.* 247. Pick up with △ left needle, inserting this through the △ *front* of every Knit stitch as shown and just described.

If the yarn is on the LEFT side of the fabric, then the un-ravelling will have stopped at the Knit row. The next will be a Purl row, so the stitches must be picked up from the △ back of the fabric, travelling towards the knitting yarn as shown. The procedure is exactly the same, the needle being inserted from △ front to back through each stitch as shown in *Fig.* 248, and *not* as in the shaded diagram above, which is incorrect as previously described.

TEASLE BRUSH

A fine wire brush designed for brushing up the surface of a knitted fabric constructed of such yarns as teasle or angora. The fabric is brushed △ on the front only. The old teasle brushes were constructed of the burrs or heads of the teasle plant and such as this was used to brush a knitted and felted fabric (*see page* 3).

WIDTH, EXTRA

Extra width can be added to knitting already commenced by knitting a separate strip, on separate needles, to the width required, sufficient to make up the deficiency. When the strip is as long as the fabric already knitted, add this to the main portion by knitting straight across as one piece. The separate portions are later joined together, as in seaming. (*See Fig.* 185, *page* 185.)

YARN, INSUFFICIENT

If the yarn proves insufficient for long sleeves, then make short. Divide the yarn which is left in two equal lengths for the two sleeves, and commence the sleeve from the top, and knit as deep as the yarn will permit. In commencing the sleeve thus, all the decreases must be read as increases, and vice versa, when working to written instructions. Working from a pattern (*see page* 151), increase according to shape.

△ Always buy sufficient yarn to complete any garment. Dyes vary, and are sometimes not repeated.

LIST OF ILLUSTRATIONS

KNITTING HINTS

INDEX

255

A CATALOG OF SELECTED
DOVER BOOKS
IN ALL FIELDS OF INTEREST

A CATALOG OF SELECTED DOVER
BOOKS IN ALL FIELDS OF INTEREST

CONCERNING THE SPIRITUAL IN ART, Wassily Kandinsky. Pioneering work by father of abstract art. Thoughts on color theory, nature of art. Analysis of earlier masters. 12 illustrations. 80pp. of text. 5⅜ × 8½.   23411-8 Pa. $3.95

ANIMALS: 1,419 Copyright-Free Illustrations of Mammals, Birds, Fish, Insects, etc., Jim Harter (ed.). Clear wood engravings present, in extremely lifelike poses, over 1,000 species of animals. One of the most extensive pictorial sourcebooks of its kind. Captions. Index. 284pp. 9 × 12.   23766-4 Pa. $12.95

CELTIC ART: The Methods of Construction, George Bain. Simple geometric techniques for making Celtic interlacements, spirals, Kells-type initials, animals, humans, etc. Over 500 illustrations. 160pp. 9 × 12. (USO)   22923-8 Pa. $9.95

AN ATLAS OF ANATOMY FOR ARTISTS, Fritz Schider. Most thorough reference work on art anatomy in the world. Hundreds of illustrations, including selections from works by Vesalius, Leonardo, Goya, Ingres, Michelangelo, others. 593 illustrations. 192pp. 7⅞ × 10¼.   20241-0 Pa. $9.95

CELTIC HAND STROKE-BY-STROKE (Irish Half-Uncial from "The Book of Kells"): An Arthur Baker Calligraphy Manual, Arthur Baker. Complete guide to creating each letter of the alphabet in distinctive Celtic manner. Covers hand position, strokes, pens, inks, paper, more. Illustrated. 48pp. 8¼ × 11.

24336-2 Pa. $3.95

EASY ORIGAMI, John Montroll. Charming collection of 32 projects (hat, cup, pelican, piano, swan, many more) specially designed for the novice origami hobbyist. Clearly illustrated easy-to-follow instructions insure that even beginning papercrafters will achieve successful results. 48pp. 8¼ × 11.   27298-2 Pa. $2.95

THE COMPLETE BOOK OF BIRDHOUSE CONSTRUCTION FOR WOOD-WORKERS, Scott D. Campbell. Detailed instructions, illustrations, tables. Also data on bird habitat and instinct patterns. Bibliography. 3 tables. 63 illustrations in 15 figures. 48pp. 5¼ × 8½.   24407-5 Pa. $1.95

BLOOMINGDALE'S ILLUSTRATED 1886 CATALOG: Fashions, Dry Goods and Housewares, Bloomingdale Brothers. Famed merchants' extremely rare catalog depicting about 1,700 products: clothing, housewares, firearms, dry goods, jewelry, more. Invaluable for dating, identifying vintage items. Also, copyright-free graphics for artists, designers. Co-published with Henry Ford Museum & Green-field Village. 160pp. 8¼ × 11.   25780-0 Pa. $9.95

HISTORIC COSTUME IN PICTURES, Braun & Schneider. Over 1,450 costumed figures in clearly detailed engravings—from dawn of civilization to end of 19th century. Captions. Many folk costumes. 256pp. 8⅜ × 11¾.   23150-X Pa. $11.95

PERSPECTIVE FOR ARTISTS, Rex Vicat Cole. Depth, perspective of sky and sea, shadows, much more, not usually covered. 391 diagrams, 81 reproductions of drawings and paintings. 279pp. 5⅜ × 8½. 22487-2 Pa. $6.95

DRAWING THE LIVING FIGURE, Joseph Sheppard. Innovative approach to artistic anatomy focuses on specifics of surface anatomy, rather than muscles and bones. Over 170 drawings of live models in front, back and side views, and in widely varying poses. Accompanying diagrams. 177 illustrations. Introduction. Index. 144pp. 8⅜ × 11¼. 26723-7 Pa. $8.95

GOTHIC AND OLD ENGLISH ALPHABETS: 100 Complete Fonts, Dan X. Solo. Add power, elegance to posters, signs, other graphics with 100 stunning copyright-free alphabets: Blackstone, Dolbey, Germania, 97 more—including many lower-case, numerals, punctuation marks. 104pp. 8⅛ × 11. 24695-7 Pa. $8.95

HOW TO DO BEADWORK, Mary White. Fundamental book on craft from simple projects to five-bead chains and woven works. 106 illustrations. 142pp. 5⅜ × 8. 20697-1 Pa. $4.95

THE BOOK OF WOOD CARVING, Charles Marshall Sayers. Finest book for beginners discusses fundamentals and offers 34 designs. "Absolutely first rate . . . well thought out and well executed."—E. J. Tangerman. 118pp. 7¾ × 10⅝. 23654-4 Pa. $5.95

ILLUSTRATED CATALOG OF CIVIL WAR MILITARY GOODS: Union Army Weapons, Insignia, Uniform Accessories, and Other Equipment, Schuyler, Hartley, and Graham. Rare, profusely illustrated 1846 catalog includes Union Army uniform and dress regulations, arms and ammunition, coats, insignia, flags, swords, rifles, etc. 226 illustrations. 160pp. 9 × 12. 24939-5 Pa. $10.95

WOMEN'S FASHIONS OF THE EARLY 1900s: An Unabridged Republication of "New York Fashions, 1909," National Cloak & Suit Co. Rare catalog of mail-order fashions documents women's and children's clothing styles shortly after the turn of the century. Captions offer full descriptions, prices. Invaluable resource for fashion, costume historians. Approximately 725 illustrations. 128pp. 8⅜ × 11¼. 27276-1 Pa. $11.95

THE 1912 AND 1915 GUSTAV STICKLEY FURNITURE CATALOGS, Gustav Stickley. With over 200 detailed illustrations and descriptions, these two catalogs are essential reading and reference materials and identification guides for Stickley furniture. Captions cite materials, dimensions and prices. 112pp. 6½ × 9¼. 26676-1 Pa. $9.95

EARLY AMERICAN LOCOMOTIVES, John H. White, Jr. Finest locomotive engravings from early 19th century: historical (1804–74), main-line (after 1870), special, foreign, etc. 147 plates. 142pp. 11⅜ × 8¼. 22772-3 Pa. $10.95

THE TALL SHIPS OF TODAY IN PHOTOGRAPHS, Frank O. Braynard. Lavishly illustrated tribute to nearly 100 majestic contemporary sailing vessels: Amerigo Vespucci, Clearwater, Constitution, Eagle, Mayflower, Sea Cloud, Victory, many more. Authoritative captions provide statistics, background on each ship. 190 black-and-white photographs and illustrations. Introduction. 128pp. 8⅞ × 11¾. 27163-3 Pa. $13.95

BRASS INSTRUMENTS: Their History and Development, Anthony Baines. Authoritative, updated survey of the evolution of trumpets, trombones, bugles, cornets, French horns, tubas and other brass wind instruments. Over 140 illustrations and 48 music examples. Corrected and updated by author. New preface. Bibliography. 320pp. 5⅜ × 8½. 27574-4 Pa. $9.95

HOLLYWOOD GLAMOR PORTRAITS, John Kobal (ed.). 145 photos from 1926–49. Harlow, Gable, Bogart, Bacall; 94 stars in all. Full background on photographers, technical aspects. 160pp. 8⅜ × 11¼. 23352-9 Pa. $11.95

MAX AND MORITZ, Wilhelm Busch. Great humor classic in both German and English. Also 10 other works: "Cat and Mouse," "Plisch and Plumm," etc. 216pp. 5⅜ × 8½. 20181-3 Pa. $5.95

THE RAVEN AND OTHER FAVORITE POEMS, Edgar Allan Poe. Over 40 of the author's most memorable poems: "The Bells," "Ulalume," "Israfel," "To Helen," "The Conqueror Worm," "Eldorado," "Annabel Lee," many more. Alphabetic lists of titles and first lines. 64pp. 5³⁄₁₆ × 8¼. 26685-0 Pa. $1.00

SEVEN SCIENCE FICTION NOVELS, H. G. Wells. The standard collection of the great novels. Complete, unabridged. First Men in the Moon, Island of Dr. Moreau, War of the Worlds, Food of the Gods, Invisible Man, Time Machine, In the Days of the Comet. Total of 1,015pp. 5⅜ × 8½. (USO) 20264-X Clothbd. $29.95

AMULETS AND SUPERSTITIONS, E. A. Wallis Budge. Comprehensive discourse on origin, powers of amulets in many ancient cultures: Arab, Persian, Babylonian, Assyrian, Egyptian, Gnostic, Hebrew, Phoenician, Syriac, etc. Covers cross, swastika, crucifix, seals, rings, stones, etc. 584pp. 5⅜ × 8½. 23573-4 Pa. $12.95

RUSSIAN STORIES/PYCCKNE PACCKA3bl: A Dual-Language Book, edited by Gleb Struve. Twelve tales by such masters as Chekhov, Tolstoy, Dostoevsky, Pushkin, others. Excellent word-for-word English translations on facing pages, plus teaching and study aids, Russian/English vocabulary, biographical/critical introductions, more. 416pp. 5⅜ × 8½. 26244-8 Pa. $8.95

PHILADELPHIA THEN AND NOW: 60 Sites Photographed in the Past and Present, Kenneth Finkel and Susan Oyama. Rare photographs of City Hall, Logan Square, Independence Hall, Betsy Ross House, other landmarks juxtaposed with contemporary views. Captures changing face of historic city. Introduction. Captions. 128pp. 8¼ × 11. 25790-8 Pa. $9.95

AIA ARCHITECTURAL GUIDE TO NASSAU AND SUFFOLK COUNTIES, LONG ISLAND, The American Institute of Architects, Long Island Chapter, and the Society for the Preservation of Long Island Antiquities. Comprehensive, well-researched and generously illustrated volume brings to life over three centuries of Long Island's great architectural heritage. More than 240 photographs with authoritative, extensively detailed captions. 176pp. 8¼ × 11. 26946-9 Pa. $14.95

NORTH AMERICAN INDIAN LIFE: Customs and Traditions of 23 Tribes, Elsie Clews Parsons (ed.). 27 fictionalized essays by noted anthropologists examine religion, customs, government, additional facets of life among the Winnebago, Crow, Zuni, Eskimo, other tribes. 480pp. 6⅛ × 9¼. 27377-6 Pa. $10.95

CATALOG OF DOVER BOOKS

MY BONDAGE AND MY FREEDOM, Frederick Douglass. Born a slave, Douglass became outspoken force in antislavery movement. The best of Douglass' autobiographies. Graphic description of slave life. 464pp. 5⅜ × 8½. 22457-0 Pa. $8.95

FOLLOWING THE EQUATOR: A Journey Around the World, Mark Twain. Fascinating humorous account of 1897 voyage to Hawaii, Australia, India, New Zealand, etc. Ironic, bemused reports on peoples, customs, climate, flora and fauna, politics, much more. 197 illustrations. 720pp. 5⅜ × 8½. 26113-1 Pa. $15.95

THE PEOPLE CALLED SHAKERS, Edward D. Andrews. Definitive study of Shakers: origins, beliefs, practices, dances, social organization, furniture and crafts, etc. 33 illustrations. 351pp. 5⅜ × 8½. 21081-2 Pa. $8.95

THE MYTHS OF GREECE AND ROME, H. A. Guerber. A classic of mythology, generously illustrated, long prized for its simple, graphic, accurate retelling of the principal myths of Greece and Rome, and for its commentary on their origins and significance. With 64 illustrations by Michelangelo, Raphael, Titian, Rubens, Canova, Bernini and others. 480pp. 5⅜ × 8½. 27584-1 Pa. $9.95

PSYCHOLOGY OF MUSIC, Carl E. Seashore. Classic work discusses music as a medium from psychological viewpoint. Clear treatment of physical acoustics, auditory apparatus, sound perception, development of musical skills, nature of musical feeling, host of other topics. 88 figures. 408pp. 5⅜ × 8½. 21851-1 Pa. $9.95

THE PHILOSOPHY OF HISTORY, Georg W. Hegel. Great classic of Western thought develops concept that history is not chance but rational process, the evolution of freedom. 457pp. 5⅜ × 8½. 20112-0 Pa. $9.95

THE BOOK OF TEA, Kakuzo Okakura. Minor classic of the Orient: entertaining, charming explanation, interpretation of traditional Japanese culture in terms of tea ceremony. 94pp. 5⅜ × 8½. 20070-1 Pa. $3.95

LIFE IN ANCIENT EGYPT, Adolf Erman. Fullest, most thorough, detailed older account with much not in more recent books, domestic life, religion, magic, medicine, commerce, much more. Many illustrations reproduce tomb paintings, carvings, hieroglyphs, etc. 597pp. 5⅜ × 8½. 22632-8 Pa. $10.95

SUNDIALS, Their Theory and Construction, Albert Waugh. Far and away the best, most thorough coverage of ideas, mathematics concerned, types, construction, adjusting anywhere. Simple, nontechnical treatment allows even children to build several of these dials. Over 100 illustrations. 230pp. 5⅜ × 8½. 22947-5 Pa. $7.95

DYNAMICS OF FLUIDS IN POROUS MEDIA, Jacob Bear. For advanced students of ground water hydrology, soil mechanics and physics, drainage and irrigation engineering, and more. 335 illustrations. Exercises, with answers. 784pp. 6⅛ × 9¼. 65675-6 Pa. $19.95

SONGS OF EXPERIENCE: Facsimile Reproduction with 26 Plates in Full Color, William Blake. 26 full-color plates from a rare 1826 edition. Includes "The Tyger," "London," "Holy Thursday," and other poems. Printed text of poems. 48pp. 5¼ × 7. 24636-1 Pa. $4.95

OLD-TIME VIGNETTES IN FULL COLOR, Carol Belanger Grafton (ed.). Over 390 charming, often sentimental illustrations, selected from archives of Victorian graphics—pretty women posing, children playing, food, flowers, kittens and puppies, smiling cherubs, birds and butterflies, much more. All copyright-free. 48pp. 9¼ × 12¼. 27269-9 Pa. $5.95

PHOTOGRAPHIC SKETCHBOOK OF THE CIVIL WAR, Alexander Gardner. 100 photos taken on field during the Civil War. Famous shots of Manassas, Harper's Ferry, Lincoln, Richmond, slave pens, etc. 244pp. 10⅝ × 8¼.
22731-6 Pa. $9.95

FIVE ACRES AND INDEPENDENCE, Maurice G. Kains. Great back-to-the-land classic explains basics of self-sufficient farming. The one book to get. 95 illustrations. 397pp. 5⅜ × 8½.
20974-1 Pa. $7.95

SONGS OF EASTERN BIRDS, Dr. Donald J. Borror. Songs and calls of 60 species most common to eastern U.S.: warblers, woodpeckers, flycatchers, thrushes, larks, many more in high-quality recording.
Cassette and manual 99912-2 $8.95

A MODERN HERBAL, Margaret Grieve. Much the fullest, most exact, most useful compilation of herbal material. Gigantic alphabetical encyclopedia, from aconite to zedoary, gives botanical information, medical properties, folklore, economic uses, much else. Indispensable to serious reader. 161 illustrations. 888pp. 6½ × 9¼. 2-vol. set. (USO)
Vol. I: 22798-7 Pa. $9.95
Vol. II: 22799-5 Pa. $9.95

HIDDEN TREASURE MAZE BOOK, Dave Phillips. Solve 34 challenging mazes accompanied by heroic tales of adventure. Evil dragons, people-eating plants, bloodthirsty giants, many more dangerous adversaries lurk at every twist and turn. 34 mazes, stories, solutions. 48pp. 8¼ × 11.
24566-7 Pa. $2.95

LETTERS OF W. A. MOZART, Wolfgang A. Mozart. Remarkable letters show bawdy wit, humor, imagination, musical insights, contemporary musical world; includes some letters from Leopold Mozart. 276pp. 5⅜ × 8½.
22859-2 Pa. $7.95

BASIC PRINCIPLES OF CLASSICAL BALLET, Agrippina Vaganova. Great Russian theoretician, teacher explains methods for teaching classical ballet. 118 illustrations. 175pp. 5⅜ × 8½.
22036-2 Pa. $4.95

THE JUMPING FROG, Mark Twain. Revenge edition. The original story of The Celebrated Jumping Frog of Calaveras County, a hapless French translation, and Twain's hilarious "retranslation" from the French. 12 illustrations. 66pp. 5⅜ × 8½.
22686-7 Pa. $3.95

BEST REMEMBERED POEMS, Martin Gardner (ed.). The 126 poems in this superb collection of 19th- and 20th-century British and American verse range from Shelley's "To a Skylark" to the impassioned "Renascence" of Edna St. Vincent Millay and to Edward Lear's whimsical "The Owl and the Pussycat." 224pp. 5⅜ × 8½.
27165-X Pa. $4.95

COMPLETE SONNETS, William Shakespeare. Over 150 exquisite poems deal with love, friendship, the tyranny of time, beauty's evanescence, death and other themes in language of remarkable power, precision and beauty. Glossary of archaic terms. 80pp. 5³⁄₁₆ × 8¼.
26686-9 Pa. $1.00

BODIES IN A BOOKSHOP, R. T. Campbell. Challenging mystery of blackmail and murder with ingenious plot and superbly drawn characters. In the best tradition of British suspense fiction. 192pp. 5⅜ × 8½.
24720-1 Pa. $5.95

ANATOMY: A Complete Guide for Artists, Joseph Sheppard. A master of figure drawing shows artists how to render human anatomy convincingly. Over 460 illustrations. 224pp. 8⅜ × 11¼.　　　　　　　　　　　　　27279-6 Pa. $10.95

MEDIEVAL CALLIGRAPHY: Its History and Technique, Marc Drogin. Spirited history, comprehensive instruction manual covers 13 styles (ca. 4th century thru 15th). Excellent photographs; directions for duplicating medieval techniques with modern tools. 224pp. 8⅜ × 11¼.　　　　　　　　　　　　26142-5 Pa. $11.95

DRIED FLOWERS: How to Prepare Them, Sarah Whitlock and Martha Rankin. Complete instructions on how to use silica gel, meal and borax, perlite aggregate, sand and borax, glycerine and water to create attractive permanent flower arrangements. 12 illustrations. 32pp. 5⅜ × 8½.　　　　　　21802-3 Pa. $1.00

EASY-TO-MAKE BIRD FEEDERS FOR WOODWORKERS, Scott D. Campbell. Detailed, simple-to-use guide for designing, constructing, caring for and using feeders. Text, illustrations for 12 classic and contemporary designs. 96pp. 5⅜ × 8½.
25847-5 Pa. $2.95

OLD-TIME CRAFTS AND TRADES, Peter Stockham. An 1807 book created to teach children about crafts and trades open to them as future careers. It describes in detailed, nontechnical terms 24 different occupations, among them coachmaker, gardener, hairdresser, lacemaker, shoemaker, wheelwright, copper-plate printer, milliner, trunkmaker, merchant and brewer. Finely detailed engravings illustrate each occupation. 192pp. 4⅝ × 6.　　　　　　　　　　　　27398-9 Pa. $4.95

THE HISTORY OF UNDERCLOTHES, C. Willett Cunnington and Phyllis Cunnington. Fascinating, well-documented survey covering six centuries of English undergarments, enhanced with over 100 illustrations: 12th-century laced-up bodice, footed long drawers (1795), 19th-century bustles, 19th-century corsets for men, Victorian "bust improvers," much more. 272pp. 5⅜ × 8¼.　27124-2 Pa. $9.95

ARTS AND CRAFTS FURNITURE: The Complete Brooks Catalog of 1912, Brooks Manufacturing Co. Photos and detailed descriptions of more than 150 now very collectible furniture designs from the Arts and Crafts movement depict davenports, settees, buffets, desks, tables, chairs, bedsteads, dressers and more, all built of solid, quarter-sawed oak. Invaluable for students and enthusiasts of antiques, Americana and the decorative arts. 80pp. 6½ × 9¼.　　27471-3 Pa. $7.95

HOW WE INVENTED THE AIRPLANE: An Illustrated History, Orville Wright. Fascinating firsthand account covers early experiments, construction of planes and motors, first flights, much more. Introduction and commentary by Fred C. Kelly. 76 photographs. 96pp. 8¼ × 11.　　　　　　　　　　　　25662-6 Pa. $8.95

THE ARTS OF THE SAILOR: Knotting, Splicing and Ropework, Hervey Garrett Smith. Indispensable shipboard reference covers tools, basic knots and useful hitches; handsewing and canvas work, more. Over 100 illustrations. Delightful reading for sea lovers. 256pp. 5⅜ × 8½.　　　　　　　　　26440-8 Pa. $7.95

FRANK LLOYD WRIGHT'S FALLINGWATER: The House and Its History, Second, Revised Edition, Donald Hoffmann. A total revision—both in text and illustrations—of the standard document on Fallingwater, the boldest, most personal architectural statement of Wright's mature years, updated with valuable new material from the recently opened Frank Lloyd Wright Archives. "Fascinating"—*The New York Times.* 116 illustrations. 128pp. 9¼ × 10¾.
27430-6 Pa. $10.95

THE BEST TALES OF HOFFMANN, E. T. A. Hoffmann. 10 of Hoffmann's most important stories: "Nutcracker and the King of Mice," "The Golden Flowerpot," etc. 458pp. 5⅜ × 8½. 21793-0 Pa. $8.95

FROM FETISH TO GOD IN ANCIENT EGYPT, E. A. Wallis Budge. Rich detailed survey of Egyptian conception of "God" and gods, magic, cult of animals, Osiris, more. Also, superb English translations of hymns and legends. 240 illustrations. 545pp. 5⅜ × 8½. 25803-3 Pa. $11.95

FRENCH STORIES/CONTES FRANÇAIS: A Dual-Language Book, Wallace Fowlie. Ten stories by French masters, Voltaire to Camus: "Micromegas" by Voltaire; "The Atheist's Mass" by Balzac; "Minuet" by de Maupassant; "The Guest" by Camus, six more. Excellent English translations on facing pages. Also French-English vocabulary list, exercises, more. 352pp. 5⅜ × 8½. 26443-2 Pa. $8.95

CHICAGO AT THE TURN OF THE CENTURY IN PHOTOGRAPHS: 122 Historic Views from the Collections of the Chicago Historical Society, Larry A. Viskochil. Rare large-format prints offer detailed views of City Hall, State Street, the Loop, Hull House, Union Station, many other landmarks, circa 1904–1913. Introduction. Captions. Maps. 144pp. 9⅜ × 12¼. 24656-6 Pa. $12.95

OLD BROOKLYN IN EARLY PHOTOGRAPHS, 1865–1929, William Lee Younger. Luna Park, Gravesend race track, construction of Grand Army Plaza, moving of Hotel Brighton, etc. 157 previously unpublished photographs. 165pp. 8⅞ × 11¾. 23587-4 Pa. $13.95

THE MYTHS OF THE NORTH AMERICAN INDIANS, Lewis Spence. Rich anthology of the myths and legends of the Algonquins, Iroquois, Pawnees and Sioux, prefaced by an extensive historical and ethnological commentary. 36 illustrations. 480pp. 5⅜ × 8½. 25967-6 Pa. $8.95

AN ENCYCLOPEDIA OF BATTLES: Accounts of Over 1,560 Battles from 1479 B.C. to the Present, David Eggenberger. Essential details of every major battle in recorded history from the first battle of Megiddo in 1479 B.C. to Grenada in 1984. List of Battle Maps. New Appendix covering the years 1967–1984. Index. 99 illustrations. 544pp. 6½ × 9¼. 24913-1 Pa. $14.95

SAILING ALONE AROUND THE WORLD, Captain Joshua Slocum. First man to sail around the world, alone, in small boat. One of great feats of seamanship told in delightful manner. 67 illustrations. 294pp. 5⅜ × 8½. 20326-3 Pa. $5.95

ANARCHISM AND OTHER ESSAYS, Emma Goldman. Powerful, penetrating, prophetic essays on direct action, role of minorities, prison reform, puritan hypocrisy, violence, etc. 271pp. 5⅜ × 8½. 22484-8 Pa. $5.95

MYTHS OF THE HINDUS AND BUDDHISTS, Ananda K. Coomaraswamy and Sister Nivedita. Great stories of the epics; deeds of Krishna, Shiva, taken from puranas, Vedas, folk tales; etc. 32 illustrations. 400pp. 5⅜ × 8½. 21759-0 Pa. $9.95

BEYOND PSYCHOLOGY, Otto Rank. Fear of death, desire of immortality, nature of sexuality, social organization, creativity, according to Rankian system. 291pp. 5⅜ × 8½. 20485-5 Pa. $8.95

A THEOLOGICO-POLITICAL TREATISE, Benedict Spinoza. Also contains unfinished Political Treatise. Great classic on religious liberty, theory of government on common consent. R. Elwes translation. Total of 421pp. 5⅜ × 8½. 20249-6 Pa. $8.95

FRANK LLOYD WRIGHT'S HOLLYHOCK HOUSE, Donald Hoffmann. Lavishly illustrated, carefully documented study of one of Wright's most controversial residential designs. Over 120 photographs, floor plans, elevations, etc. Detailed perceptive text by noted Wright scholar. Index. 128pp. 9¼ × 10¾.
27133-1 Pa. $11.95

THE MALE AND FEMALE FIGURE IN MOTION: 60 Classic Photographic Sequences, Eadweard Muybridge. 60 true-action photographs of men and women walking, running, climbing, bending, turning, etc., reproduced from rare 19th-century masterpiece. vi + 121pp. 9 × 12. 24745-7 Pa. $10.95

1001 QUESTIONS ANSWERED ABOUT THE SEASHORE, N. J. Berrill and Jacquelyn Berrill. Queries answered about dolphins, sea snails, sponges, starfish, fishes, shore birds, many others. Covers appearance, breeding, growth, feeding, much more. 305pp. 5¼ × 8¼. 23366-9 Pa. $7.95

GUIDE TO OWL WATCHING IN NORTH AMERICA, Donald S. Heintzelman. Superb guide offers complete data and descriptions of 19 species: barn owl, screech owl, snowy owl, many more. Expert coverage of owl-watching equipment, conservation, migrations and invasions, etc. Guide to observing sites. 84 illustrations. xiii + 193pp. 5⅜ × 8½. 27344-X Pa. $8.95

MEDICINAL AND OTHER USES OF NORTH AMERICAN PLANTS: A Historical Survey with Special Reference to the Eastern Indian Tribes, Charlotte Erichsen-Brown. Chronological historical citations document 500 years of usage of plants, trees, shrubs native to eastern Canada, northeastern U.S. Also complete identifying information. 343 illustrations. 544pp. 6½ × 9¼. 25951-X Pa. $12.95

STORYBOOK MAZES, Dave Phillips. 23 stories and mazes on two-page spreads: Wizard of Oz, Treasure Island, Robin Hood, etc. Solutions. 64pp. 8¼ × 11.
23628-5 Pa. $2.95

NEGRO FOLK MUSIC, U.S.A., Harold Courlander. Noted folklorist's scholarly yet readable analysis of rich and varied musical tradition. Includes authentic versions of over 40 folk songs. Valuable bibliography and discography. xi + 324pp. 5⅜ × 8½. 27350-4 Pa. $7.95

MOVIE-STAR PORTRAITS OF THE FORTIES, John Kobal (ed.). 163 glamor, studio photos of 106 stars of the 1940s: Rita Hayworth, Ava Gardner, Marlon Brando, Clark Gable, many more. 176pp. 8⅜ × 11¼. 23546-7 Pa. $11.95

BENCHLEY LOST AND FOUND, Robert Benchley. Finest humor from early 30s, about pet peeves, child psychologists, post office and others. Mostly unavailable elsewhere. 73 illustrations by Peter Arno and others. 183pp. 5⅜ × 8½.
22410-4 Pa. $5.95

YEKL and THE IMPORTED BRIDEGROOM AND OTHER STORIES OF YIDDISH NEW YORK, Abraham Cahan. Film Hester Street based on Yekl (1896). Novel, other stories among first about Jewish immigrants on N.Y.'s East Side. 240pp. 5⅜ × 8½. 22427-9 Pa. $6.95

SELECTED POEMS, Walt Whitman. Generous sampling from *Leaves of Grass*. Twenty-four poems include "I Hear America Singing," "Song of the Open Road," "I Sing the Body Electric," "When Lilacs Last in the Dooryard Bloom'd," "O Captain! My Captain!"—all reprinted from an authoritative edition. Lists of titles and first lines. 128pp. 5³⁄₁₆ × 8¼. 26878-0 Pa. $1.00

PIANO TUNING, J. Cree Fischer. Clearest, best book for beginner, amateur. Simple repairs, raising dropped notes, tuning by easy method of flattened fifths. No previous skills needed. 4 illustrations. 201pp. 5⅜ × 8½.   23267-0 Pa. $5.95

A SOURCE BOOK IN THEATRICAL HISTORY, A. M. Nagler. Contemporary observers on acting, directing, make-up, costuming, stage props, machinery, scene design, from Ancient Greece to Chekhov. 611pp. 5⅜ × 8½.   20515-0 Pa. $11.95

THE COMPLETE NONSENSE OF EDWARD LEAR, Edward Lear. All nonsense limericks, zany alphabets, Owl and Pussycat, songs, nonsense botany, etc., illustrated by Lear. Total of 320pp. 5⅜ × 8½. (USO)   20167-8 Pa. $6.95

VICTORIAN PARLOUR POETRY: An Annotated Anthology, Michael R. Turner. 117 gems by Longfellow, Tennyson, Browning, many lesser-known poets. "The Village Blacksmith," "Curfew Must Not Ring Tonight," "Only a Baby Small," dozens more, often difficult to find elsewhere. Index of poets, titles, first lines. xxiii + 325pp. 5⅜ × 8¼.   27044-0 Pa. $8.95

DUBLINERS, James Joyce. Fifteen stories offer vivid, tightly focused observations of the lives of Dublin's poorer classes. At least one, "The Dead," is considered a masterpiece. Reprinted complete and unabridged from standard edition. 160pp. 5³⁄₁₆ × 8¼.   26870-5 Pa. $1.00

THE HAUNTED MONASTERY and THE CHINESE MAZE MURDERS, Robert van Gulik. Two full novels by van Gulik, set in 7th-century China, continue adventures of Judge Dee and his companions. An evil Taoist monastery, seemingly supernatural events; overgrown topiary maze hides strange crimes. 27 illustrations. 328pp. 5⅜ × 8½.   23502-5 Pa. $7.95

THE BOOK OF THE SACRED MAGIC OF ABRAMELIN THE MAGE, translated by S. MacGregor Mathers. Medieval manuscript of ceremonial magic. Basic document in Aleister Crowley, Golden Dawn groups. 268pp. 5⅜ × 8½.
23211-5 Pa. $8.95

NEW RUSSIAN-ENGLISH AND ENGLISH-RUSSIAN DICTIONARY, M. A. O'Brien. This is a remarkably handy Russian dictionary, containing a surprising amount of information, including over 70,000 entries. 366pp. 4½ × 6⅛.
20208-9 Pa. $9.95

HISTORIC HOMES OF THE AMERICAN PRESIDENTS, Second, Revised Edition, Irvin Haas. A traveler's guide to American Presidential homes, most open to the public, depicting and describing homes occupied by every American President from George Washington to George Bush. With visiting hours, admission charges, travel routes. 175 photographs. Index. 160pp. 8¼ × 11. 26751-2 Pa. $10.95

NEW YORK IN THE FORTIES, Andreas Feininger. 162 brilliant photographs by the well-known photographer, formerly with *Life* magazine. Commuters, shoppers, Times Square at night, much else from city at its peak. Captions by John von Hartz. 181pp. 9¼ × 10¾.   23585-8 Pa. $12.95

INDIAN SIGN LANGUAGE, William Tomkins. Over 525 signs developed by Sioux and other tribes. Written instructions and diagrams. Also 290 pictographs. 111pp. 6⅛ × 9¼.   22029-X Pa. $3.50

EARLY NINETEENTH-CENTURY CRAFTS AND TRADES, Peter Stockham (ed.). Extremely rare 1807 volume describes to youngsters the crafts and trades of the day: brickmaker, weaver, dressmaker, bookbinder, ropemaker, saddler, many more. Quaint prose, charming illustrations for each craft. 20 black-and-white line illustrations. 192pp. 4⅝ × 6. 27293-1 Pa. $4.95

VICTORIAN FASHIONS AND COSTUMES FROM HARPER'S BAZAR, 1867–1898, Stella Blum (ed.). Day costumes, evening wear, sports clothes, shoes, hats, other accessories in over 1,000 detailed engravings. 320pp. 9⅜ × 12¼. 22990-4 Pa. $13.95

GUSTAV STICKLEY, THE CRAFTSMAN, Mary Ann Smith. Superb study surveys broad scope of Stickley's achievement, especially in architecture. Design philosophy, rise and fall of the Craftsman empire, descriptions and floor plans for many Craftsman houses, more. 86 black-and-white halftones. 31 line illustrations. Introduction. 208pp. 6½ × 9¼. 27210-9 Pa. $9.95

THE LONG ISLAND RAIL ROAD IN EARLY PHOTOGRAPHS, Ron Ziel. Over 220 rare photos, informative text document origin (1844) and development of rail service on Long Island. Vintage views of early trains, locomotives, stations, passengers, crews, much more. Captions. 8⅞ × 11¾. 26301-0 Pa. $13.95

THE BOOK OF OLD SHIPS: From Egyptian Galleys to Clipper Ships, Henry B. Culver. Superb, authoritative history of sailing vessels, with 80 magnificent line illustrations. Galley, bark, caravel, longship, whaler, many more. Detailed, informative text on each vessel by noted naval historian. Introduction. 256pp. 5⅜ × 8½. 27332-6 Pa. $6.95

TEN BOOKS ON ARCHITECTURE, Vitruvius. The most important book ever written on architecture. Early Roman aesthetics, technology, classical orders, site selection, all other aspects. Morgan translation. 331pp. 5⅜ × 8½. 20645-9 Pa. $8.95

THE HUMAN FIGURE IN MOTION, Eadweard Muybridge. More than 4,500 stopped-action photos, in action series, showing undraped men, women, children jumping, lying down, throwing, sitting, wrestling, carrying, etc. 390pp. 7⅞ × 10⅝. 20204-6 Clothbd. $24.95

TREES OF THE EASTERN AND CENTRAL UNITED STATES AND CANADA, William M. Harlow. Best one-volume guide to 140 trees. Full descriptions, woodlore, range, etc. Over 600 illustrations. Handy size. 288pp. 4½ × 6⅜. 20395-6 Pa. $5.95

SONGS OF WESTERN BIRDS, Dr. Donald J. Borror. Complete song and call repertoire of 60 western species, including flycatchers, juncoes, cactus wrens, many more—includes fully illustrated booklet. Cassette and manual 99913-0 $8.95

GROWING AND USING HERBS AND SPICES, Milo Miloradovich. Versatile handbook provides all the information needed for cultivation and use of all the herbs and spices available in North America. 4 illustrations. Index. Glossary. 236pp. 5⅜ × 8½. 25058-X Pa. $6.95

BIG BOOK OF MAZES AND LABYRINTHS, Walter Shepherd. 50 mazes and labyrinths in all—classical, solid, ripple, and more—in one great volume. Perfect inexpensive puzzler for clever youngsters. Full solutions. 112pp. 8⅛ × 11. 22951-3 Pa. $4.95

CATALOG OF DOVER BOOKS

STICKLEY CRAFTSMAN FURNITURE CATALOGS, Gustav Stickley and L. & J. G. Stickley. Beautiful, functional furniture in two authentic catalogs from 1910. 594 illustrations, including 277 photos, show settles, rockers, armchairs, reclining chairs, bookcases, desks, tables. 183pp. 6½ × 9¼. 23838-5 Pa. $9.95

AMERICAN LOCOMOTIVES IN HISTORIC PHOTOGRAPHS: 1858 to 1949, Ron Ziel (ed.). A rare collection of 126 meticulously detailed official photographs, called "builder portraits," of American locomotives that majestically chronicle the rise of steam locomotive power in America. Introduction. Detailed captions. xi + 129pp. 9 × 12. 27393-8 Pa. $12.95

AMERICA'S LIGHTHOUSES: An Illustrated History, Francis Ross Holland, Jr. Delightfully written, profusely illustrated fact-filled survey of over 200 American lighthouses since 1716. History, anecdotes, technological advances, more. 240pp. 8 × 10¾. 25576-X Pa. $11.95

TOWARDS A NEW ARCHITECTURE, Le Corbusier. Pioneering manifesto by founder of "International School." Technical and aesthetic theories, views of industry, economics, relation of form to function, "mass-production split" and much more. Profusely illustrated. 320pp. 6⅛ × 9¼. (USO) 25023-7 Pa. $9.95

HOW THE OTHER HALF LIVES, Jacob Riis. Famous journalistic record, exposing poverty and degradation of New York slums around 1900, by major social reformer. 100 striking and influential photographs. 233pp. 10 × 7⅞.
22012-5 Pa $10.95

FRUIT KEY AND TWIG KEY TO TREES AND SHRUBS, William M. Harlow. One of the handiest and most widely used identification aids. Fruit key covers 120 deciduous and evergreen species; twig key 160 deciduous species. Easily used. Over 300 photographs. 126pp. 5⅜ × 8½. 20511-8 Pa. $3.95

COMMON BIRD SONGS, Dr. Donald J. Borror. Songs of 60 most common U.S. birds: robins, sparrows, cardinals, bluejays, finches, more—arranged in order of increasing complexity. Up to 9 variations of songs of each species.
Cassette and manual 99911-4 $8.95

ORCHIDS AS HOUSE PLANTS, Rebecca Tyson Northen. Grow cattleyas and many other kinds of orchids—in a window, in a case, or under artificial light. 63 illustrations. 148pp. 5⅜ × 8½. 23261-1 Pa. $4.95

MONSTER MAZES, Dave Phillips. Masterful mazes at four levels of difficulty. Avoid deadly perils and evil creatures to find magical treasures. Solutions for all 32 exciting illustrated puzzles. 48pp. 8¼ × 11. 26005-4 Pa. $2.95

MOZART'S DON GIOVANNI (DOVER OPERA LIBRETTO SERIES), Wolfgang Amadeus Mozart. Introduced and translated by Ellen H. Bleiler. Standard Italian libretto, with complete English translation. Convenient and thoroughly portable—an ideal companion for reading along with a recording or the performance itself. Introduction. List of characters. Plot summary. 121pp. 5¼ × 8½.
24944-1 Pa. $2.95

TECHNICAL MANUAL AND DICTIONARY OF CLASSICAL BALLET, Gail Grant. Defines, explains, comments on steps, movements, poses and concepts. 15-page pictorial section. Basic book for student, viewer. 127pp. 5⅜ × 8½.
21843-0 Pa. $4.95

THE INFLUENCE OF SEA POWER UPON HISTORY, 1660–1783, A. T. Mahan. Influential classic of naval history and tactics still used as text in war colleges. First paperback edition. 4 maps. 24 battle plans. 640pp. 5⅜ × 8½.
25509-3 Pa. $12.95

THE STORY OF THE TITANIC AS TOLD BY ITS SURVIVORS, Jack Winocour (ed.). What it was really like. Panic, despair, shocking inefficiency, and a little heroism. More thrilling than any fictional account. 26 illustrations. 320pp. 5⅜ × 8½. **20610-6 Pa. $8.95**

FAIRY AND FOLK TALES OF THE IRISH PEASANTRY, William Butler Yeats (ed.). Treasury of 64 tales from the twilight world of Celtic myth and legend: "The Soul Cages," "The Kildare Pooka," "King O'Toole and his Goose," many more. Introduction and Notes by W. B. Yeats. 352pp. 5⅜ × 8½. **26941-8 Pa. $8.95**

BUDDHIST MAHAYANA TEXTS, E. B. Cowell and Others (eds.). Superb, accurate translations of basic documents in Mahayana Buddhism, highly important in history of religions. The Buddha-karita of Asvaghosha, Larger Sukhavativyuha, more. 448pp. 5⅜ × 8½. 25552-2 Pa. $9.95

ONE TWO THREE . . . INFINITY: Facts and Speculations of Science, George Gamow. Great physicist's fascinating, readable overview of contemporary science: number theory, relativity, fourth dimension, entropy, genes, atomic structure, much more. 128 illustrations. Index. 352pp. 5⅜ × 8½. **25664-2 Pa. $8.95**

ENGINEERING IN HISTORY, Richard Shelton Kirby, et al. Broad, nontechnical survey of history's major technological advances: birth of Greek science, industrial revolution, electricity and applied science, 20th-century automation, much more. 181 illustrations. ". . . excellent . . ."—Isis. Bibliography. vii + 530pp. 5⅜ × 8¼.
26412-2 Pa. $14.95

Prices subject to change without notice.

Available at your book dealer or write for free catalog to Dept. GI, Dover Publications, Inc., 31 East 2nd St., Mineola, N.Y. 11501. Dover publishes more than 500 books each year on science, elementary and advanced mathematics, biology, music, art, literary history, social sciences and other areas.